SMART CITIES
DIGITAL NATIONS

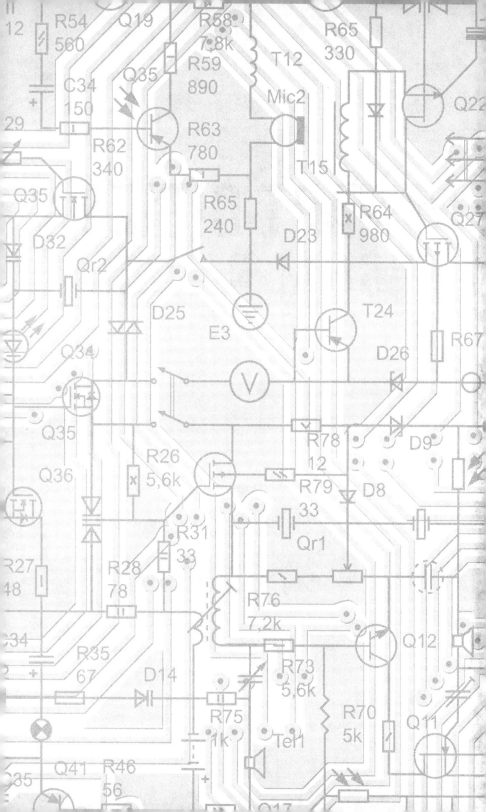

SMART CITIES
DIGITAL NATIONS

HOW DIGITAL URBAN INFRASTRUCTURE CAN DELIVER
A BETTER LIFE IN TOMORROW'S CROWDED WORLD

CASPAR HERZBERG

Foreword by JOHN CHAMBERS, Executive Chairman, Cisco

Roundtree Press

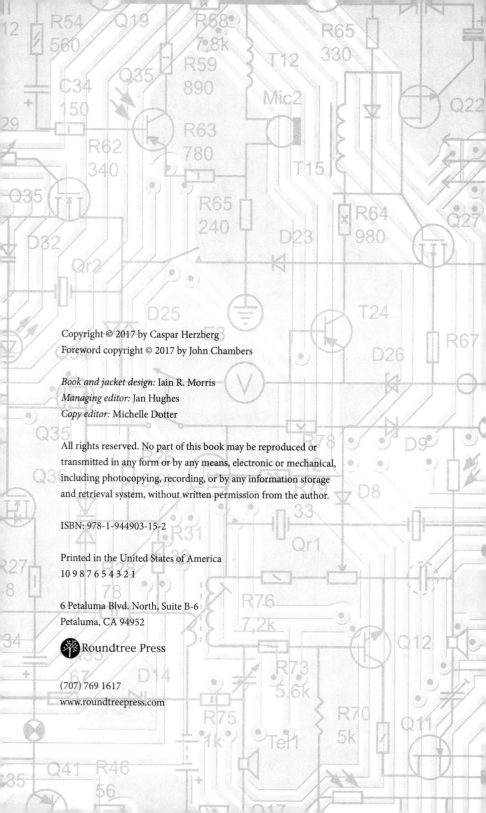

Book and jacket design: Iain R. Morris
Managing editor: Jan Hughes
Copy editor: Michelle Dotter

ISBN: 978-1-944903-15-2

Printed in the United States of America
10 9 8 7 6 5 4 3 2 1

6 Petaluma Blvd. North, Suite B-6
Petaluma, CA 94952

Roundtree Press

(707) 769 1617
www.roundtreepress.com

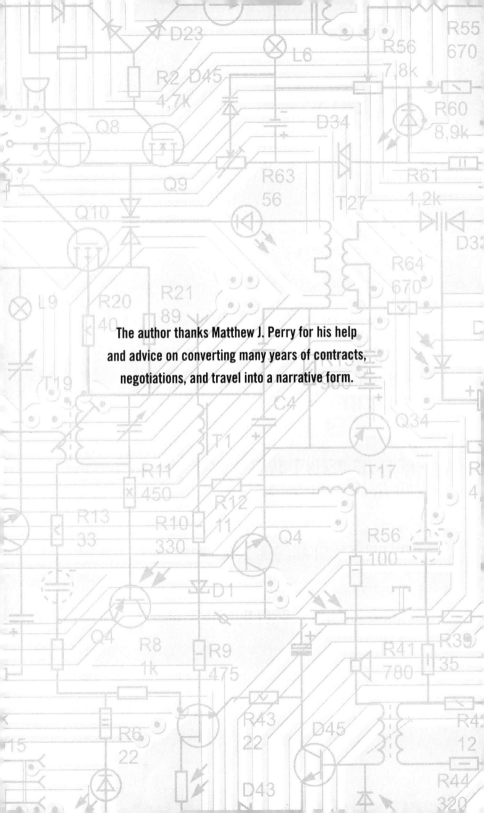

The author thanks Matthew J. Perry for his help
and advice on converting many years of contracts,
negotiations, and travel into a narrative form.

CONTENTS

FOREWORD
BY JOHN CHAMBERS • 9

MAP
KEY SMART CITY PROJECTS, 2006-2017 • 12

CHAPTER 1
THE OPPORTUNITY AND NECESSITY OF THE SMART CITY • 15

CHAPTER 2
THE FLUID DEFINITION OF A SMART CITY— AND WHAT IT DOES • 31

CHAPTER 3
GENESIS: SAUDI ARABIA, 2005–2008 • 41

CHAPTER 4
SECOND CHANCE: SONGDO, KOREA, AND THE CITY LAB OF TOMORROW • 61

CHAPTER 5
ENTER THE DRAGON: CHINA'S CITIES OF THE
FUTURE, TODAY • 91

CHAPTER 6
TRANSFORMING INDIA INTO A DIGITAL NATION,
THE DEMOCRATIC WAY • 123

CHAPTER 7
THE INTERNET OF EVERYTHING TRANSFORMS
BROWNFIELDS AND BEYOND • 147

CHAPTER 8
EGYPT, 2015: THE SMART CITY AS A PROMISING
PERSPECTIVE • 163

CHAPTER 9
THEORIES ON SMART CITIES: SUSTAINABILITY
IN A CROWDED WORLD • 171

CHAPTER 10
BEYOND SONGDO AND THE FUTURE OF
THE CITY • 193

CONCLUSION • 213

INDEX • 217

ACKNOWLEDGMENTS • 224

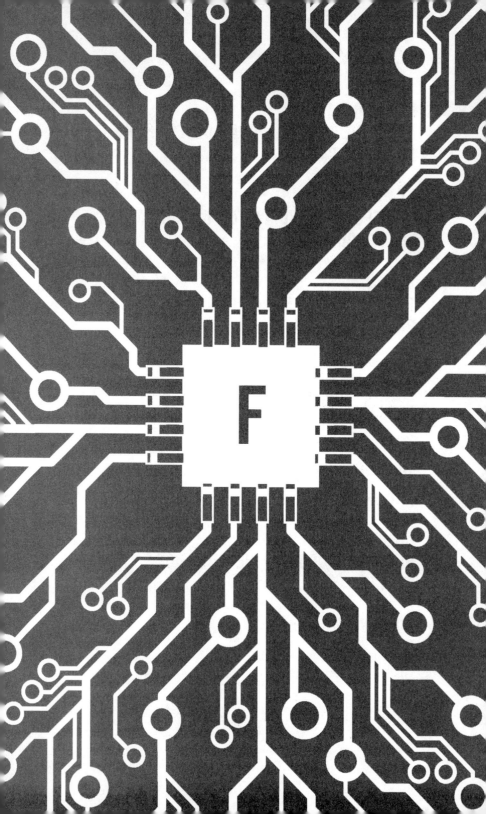

FOREWORD

OR THE HUMAN RACE TO SUCCEED, our cities must succeed. The "urbanization" of our planet is well documented, as people are increasingly drawn from rural areas to cities seeking better opportunities and quality of life. By 2050, about two-thirds of the world's population will live in or near urban centers.[1] If we don't get our cities right, we're in big trouble.

But there's good news. Urban centers are incredible test beds for the Internet of Everything, the increasing connections between all of us, and digitization. Some of our most promising innovation is being fueled by cities working to create a better future for their citizens.

We're early in the journey, but there is a lot of progress being made. With the Internet of Everything, I believe the cities of the world have all the tools they need to become self-sustaining, more efficient, healthier, and safer for all their citizens. This takes foresight, courage, and the right partners to capture these opportunities and truly transform. As beacons for young and aspiring talent, cities must function effectively to help the best ideas and practices rise to the top and define each nation's place in the global economy.

Digitization is essential for cities to reap the benefits of the Internet of Everything, which requires hardware, data storage, complex and interlocked networks and platforms. If you live in a city, you may already be well aware of how cameras, sensors, and data networks have changed the way you live, work, and travel. Smart appliances, thermostats, or security systems may have already made your home more responsive to your preferences and needs. This is just the beginning.

Sensors can alert systems managers when there is a service disruption, a leak in a water main, or when traffic problems occur.

Networked devices embedded in the electric grid, gas lines, street-lights, security cameras, and more now capture and share information that can be analyzed and used to create a greater citywide intelligence and memory.

Imagine a world where citizens don't have to drive laps around a city to find a parking space and instead can monitor the available spots in their neighborhood with a mobile app. Or streetlights that only come on when a person is in the vicinity, saving electricity and costs while also keeping our cities safe. What if there were ways in which citizens could connect with communities around the world via video telepresence equipment, and students could be tutored on Spanish from a teacher based in Spain.

This is not the future. This is today. Young cities that have implemented digital capabilities in their master plans serve as the laboratories from which we can glean the challenges and possibilities presented by our technological advances. Cities with centuries of infrastructure are discovering ways to reinvent entire districts through digital transformation.

Networked digital solutions are helping cities conserve resources, generate new sources of municipal revenue, ease traffic, and enable citizens to work from anywhere they choose. Any of these improvements have a measurable impact on quality of life. But digital transformation is a tide that lifts many boats. It provides the capacity to take efficiency, speed, and safety to new levels.

And yet, the future of digital cities is still an open question. India, for example, is anticipating the construction of 100 new cities in the next few decades. Saudi Arabia, Malaysia, and other developing nations with young populations are in need of new, vibrant economic centers where the next generation can receive training and find job opportunities. Meanwhile, the established nations around the world must reinvigorate their legacy cities so they are not left behind in a digital global economy.

How can cities and nations afford these improvements? Which should be implemented first? How will these networks and sensors deliver revenue, as well as speed and convenience?

These are just some of the questions answered in *Smart Cities*,

Digital Nations. This is a comprehensive view of how urban centers are changing and must change, written by someone who has been involved from the beginning in Cisco's efforts to positively transform the world's cities. It recounts several important engagements with municipalities around the world over the past fifteen years as we worked to reinvent our definition of what a city is and can be. So read on, and learn how—through the power of the network and digital transformation—the cities of the future will be centers of health and prosperity for many generations to come.

—*John Chambers* served as CEO of Cisco from January 1995 to July 2015, and remains with the company as executive chairman of the board.

---

[1] United Nations, Department of Economic and Social Affairs, Population Division (2014). *World Urbanization Prospects: The 2014 Revision, Highlights* (ST/ESA/SER.A/352): https://esa.un.org/unpd/wup/Publications/Files/WUP2014-Highlights.pdf. Estimates vary, even among reputable sources, but as of this writing, it is accepted that more than half the people in the world live in urban areas.

KEY SMART CITY PROJECTS, 2006-2017

BARCELONA,
SPAIN

GUAYAQUIL,
ECUADOR

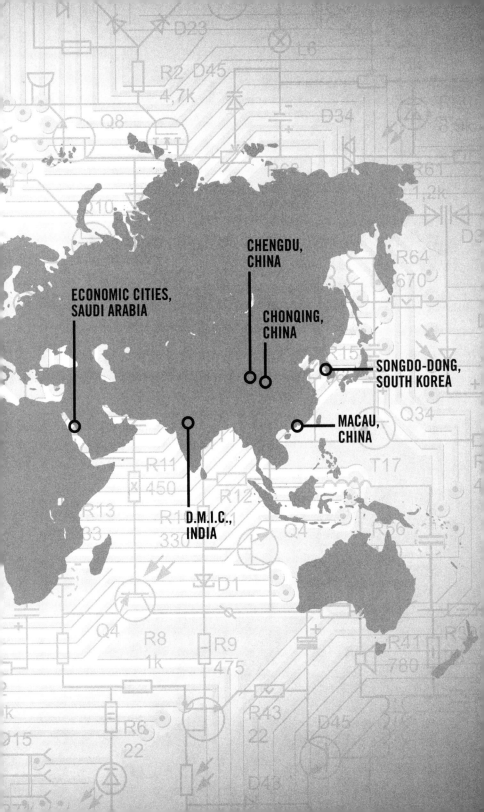

ECONOMIC CITIES,
SAUDI ARABIA

CHENGDU,
CHINA

CHONQING,
CHINA

SONGDO-DONG,
SOUTH KOREA

MACAU,
CHINA

D.M.I.C.,
INDIA

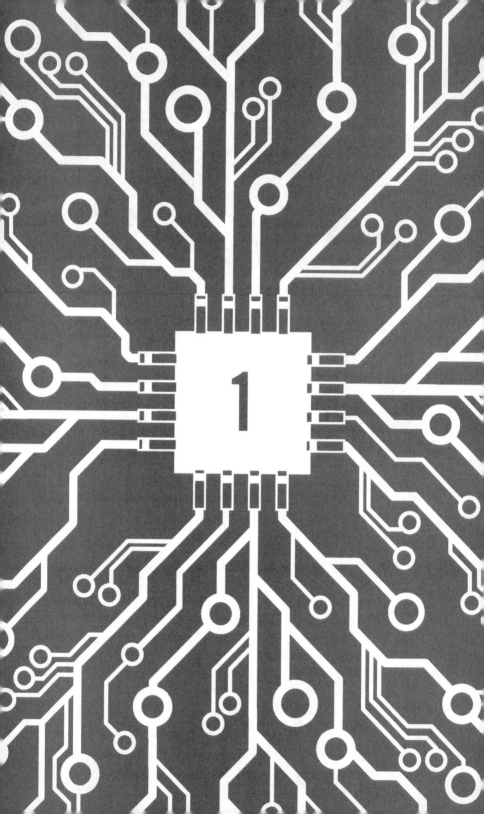

THE OPPORTUNITY AND NECESSITY OF THE SMART CITY

EVERYONE HAS AN IDEA OF WHAT A CITY IS. For some of us, it's a place of constant activity, concentrated work energy, and tremendous innovation. Others see a playground filled with tempting and expensive opportunities for consumption and exploration. Detractors hear the noise, resent the crowds, and complain about congestion, unsanitary conditions, and overcrowded residential areas. Urban planners see great potential for both progress and problems. Corporations analyze the opportunities for growth and a favorable business climate. Most everyone senses the future already exists, in some budding form, within cities, but whether one sees a paradise, a dystopia, or something in between depends greatly on economic status, geographical location, and personal experience.

These variations in perspective are nothing new. Cities have been inspiring and horrifying us in turn for generations. While the city experience is one that defies any quick description or assessment, much of the horror comes from being shocked by what is new and challenging to our way of life. The problems of urban life are real, complex, and difficult to resolve, yet the opportunities created by successful resolutions are multifaceted, far-reaching, and potentially game-changing. And with each passing year of the twenty-first century, they become unavoidable.

POPULATION AND DATA EXPLOSION IN EMERGING COUNTRIES: CAN WE MANAGE THE TWO-PRONGED CHALLENGE?

Cities today are confronting a pair of irrepressible onslaughts: unprecedented population growth and vast amounts of data that demand digital capabilities. While both have benefits, both are, by definition, ubiquitous threats to urban life quality in many countries, especially in emerging countries.

The first threat, physically real and vital, is people—many more people. The world population in 2014 was more than seven billion, 54 percent of which was urban, up from 34 percent in 1960. Over the next fifteen years, that percentage could increase by 1.84 to 1.44 percent each year.[1] This means hundreds of millions more city-dwellers and transients, huge increases in demand for energy and resources, and escalating pressure on existing infrastructure meant to provide for far fewer people.

Despite reports of Chinese uninhabited "ghost towns" and declining populations in Japan, Europe, and the Rust Belt cities of the United States, China and India alone will account for a five-hundred-million-person increase in urban population over the next quarter century—even as they struggle to sustain record growth and reconfigure the balance of global power.

Most of today's cities are underequipped to deal with a huge urban population increase. Available space is not used efficiently. Dated, expensive, and dirty means of transportation as well as dilapidated water-supply and sewage systems are still the norm. The twentieth-century model of the city, much of it running off nineteenth-century infrastructure, is grossly outdated. It does not deliver services efficiently, nor does it utilize modern technology in ways that can both reduce operating costs and improve living standards. And yet, unchecked consumption is still a key principle for growth: more people, requiring more space, more goods, more services. The deck is stacked against cities that cannot adapt to the new global reality.

Thanks to technological innovation, however, a new urban dynamism is in progress. Modern master plans for cities that recycle more, monitor usage better, and provide cleaner, more efficient living standards are on the drawing board—and some have been implemented. Brand-new cities, attuned to current needs, are taking shape, utilizing digital technology that revolutionizes how cities operate and provide for their citizens. Sensors, data, and machine intelligence are changing our perceptions of what a city does and how much energy it needs, giving rise to state-of-the-art urban centers known as "smart cities."

The smart city can be both a literal and figurative description, sometimes within the same urban space, but without exception, it is a place where citizens have embraced digital technology as a leading part of a city's future. These cities will arise in many forms and by varying degrees, but the key principle is merging city services into one platform; services that have been historically disparate and inefficient can be interconnected and improved through digitization. Some smart cities, such as Songdo, South Korea, and King Abdullah Economic City, Saudi Arabia, are early test beds for Internet-driven city services. Others, such as Barcelona, Hamburg, and Guayaquil, are becoming smarter gradually, bringing intelligence to their streets, utilities, education, and health infrastructures, and in some cases, creating brand-new districts that offer the full array of digital services. So while there is no single formula for successful digital modernization, ground has been broken on many new smart cities, and many more are planned in nations that desperately need them.

This book identifies the challenges of smart cities and then explores their design and implementation, illustrated by firsthand experiences. And while much of the literature on smart cities focuses on what happens in the West, important contributions to the emergence of smart and globally connected cities have been made by a couple of daring, ambitious new cities in emerging and newly emerged countries.

These new smart cities engage high-tech industrial pioneers to provide the digital infrastructure, and companies such as Cisco are finding success providing the Internet "plumbing" in this age of massive digital expansion. The countries and cities explored in this book are perfect examples with which to trace the development of smart cities and analyze the lessons learned in making them work. This, in turn, forms the basis for the "Internet of Things" (IoT), a network that enables physical objects to collect and exchange data, and the "Internet of Everything" (IoE), a future wherein devices, appliances, people, and process are connected via the global Internet. The IoE is a value proposition that is estimated to be worth trillions of dollars to the technology industry and the early adopters in business and the public sector.

This new digital technology is also the source of the second challenge that threatens to overwhelm the modern city: data. Sensors, machines, vehicles, departments, and people will soon generate amounts of information that are almost incalculable. Data is the stuff of modern life, the derivative of just about any activity imaginable, and it continues to improve our lives and experiences. But the computer chips that direct and compile this data, and the algorithms that sort through it, will not fall into place by some natural order. The demand for hardware, software, engineers, and coders is staggering; it will become chronic as more city systems go digital and come to count on a steady stream of information.

Even more alarming is the fact that for every IP address embedded in every sensor, there is a potential security breach. It is perhaps human inclination to invent and implement first and ask questions later. Many early developers and users of smart technology have routinely ignored the potential threats to an ever-widening network of sensors and devices. But as hacking incidents become commonplace and more sophisticated tools are used to access critical information, the need for reliable defenses and quick responses to breaches will keep city security professionals busy for many years.

In response, future-proofed security features, inputs for alternative-energy systems, and video capabilities must be developed, and nearly every feature will have to be refined as more smart services and applications are patched in. Success requires more than the ingenuity and insight of tech developers and engineers. It requires every responsible citizen to participate in defining what the technology is used for and when. No one can afford to be a bystander.

THE FUTURE: SEEN FROM THE EAST, COMING TO THE WEST

History repeatedly tells us what happens when too many people are trying to live with insufficient land, resources, or jobs. And while data may be a new concern with regard to population growth, it poses unforeseen threats, in addition to the opportunities it creates. It could be argued that there has never been a time in history when "too much information" was even possible at the city level. But as the Internet of Things becomes the Internet of Everything, we will enter a new, information-laden reality. The systems and platforms implemented today will harness more or less of that data, depending on how systematically it is captured and how aware people are of its potential uses. Data, like fire, is agnostic when it comes to humans—its value, or danger, depends wholly on who uses it and how they use it. We must keep our data under control even as we discover new sources and uses for it, which will create a delicate balancing act.

As it turns out, the most ambitious attempts to build a data-driven city, the first indisputably modern city of the twenty-first century, are not Western endeavors. They are created, for the most part, in countries with great need to combat the rising tide of urbanization. These are nations with young populations, widespread poverty, and insufficient investment in the economic infrastructure to create jobs. For nations such as India, Korea, China, Malaysia, and Saudi Arabia, the timing of development is urgent. Their urban populations are growing at an extraordinary pace, giving rise to conditions that threaten to shatter aging infrastructure. For these nations and cities to provide for more people with fewer resources, in harsher conditions, they cannot be followers in the urban digital revolution—they must lead.

New cities in Saudi Arabia, India, China, and South Korea promise to revise the definition of how a city operates. Digital networks will run as a de facto "fifth utility" that interweaves electricity, water, waste, and gas systems, creating a unified matrix of urban operations and explosive growth in information sharing. As more sensors, cameras, routers, and data storage facilities are added, these cities can actually expand their fundamental intelligence as they grow and add residents. But digital technology in and of itself is no guarantee for streamlined function, increased revenue, cost savings, and residual benefits. Without foresight and careful planning, digitized services could create more problems than they solve or leave too many citizens cut off from the spoils. There is no one-size-fits-all solution, either. Each city and nation will have to shape their new cities to meet their own needs. The technology purveyors must be endlessly resourceful and willing to create business cases that fit the specifics of each economic market.

We *can* build smart cities today—and we *must*. Thousands of developed cities will need to build in digital technology in increments, fitting them to legacy assets and staying competitive with newer, streamlined cities. Even as the IoE explodes before our eyes, we must create solutions that contain the data and allow millions more residents to live in safety, with reliable Internet connectivity and power delivery. It is an enormous engineering challenge, but the way forward is clear. The West will need to take its cues from the East. IoE technology is tilting the playing field; suddenly nations and cities that were left behind in the twentieth century can catch up and push ahead. Western nations presently at the pinnacle of development cannot stand pat: U.S. and European cities must devise their own smart solutions to the challenges of modern commerce and communication. They are just as dependent on digitalized services as those with more poverty and immediate needs to fill.

THE PRIMARY GOAL OF NEW CITIES: COMBATING THE THREAT OF OVERPOPULATION AND RESOURCE SCARCITY

The threats currently facing our cities have existed as far back in history as they likely will extend into the future. The worst slums created in Western nations during the Industrial Revolution have been eradicated, but those oppressive conditions have been duplicated and extended in many developing nations. Meanwhile, developed cities are faced with the challenges of modernization as they attempt to combat congestion, develop better services for residents and businesses, conserve resources, and remain economically vital. There are more cities and megacities than at any point in history, and many more will rise in the coming decades.

The world is faced with a choice. City development can progress in a manner that makes the most of new technologies and commits resources to upgrading old and obsolete features, or it can adopt technology in a haphazard, insecure manner that does little to combat the grave population and environmental problems we face. Political will and investment capital are essential to the creation of communities and urban centers that are "smart," in the best sense of the word. As with any aspect of urban development, diverse and at times competing stakeholders must manage to work in mutually beneficial arrangements, meeting short-term needs while clearing the way for continued growth.

THE NETWORK AND THE SMART AND CONNECTED CITY

While cities have always been repositories for intelligence and creativity, the modern sense of a "smart city" adds a new layer of complexity to this scenario. Cities no longer are simply places where excellent minds, companies, artists, and schools cluster—the infrastructure of the city can now be imbued with an actual intelligence of its own. The smart city creates an urban reality that is greater than the sum of its intellectual parts.

One of the primary tasks of making urban life possible has concerned the delivery and maintenance of utilities, which in the last century meant power, water, and heat. The new utility is the network that weaves all other utilities, as well as information and data from dozens of other sources, into a single architecture. That network represents a quantum jump in the complexity of urban planning, and it will define the difference between city services that are merely responsive and those endowed with an actual, measurable intelligence. This intelligence will be the key to creating work and living environments that respond to the great challenges of rapidly increasing population, resource conservation, climate change, and the lack of sufficient bricks and mortar to house and provide for urban denizens in accordance with modern standards. Creating "smart" cityscapes is a daunting uphill climb, but the need for them has never been more acute.

Because of this, companies that lay the groundwork play an important role in both shaping and implementing the visions of smart and connected communities. Described earlier as "plumbers" connecting siloed elements of the IT grid, these firms have had a vested interest in building smarter cities from the get-go. Cisco, for example, was thrust into the position of facilitating development and acting as a leader when disparate stakeholders—drawn from private and public agencies—came to the table during sprawling development projects. The company's technological strength is essential to municipal planning and business modeling, and ultimately helps civic leaders implement better systems for their constituents and ensure more sustainable futures for growing populations.

The opportunity presented by this timing cannot be underestimated, but it would not be entirely accurate to say Cisco created its own luck. A decade ago, like many multinational corporations, the company needed to react to globalization trends that were shifting a great deal of potential business from West to East. As India, the Middle East, the Asia-Pacific region, and China grew into economic powerhouses, it became imperative to consider how Cisco's products and advisory services could help transform the private and public sectors across these rapidly growing markets.

The firm is now bringing its expertise to the enormous challenges faced by populations in which the concept of wealth and a sustainable living standard are at dramatic variance with Western standards—for the time being. Energy demand in Asia and the Pacific region is expected to outpace the world average over the next twenty years (2.1 percent annual growth rate increase between 2010 and 2035, compared to the world average of 1.5 percent).[2] The urban population of these regions, as of 2010, was the second lowest in the world, but it was growing at the second-fastest rate. The year 2010 was also when the world's urban population topped 50 percent of the globe's total. The future, to a great extent, is to be found in Asian-Pacific and Latin American cities and megacities, and it will be shaped by the consumption and efficiency standards adopted during this explosive growth. A recent study by PricewaterhouseCoopers sees Brazil, Mexico, and Indonesia in the top ten countries as measured by GDP in 2050, joining China, India, and Japan to change the global economic balance substantially from where it is today.

An important premise of this book is that one's conception of the smart and connected city—as with cities in general—depends greatly on one's vantage point. Today, cities such as Barcelona, Bilbao, Kansas City, Guayaquil, and Sao Paolo are galvanizing their municipal services by employing IT network architecture step by step. These brownfield (land previously used for industrial purposes) projects spark our imagination as they attack problems caused by congestion and population density. Once it becomes easier to park a car in Barcelona, be diagnosed at telemedicine kiosks in Guayaquil, and reduce energy costs through smart lighting in Kansas City, further quality-of-life enhancements can follow. Success in one service vertical facilitates greater experimentation with information technology in others. Through innovation and knowledge sharing, a long-established urban environment can become smarter by degrees.

Contrast this view with population centers rising literally out of the bare earth. In India, Korea, China, and Saudi Arabia, as we shall see, cities begin on the design board and take shape with an IT architecture connecting all services. The power and intelligence generated by the Internet of Everything, which is not a distinct technology but rather the convergence of multiple technologies, will not appear in increments; it will define the entire urban ecosystem. In Songdo, South Korea, and other business/mixed-use zones in rapidly expanding cities, IoE technology will create enviable real estate options for companies looking for an advantageous location in busy economic regions. In cities already teeming with new arrivals and struggling against macroeconomic forces that produce great poverty and slum conditions as quickly as they can create great fortunes, IoE technology and smart and connected (S+CC) building plans may be the only hope for an ongoing increase in living standards.

The Internet of Everything, which is a classic example of a tool that first is shaped and then shapes its users and environment, has developed rapidly in the crucible of smart and connected city projects. John Chambers, executive chairman of Cisco, summarizes it as "cheap and ubiquitous sensors, tied together by widespread high-speed wireless networks, generating data stored in the cloud, crunched by increasingly valuable analytics, and accessible via simple apps by billions of smartphones and tablets."[3] The key words in this description are *ubiquitous* and *billions*—neither is an over-statement. IoE technology will be the underpinning feature of urban planning, but the sheer reach of its technology and the level of complexity are difficult to imagine—and the engineering challenge of keeping up with the potential demand for connectivity is formidable. Coupled with the worldwide urbanization trend, it is one reason why the triumph of IoE technology cannot be assumed. People and things are literally flooding many cities at a pace that sometimes cannot be matched with available know-how, human hours, funding, and political will. Meanwhile, the advisory and product services of Cisco and other technology companies must remain profitable. In economic downturns, sustaining IoE and smart city momentum, even in the face of great need, can be daunting.

Smart and connected city development has already endured a series of booms and downturns typical of frontier-defining advancement. From the corporate side, it can be very tricky to justify market returns that require investments measured in years rather than quarters. Political and business leaders must contend with the pressure of attracting both investment and talent to new cities and often must fight to secure the funds necessary to implement the technological infrastructure. Business modeling must incorporate methods to adjust forecasts that may well prove too optimistic.

This means the smart and connected city concept, however much it may signify the future, must be championed and defended. The architects must weigh a diverse and extensive set of variables when creating a new blueprint. Investors, residents, and administrators of these new urban landscapes will need to be convinced of the technology's necessity through many business quarters to come.

THE SMART AND CONNECTED CITY JOURNEY

The first chapters of this book are chronological. They re-create the great promise and excitement generated when Saudi Arabia took its first bold steps toward building new economic cities out of the desert in 2006–2008. The Internet of Everything was in its conceptual infancy, and the idea of building cities from scratch was perhaps unduly brash. Still, a nation determined to raise its profile as an intellectual leader was motivated to invest in cutting-edge technology to create brand-new "knowledge cities" from a slate that was—in geographical, historical, and technological senses—almost blank. It was a time of ambitious projections and expectations. Like most first stabs at a brave new future, this one did not immediately live up to the envisioned promise. But it nonetheless provided invaluable insights into how smart and connected cities could develop. Hindsight allows one to see how much went well and how companies can continue to work off the blueprints drafted during those first "boom" years.

From the Middle East, the journey will progress to the Songdo International Business District, which is part of the Incheon Free Economic Zone in South Korea. Here the first verifiable, demonstrable example of a brand-new "smart" community rose out of a landfill, and at last, civic leaders and developers from many other nations could see the technology at work in real time. This was a landmark for the technology and for Cisco; the firm could highlight, promote, and share its designs with potential partners and customers. To date, Songdo remains a pivotal and advanced greenfield (land not previously developed) development. After overcoming many pioneering challenges, by 2015, Songdo had become a fantastic success. The project was also a springboard for the firm's involvement in many other smart and connected projects in China, India, South America, the southern Pacific, and Europe, which will be detailed in subsequent chapters.

The book then addresses particular challenges of smart and connected city development, ranging from technological impediments, project leadership, integration of existing technologies, insights into enfranchising local partners, and the delicate negotiations required to keep a project's stakeholders on board. It concludes with an exploration of what the smart and connected city of the future, perhaps in 2035, will look like, as well as speculation on the challenges that the next generation of engineers and decision-makers will be facing as they attempt to provide advanced services and quality of life to billions of urban dwellers.

GAUGING THE INTELLIGENCE OF CITIES

I t is beyond the scope of this book to synthesize all the world's urbanization trends, but a few distinctions of terminology will help to clarify. A company's involvement in smart and connected city projects can range from advisory services focused on developing a smart city vision, to the design of a smart city's network, to the provision of switches, routers, and third-party hardware. Cisco, for example, has led S+CC initiatives in both greenfield projects, where new business parks or entire cities begin on a drawing board, to a wide variety of work in brownfield environments and cities with longstanding infrastructure that are incrementally introducing IT refinements to existing services or are looking to add smart or digital services. Both brownfield and greenfield projects can be attractive investments from a corporate standpoint; each is defined in part by particular challenges to development and execution, as we shall see in later chapters. The motivations behind these infrastructure developments also have varied origin. Many of the first smart and connected projects sprang out of private-sector real estate ventures. By now, tech companies are likely to engage with municipal governments seeking to ignite new opportunities independent from, if not contrasting with, national aims. In other cases, these municipalities might be executing in accord with a well-defined national digital strategy. China's Internet "Plus" initiative, which was launched in 2015 and aims to integrate the Internet with traditional industries, would be such an example.

But in the end, almost all successful smart and connected initiatives will feature a mesh of varied interests. Network architects will need to model not just business outcomes but sustainable partnerships, in which the benefits for all stakeholders remain top of mind. At the same time, technology experts and engineers must advocate for global open standards to ensure that positive results can be reproduced in other cities and markets. But while consistent technological operational standards may be an important goal, decision-makers also must be responsive to the preferences of the people who are meant to benefit from smart systems. Since public enthusiasm waxes and wanes, smart and connected initiatives require strong political will combined with skillful leadership, as well as plenty of money. Stakeholders must be attuned to the response these technological upgrades evoke.

Particularly in brownfield developments, technology teams must help stakeholders make choices when funds for improvement are limited. Gap analysis and market comparisons can help cities determine which of their services will deliver benefits in maximum ratio to cost. When cities need to improve services in sanitation, transportation, offsite education and healthcare, energy efficiency, and utility usage, yet available funds total many millions less than those required, where is the starting point? Far from being a simple technology provider, tech companies are routinely tasked with facilitating this difficult analysis.

All cities will become smarter as the Internet of Everything suggests new ways to monitor services and generate less waste, inefficiency, and energy usage. But it is important to note that the future likely does not belong primarily to the megacities (generally defined as cities with populations in excess of ten million). The McKinsey Global Institute notes that while we may expect six hundred cities to generate 60 percent of the global GDP into the foreseeable future, much of the growth will occur in cities that are quickly developing after years of backwater existence. These urban centers, with populations between 150,000 and one million, are forecast to generate economic activity at the expense of established megacities over the next decade. Some will become megacities in their own right, but many more will be characterized by less sprawl, poverty, and slum conditions. The lion's share of these cities will in fact be in emerging countries.[4] It is in these environments that the most efficient and far-reaching smart and connected developments are expected. While megacities will continue to play an outsized role in the global economy, many analysts believe that the best hope for quality urban life lies beyond their vast perimeters, at least until smart and connected development has become so reproducible and essential to urban activity that problems of resource scarcity can be overcome. Indeed, the problems of adequate sanitation, potable water, and reliable electricity are still primary to urban experience in the developing world.

Figuring out how to solve the many urban problems of a metro in Manila, Jakarta, or Rio de Janeiro by deploying the analytical and execution capabilities of a smart city network, full of IoE technology and sensors, will go a long way to making the world a better, more hospitable, and more equitable place. When considering what smart and connected city initiatives mean in a global sense, it is important to remember that in many markets, including those with impressive GDP growth and wealth creation, delivering basic services still tops the long list of tasks.

It is impossible to ignore the importance of IT technology and architecture to a future in which billions more people must make do with scarcer resources. Creating city services that can intelligently adjust to changing weather patterns and recover after utility disruptions will be a primary component to urban expansion. And while the prevailing perspective is geared toward "smart" rather than just "green" development, increasingly the two points of view must overlap, particularly in vulnerable coastal cities. By its very nature, IoE technology is focused on efficient delivery of utilities and services and reduction of waste, which surely are goals that will resonate with advocates for restrictions on carbon. As with most elements of the technology, improvements will be measured in increments as S+CC architecture becomes ever more modular and less improvised. While there is a great deal more to be done, the progress is undeniable.

Like most other game-changing technological advances, a smart and connected city can look like a boom or a bust depending on which business quarter is studied. The first smart cities were frontiers, characterized by a blend of sudden successes and unforeseen roadblocks. IoE technology, which will influence commerce and living standards far beyond the limits of cities large and small, was a direct result of pioneering tech companies' work and vision for the future. The journey is far from over. Yet it is reasonable to be bullish about the future and have many reasons to believe that tomorrow's incarnations of city life will be richer and more connected, intelligent, enjoyable, and profitable.

[1] "Global Health Observatory (GHO) data," World Health Organization, 2016, www.who.int/gho/urban_health/situation_trends/urban_population_growth_text/en/.

[2] "Energy Outlook for Asia and the Pacific," Asia-Pacific Economic Cooperation and Asian Development Bank, October 2013, www.adb.org/sites/default/file/publication/30429/energy-outlook.pdf.

[3] John Chambers and Wim Elfrink, "Cisco CEO: Why the future of the Internet is already here," *Fortune*, July 14, 2014, http://fortune.com/2014/07/16/cisco-ceo-why-the-future-of-the-internet-is-already-here/.

[4] Richard Dobbs, Sven Smit, Jaana Remes, James Manyika, Charles Roxburgh, Alejandra Restrepo, "Mapping the economic power of cities," McKinsey Global Institute, March 2011, http://www.mckinsey.com/global-themes/urbanization/urban-world-mapping-the-economic-power-of-cities.

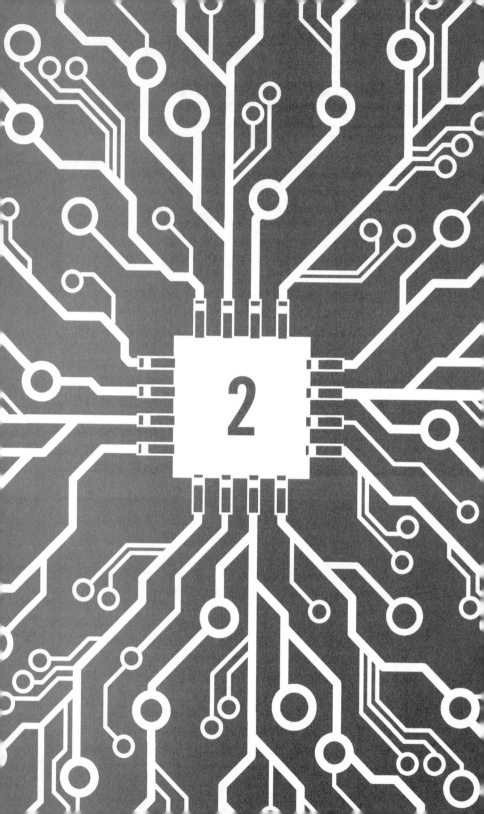

THE FLUID DEFINITION OF A SMART CITY—AND WHAT IT DOES

N 2005, the smart city was more of a concept than a reality. A decade later, we have seen the first actual smart cities take shape, with many existing cities becoming more responsive and interactive with their residents. In another five years, it will be defined in new, often unexpected ways. This is progress, not dysfunction. Creation of a new technology is often messy and tangled at the outset. Nonetheless, for our purposes, we can establish a few definitions of what the smart city is today.

The technology networking architecture companies produce and enable has far-reaching implications for every community it supports. The larger the community, the more complex the calculations and the greater the need for new definitions of city services and technology will be. The language describing smart cities will continue to change as our perceptions of the Internet of Everything and its potential become clearer.

THE CITY IS A PROCESS, NOT JUST A PLACE

Every city is a breathing, reactive organism. It has sensations, records information, responds to stimuli, and endures the normal wear and tear inflicted by its host environment and the organisms within it. For the purposes of this book, however, it is helpful to consider a city in terms of what it does: how it creates and provides services to citizens; how it houses and feeds them; how it generates and stores energy; and how it keeps itself safe.

These city functions, traditionally, have developed as independent, *siloed* networks of infrastructure, processes, and information.

Energy suppliers, traffic coordinators, medical and educational ad-ministrators, and police forces have developed their own distinct communication networks over generations. In cities of the past, where electronic sensors were nonexistent or rudimentary, there was little information to be shared beyond what hands-on technicians and operators saw in their work.

The crucial difference between a modern city and the cities of the past (and most in the present) is the how they capture data. The Internet's reach has extended beyond people to objects. Each owner of a computer is indelibly identified with an IP address; now, sensors embedded in traffic lights, appliances, vehicles, roads—just about anything you see or use in a city—can have their own IP addresses. This means, in turn, that they can assemble data, connect to a net-work of fiber-optic cables, and transmit the data to individuals or processing centers.

Data is agnostic. It can be useful to a wide variety of recipients with different purposes. In the case of a city, the data stream from a sensor network alongside a busy street or highway can be useful to myriad operators. Departments of public works can learn where road repairs are needed; motorists can know in advance where con-gestion or accidents have made certain routes unwise; police can re-cord driving violations and accidents and dispatch responders; and city planners can record traffic flows over extended periods and gen-erate models that track pollution, traffic density, and the roadway's safety record.

In the ideal smart city, the data becomes communal knowledge. Rather than existing for the benefit of a single utility, government agency, or worker set, it can be applied to many of a city's func-tions simultaneously. Silos that isolated city services are disman-tled; over time, the data sharing and compilation grows and deep-ens. Awareness of the city environment sharpens and solutions previously thought impossible proliferate. The city's elements and networks, in time, become smarter and create a virtuous chain of sophistication and efficiency that can extend beyond the city into networks that include state or national entities, other cities, and even other nations.

This is the practical application of what is now called the Internet of Things, or, more comprehensively, the Internet of Everything. Like any new concept, IoT/IoE is still being shaped, and it means different things to different interested parties. But for the purposes of this book, it is appropriate to think of the Internet of Everything as the primary outgrowth of the smart city.

With urban populations expected to boom in many nations, the existing urban landscape is not enough. Brand-new cities are needed to make room for all the people who will move out of rural environments, either because they are instructed by the government (as in China), encouraged (as in India and Saudi Arabia), or seeking better fortunes on their own (as in just about every nation and every era).

China, India, and other Asian nations simply do not have sufficient capacity to house all the people who will call a city home in the coming decades; they are tasked with building new ones from scratch. These massive infrastructure projects are referred to as greenfields. In some cases, the city is an expansion of an existing urban area, or even the revitalization of long-decayed infrastructure. IoE wireless networks and fiber-optic cables, sensors, and data collection points can be laid down as primary components of the development, along with new energy delivery systems, fresh and wastewater delivery and evacuation networks, and HVAC (heating, ventilation, and air-conditioning) systems. Everything is new; what is of critical importance is consistent application of standards and features for building. While these projects are vast, literally transforming landscapes (or even creating them in shallow water), in many ways, they are easier to plan and build out, since there is nothing, or very little, to clear away or work around. Songdo (South Korea), King Abdullah Economic City (Saudi Arabia), and Dholera (India) are all examples of greenfield developments. Each of these huge undertakings represents billions of dollars in investment and a challenge that requires multiple partners and complex financing. In the best case, they become home to pioneer occupants within several years. Others might require a decade or more to take shape, due to delays caused by economic downturns, financing disruptions, political disagreements, or delays common to real estate development.

UPGRADING EXISTING CITIES

F ar more common to Western nations are brownfield developments. When New York, Amsterdam, San Francisco, or Guayaquil isolate funds for limited expansion of services or infrastructure, usually in the low millions of dollars, there is an opportunity to introduce IoE technology throughout a single silo, or perhaps to link the services of two or more silos. When the Iskandar region of Malaysia pursues a remote, interactive health network or the municipality of Hangzhou implements smart lighting and LED usage, the benefits accrue to particular services and deliver targeted results. The city or region indeed grows "smarter," but these projects are part of an incremental process. Still, even with limited results for citizens, businesses, and governments, brownfield projects are extremely useful as proof points that help technology purveyors refine their methods. They also create business cases for future customers.

It might seem that the only smart city is the greenfield, but when cities are defined as processes rather than just bricks and mortar, the importance and relevance of brownfields become clear. The Internet of Everything is materializing in just about every aspect of modern life and commerce imaginable, but its inroads initially will be more obvious in some industries and cities than others. Nevertheless, brownfields and greenfields are part of the same process; both, in terms employed here, qualify as smart cities. In both, the intelligence of an Internet network is harnessed to provide better and more services than before. Resources, energy, and time are saved as the city's functions are refined through the benefits of increased information flow.

VISUALIZING THE FOURTH UTILITY

W hen beginning work within a brownfield, there typically is an element of discovery for municipal leaders. Although most everyone has begun to explore the possibilities of IoE technology, its practical applications are still novel to many in the private and public sectors. Even leaders who embrace the vision of a smart and connected city likely will have choices to make at the outset. Which service areas are in greatest need of an upgrade? Which can generate quick return, either as revenue or public support? Over the past ten years, these tricky questions have been posed to technology companies just as often as municipal stakeholders or real estate developers.

Smart city work teams have provided a great deal of analysis, much of it necessarily quite technical. For this discussion, the reader need not be immersed in the details of IT engineering, but it will be of great use to understand the primary components of the optimal smart city construct and the means by which services intersect and reinforce each other.

THE NETWORK

Every city gains intelligence through a variety of data gateways. Cloud computing, mobile operations, social media, Ethernet cables in local area networks, and fiber-optic cables (some ruggedized for use in harsh environmental conditions, such as hot factories, oceans, or remote utilities) are all utilized, although over time we can expect that the variety of gateways will change as the technology does. Each city has operational centers where the data is collected and analyzed, and where communications throughout the various networks are monitored. The networks have different levels, some of which will never be seen or manipulated by anyone other than technicians. On other network levels, end users will interface.

The more of these networks and data gateways that are bundled, the smarter the city is. Existing cities have the challenge of connecting an enormous number of devices and sensors to existing networks. The number of things connected to the Internet at present is huge—probably around twelve billion, depending on which estimate is used.[1] But experts predict the number of connected things could hit fifty billion by 2020 as the rate of connection multiplies—and this estimate is recognized as conservative. The point here is that our networks are smart but are expected to become far smarter within less than ten years. Each sensor and device can have its own IP address and, in time, computing abilities. Not only will the number of connections increase, the rate of information exchange, and thus decision-making, will also make startling jumps forward.

However, as greenfield developments become more common (and in Eastern nations, this is almost a fait accompli), it is reasonable to expect that service delivery platforms will become more standardized, as today's prototypes are refined and ultimately become established go-to products of IT purveyors. No matter what environment supports a city or which government controls its functions, there will always be certain service verticals: energy, water, and gas delivery; building management (smart and connected real estate); transportation; medical and educational infrastructure; and safety and security. In a greenfield city, each of these verticals will be mapped out in a master plan, its networks overlapping and communicating with those of other verticals and sharing in data access.

The sharing of data by different municipal departments likely makes intuitive sense to most of us; a department of public works, traffic monitoring, and weather forecasters, for example, all have a staked interest in knowing about road conditions. The challenge is to create the pathways by which data sharing can be automated. It also requires that developers consider what is possible from the outset. Over the years, the teams I have worked with have drawn up many diagrams that demonstrate the dynamic, cumulative possibilities of networks overlaid with networks. In the process, we are helping to create a new, interdependent concept of how a city operates.

IMPERATIVES: WHAT THE CITY NEEDS NOW

B rownfield projects begin with a problem or need as yet unmet: Does data need to become more transparent and available among citizens and city officials? Do service verticals need to become more productive, less wasteful, or better sources of revenue? How can energy consumption at the city level be reduced? Does risk or citizen safety need better management? Is a city providing sufficient resources to foster an innovative, dynamic environment that will attract business and talent? Beyond these immediate needs, there are greater questions: Is the city looking to transform its image or promote sustainability? Is it economically prosperous but not, as yet, providing the quality of life that citizens have come to expect?

The last question will remain evergreen as the Internet of Everything continues to affect our daily lives. Unsurprisingly, as people experience fluid communications and services, they like and come to expect them. There will be few singular "fixes" to most government services. For the foreseeable future, we can expect information to flow faster, more transparently, and to more service providers. Cities will be expected to keep up with technology's advancement; this is a challenge we are experiencing in real time. "Big Data," the name for the avalanche of data generated in the last few years, represents most of the information ever created by civilization. But it will become exponentially bigger.[2] The number of connections and feeds and processors required to keep up, as yet more people wield devices with massive computing power, is almost unfathomable. As fast and efficient as data analytics and storage methods are, Big Data may still be too much to handle. This point underscores the fact that smart cities are not, at their essence, about technology. What matters most are the quantifiable benefits to *citizens*, *businesses*, and *urban administration*. The choices that determine where and how accumulated data is used will be more important than the collection process itself. There is no utopia—or dystopia—on the horizon in which the potentials of IoE technology are harnessed to deliver maximum value. The natural element of chaos and spontaneity cannot be engineered out of existence. Whether cities will be better or worse places to live depends on how we use our tools, not the tools themselves.

Of course, this does not free the makers of those tools from an ever-increasing demand for computational power, ubiquity, and reliability. Cisco and other companies must answer to market mandates for sophisticated interconnectivity. The digital overlay of the urban landscape will continue to expand as more services are incorporated and silos are broken down.

Every component of society can benefit from an increase in efficiency and automated management. Libraries, museums, schools, hospitals, sports centers, private residences, and businesses will be connected to the various layers of the network. A foundational layer of storage, computing, security, and collaboration services will undergird a layer of middleware, which also interfaces with the applications used by citizens, or the surface layer of an IoE system. The applications, in the form of smart devices, kiosks, signage, telecommunications, social media, portals, cameras, and databases, comprise the smart features we will (and many already do) use every day.

Each layer, endpoint, and user of the IoE network has a relationship to the others, but the conditions vary from network to network and device to device. Again, customers and other end users, for the most part, will be unaware of anything beyond their particular device or service. But the smart city will be the one in which there are two-way connections of not just data flow but billing, monitoring, and maintenance. In today's smart and connected buildings, control centers already chart these multidimensional and value-adding services, as well as the interplay between them. The future will be a proposition of more monitors, more bundling of and within control centers, better video feed on less bandwidth, wider-reaching networks, and greater symbiosis between the center and the edges of the technological web.

PRACTICALLY SPEAKING: THE SMART CITY OF THE MID-2010S

IoE technology has helped to create services already used by millions. If your physician has enabled a patient portal through which you can access your records, submit prescription requests, and create appointments, you have benefited, to a small but appreciable effect, from the Internet's incursion into the medical field. The technology exists to take this process many steps beyond. Doctors can, via telepresence, engage with patients remotely, removing the need for many routine office visits, but also saving small amounts of the patient's energy, resources, and time. Multiplied by the population of a city, suddenly we are talking about data points that represent huge reductions in energy and congestion. Stronger databases and retrieval networks can expedite a traveler's passage through an airport or train station; multiply by the daily load of passengers at a hub such as Atlanta or Dubai, and the lines at security checkpoints are shortened dramatically. A chain of sensors embedded in a water delivery system can detect leakage and troubleshoot weak points; the resulting conservation, as it is refined, can help to reduce the huge amount of purified water that never reaches residents' taps.[3] Residents of California in 2015, or India in 2020, will have no difficulty seeing the implications of these improvements.

But one must also consider the impact on nations where explosive growth of urban populations is a certainty in years to come. Whether the cities are standalone greenfields or new extensions of existing municipalities, there is a huge, even daunting need to keep up with population growth. Couple this with the established pattern of acceptance—more and better services, and thus ongoing demand for quality—and the race against time is evident. Companies invested in the delivery of new and better information infrastructures will need to maintain a feverish pace of innovation and application to keep up with the needs and expectations of the emerging urban world.

Presently, there is no reliable method of pinpointing where the next innovation in the network will come from. As frustrating as this reality is for those who rely on planning and quotas, it is also a testament to the possibilities that exist. Cities have always been laboratories, but the quality of material and the potential for gain have never been greater.

---

[6] In 2013, Gartner forecast 4.9 billion connected things for 2015. This figure is typical of IT analysts, but projections for 2020 and beyond vary widely, in part due to differing definitions of what "things" should be counted, as well as analysis of market trends.

[7] In 2013, it was common to see sources as varied as IBM and the U.S. Chamber of Commerce declaring that 90 percent of data had been generated in just the past two years. Projections for the next two years—or twenty—require interesting comparisons. IDC, in 2014, projected a 40 percent growth in data over the coming decade; by 2020, the number of digital bits is forecast to equal the number of stars in the universe.

[8] "The Case for Fixing the Leaks," Center for Neighborhood Technology (CNT), 2013, www.cnt.org/sites/default/files/publications/CNT_CaseforFixingtheLeaks.pdf. CNT estimates that 14 to 18 percent of purified water is lost due to aged and inefficient water delivery infrastructure. While IoE sensor technology alone cannot combat these brownfield problems of leaky pipes, it can contribute to maintenance and troubleshooting as new lengths of piping are installed, or the work of isolating the worst trouble spots when incremental upgrades are the only feasible measure due to budgetary constraints.

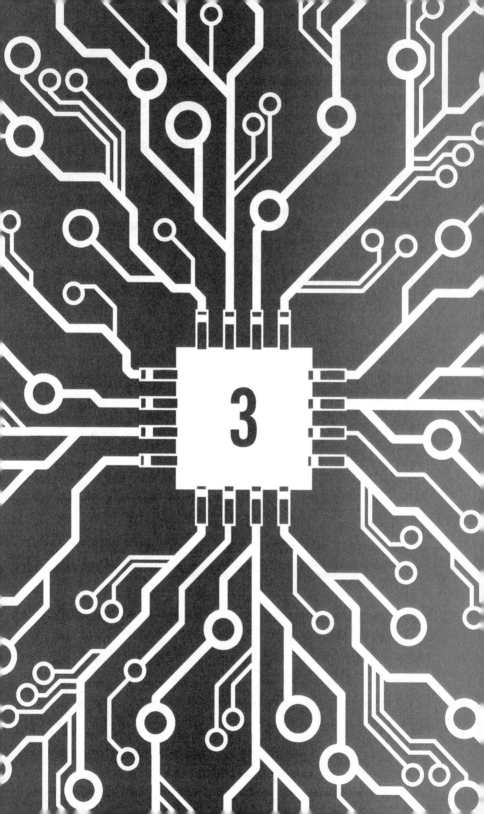

GENESIS: SAUDI ARABIA, 2005–2008

"The first generation meets with death, the second misery, and only the third will have bread."
—Saying attributed to German settlers in the New World

BY LATE 2005, tech companies were ready to commit abundant resources and manpower to the Kingdom of Saudi Arabia (KSA). Top management from Cisco, for example, was making regular visits to the kingdom, while luminaries from other multinational corporations, including Bill Gates, were also meeting with top KSA economic officers. The United Arab Emirates may have received the lion's share of international coverage for Dubai's economic and architectural ascendancy, but beneath the hum of press coverage, KSA was proposing some of the boldest infrastructure developments on the planet.

The reasons were simple. Smart people inside and outside of the country could see that trends in technology, economics, and population growth were converging to create significant, unique opportunities. From the outsider's perspective, it was clear that the kingdom's decision-makers were motivated to act. It is fair to say that few nations have attempted to modernize urban life as quickly and dramatically as Saudi Arabia in the early years of the twenty-first century. As for Cisco—one of the largest networking companies in the world, whose groundwork in creating technological infrastructure is profiled throughout this book—the real story of smart and connected cities begins here.

To be sure, other urban architecture projects preceded Cisco's work in KSA. Technological advances are too complex and variegated to be isolated in one time and place. Nevertheless, this was a crucible that produced IT network architecture blueprints still in use today. But as the epigraph at the beginning of this chapter suggests, the results of the work and collaboration were very different from what was anticipated. There were lessons learned with regard to smart and connected city building in the early stage of development: When the future looks especially bright, the horizon's details often are obscured for even the most subjective thinkers.

ECONOMIC PRESSURE AND REFORM IN THE DESERT

What made Saudi Arabia attractive to multinational investment was an exceptional confluence of growth, geography, and ambitious attempts to prepare for the future. KSA was committed to ICT development early, due to a need to diversify the economy and other factors: a trend toward deregulation allowed for greater international presence; ample ambition and the willingness of economic authorities to announce bold plans; a large, growing population of underemployed youth could not be sustained by the oil industry; and perhaps most important, the kingdom had the cash reserves to enact business proposals on a national scale. Deep though the kingdom's pockets were, the need to put oil revenues to work was urgent. With 65 percent of the population under the age of thirty, the need for jobs and housing was an earthquake that could be predicted with precision, and just as implacable as a geologic event. Great plans would be necessary to absorb the shock.

Even in 2005, after pronounced market fluctuation, Saudi Arabia was awash in oil profits. More than 51 percent of the country's GDP derived from oil rents[1] (measured by the differential between world crude prices and production costs). Its GDP growth rate, however, had spiked at 7.66 percent in 2004 and then dropped, along with oil prices, through 2005 and 2006. While the Saudi government[2] publicly announced a surplus of some 100 billion barrels of oil as defense against severe economic misfortune, the fact remained that the country's deficits were pinned to the price of oil on the world market.

The country's demographics and employment data were another source of concern. Unemployment remained above 10 percent nationally and, typically for the twenty-first century, youth unemployment was far higher. Women, although now representing almost 15 percent of the workforce, were three times as likely to be without work as men in 2007.[3] Even those with advanced degrees found it difficult to secure any work. Men and women with means and ambition often went abroad to study and then remained in their host countries. Many who stayed home complained the education they received left them uncompetitive in an increasingly technical world. Moreover, these shortcomings were hardly obscured, and the Internet was making it much easier for young Saudis to contrast their circumstances with the rest of the world. It is understandable why the combination of educational and employment concerns often elicited comparisons to a time bomb.

Compounding the labor statistics was the fact that foreign workers were awarded most of the jobs in the country. By one estimate, expatriate workers accounted for nine out of ten hires in the Saudi private sector.[4] While the kingdom was a much more reliable employer of Saudi nationals, the tendency to hire foreign workers in precisely the sector that needed growth was another serious problem. It was no certainty that a young, underemployed population in the country would lead to political unrest, but the chances were sufficiently daunting to push the political structure into action.

King Abdullah ascended the KSA throne in August 2005. Although already past his eightieth birthday, he was determined to sustain and expand a platform for nationwide reform in an attempt to combat the disparity between workers and opportunities. Reform had been the subject of fervent debate in the nation for several years prior to his ascent, and already there had been some measures to encourage greater private enterprise. In 2002, the personal computer industry was deregulated; this, coupled with a low Internet penetration, created an impetus to explore ICT technologies both through internal private enterprise and collaboration with international companies. A willingness to get out of business's way was but one aspect of the Saudi government's strategy. The kingdom pledged $2.4

billion to a multiyear modernization of the early educational system, as well as to build eighteen new universities over ten years.

These were not simple political calculations in this deeply conservative country. Although liberal intellectuals had been lobbying the government to embrace reform, this created tension within the political structure. Many conservatives were wary of the reformers' mindset; others were loyal to the traditional theological approaches to education, the role of women, and intersections of Saudi culture and foreign mind-sets. The king's power was secure, but it owed a great deal to its relationship with the powerful religious scholars, whose council provided context and support for many of the government's actions. Too much reform too quickly instituted could destabilize this alliance.

Despite the delicate political balance, KSA's ambitions were clarified in no uncertain terms when the Saudi Arabia General Investment Authority (SAGIA) rolled out its "10 x 10" program in 2006. The goal was to become one of the world's ten most competitive nations by 2010. In part, this plan addressed continuing revisions to existing policy, but it caught the world's attention with a broad stroke: SAGIA announced a plan to build six brand-new "economic cities" to stimulate the diversification process and attract new business within its newly hospitable borders. Each of these cities would be "greenfield": created from the ground up, in terrain that many would consider hostile to human habitation, let alone robust economic development.

Amr al-Dabbagh became governor of SAGIA in 2004. His business acumen and leadership made him an excellent liaison for Saudi Arabia's interests. It was clear that al-Dabbagh, while respectful of the economic objectives of his potential partners, believed the multinationals enfranchised by SAGIA must adhere to a standard higher than pure profit. As the founding chairman of the Jeddah Economic Forum (sometimes referred to as Saudi Arabia's answer to Davos and an annual speaking platform for international business leaders), al-Dabbagh proposed a vision of corporate accountability, in which multinationals acted as conscientious citizens as well as shrewd business partners. Under al-Dabbagh's guidance, SAGIA did not encourage a "big-picture" perspective; it was a requisite of doing business.

As happens with any bold project, skeptics were quick to seek out the soft points. Building cities "from scratch" was not a popular endeavor in the latter part of the twentieth century. Attempts at building large new cities, such as Brasilia or Egypt's 6th of October City and New Cairo, were not examples of the success the Saudis anticipated for King Abdullah Economic City (KAEC, pronounced "cake"). Brasilia sustained a population in excess of two million, yet Sao Paolo and Rio de Janeiro dwarfed it not only in size but also economic importance. Additionally, it left visitors underwhelmed by its productivity, convenience, and aesthetics. In the case of New Cairo and 6th October City, they were designed to relieve some of the pressure from Cairo's runaway population growth but thus far had perpetuated its striking income disparity. Rather than solving a need for stronger economic drivers, many found these developments to be suburban retreats for the wealthy and impractical for the working poor.

The entire concept of urban planning on the brand-new, citywide scale too easily invoked dystopian images of grey, lifeless structures containing none of the vitality and relevance the world now expects of city life. Meanwhile, established cities such as London and Chicago were fighting hard to retain their positions as transportation hubs; was it not presumptuous to believe that a brand-new city could divert enough air traffic to sustain economic promise?

At the same time, the technological challenges were daunting. Emaar Properties, the premiere regional real estate developer, was tasked with constructing the flagship city, which earned its name— King Abdullah Economic City—before a single tower of its business district had been completed (in response, Emaar formed a subsidiary: Emaar, the Economic City). Yet by 2020, a commercial district was to be the hub of a wheel that provided a rich array of urban experience and utility. The blueprints for KAEC also included a port with the capacity to handle the largest shipping vessels on the Red Sea; an industrial zone on the city outskirts; a university and R&D parks; and a full complement of resort amenities, from hotels to golf courses and ten miles of beachfront. The residential areas would have sufficient units accommodate up to two million people, while a series of canals would provide both efficient transportation and relief from relentless building sprawl.

The vision was breathtaking, but so was the cost—initial estimates ran to 300 billion Saudi riyal (SR), or $80 billion USD—and attendant risk. The kingdom could not afford for KAEC to become an impressive testament to its industry; it needed to become an economic powerhouse that supported international commerce and trade. Located sixty miles north of Jeddah, KAEC would be a stop on the Haramain High Speed Rail Project line, while maintaining an international airport and eventually offering some twenty-five thousand hotel rooms. These figures, liberally provided to the media, were a clear indication that this city would not simply participate in global commerce. It would help to create it by becoming a business-friendly destination in which Western and regional influences could mix (the Hajj Terminal at the seaport, once completed, was expected to accept three hundred thousand pilgrims traveling to holy Muslim cities).

KAEC was the largest jewel in a handful. The Saudis envisioned no less than six new economic cities as part of the diversification strategy. Also of prime importance was the Knowledge Economic City, announced in 2006 as an extension of the holy city of Medina. Not only would this be a center for learning and business vitality, it would also help to accommodate the millions of pilgrims visiting Medina annually. This was the ultimate example of combining economic initiatives with the religious traditions that would remain essential to the function of KSA's political regime. The emphasis on knowledge not only dovetailed with King Abdullah's announced educational reforms, it hearkened back to the wealth of Islamic intellectual accomplishment and history. To those who did not believe a government with a strong theological component could play a leading role in twenty-first century thought leadership, KEC was the defiant answer.

Also ready for the drawing board was Prince Abdulaziz bin Mousaed Economic City in Hail, slated to become a transportation hub, and Jazan Economic City in the south near the Yemeni border, which would focus on agribusiness and heavy industry. Two other cities, one near the Jordanian border in the Tabouk region, the other in the Eastern Province near the Persian Gulf, would be strategically located for KSA's increased importance as a trade and commercial hub. SAGIA's aggregate GDP forecast for these cities was $150 billion by 2020, almost half the kingdom's GDP output in 2006.[5]

Saudis found these numbers astonishing, especially when they were assigned, in great part, to what were still tracts of desert. Yet even while some questioned the national commitment or the stakeholders' ability to execute such grandiose plans, many Saudi families bought pieces of KAEC real estate as soon as they came available, hoping to purchase a slice of the future at bargain prices. Meanwhile, the push for economic diversification remained of paramount importance to the city planners. "The whole objective is job creation," al-Dabbagh told the *New York Times* in 2010. "The biggest oil refinery produces at most 1,500 jobs. We will produce a million."[6]

The KSA government's approach to reform also extended to the business climate of the economic cities. These would be regions where the standards of Westerners and Saudis could mingle without tension. The promise to let business do business tacitly confirmed that multinational corporations should expect no problems sending their best people to work in Saudi Arabia, man or woman, provided the normal amount of respect for cultural traditions was displayed. Ideally, these cities would allow Saudi Arabia to modernize and extend its global connectivity on its own terms.

Predictions of prosperity may not convince all the world's business analysts, but KSA's plans were developed sufficiently for many a multinational corporation to justify a closer look. Could this proud nation retain its power structure and traditions while encouraging business on a scale to rival that of Dubai in the United Arab Emirates? It was a question worth exploring.

THE PATH TO A MEMORANDUM OF UNDERSTANDING

S AGIA's pronouncements and KAEC's size might bring to mind a gold rush, but unlike California in the 1850s, this technical frontier opened up with a bit more caution and planning. In fact, Cisco had been building quiet relationships with KAEC stakeholders over the months following the announcement of 10 x 10. And while it was acknowledged in the industry that KAEC and the other economic cities represented great opportunity, there was considerable internal debate about how aggressively the company should respond to KSA's appeals to multinational involvement.

While Cisco's activity in Saudi Arabia at this time might be seen by some as too cautious, subsequent actions should make it clear that the kingdom's economic development plans were a manifestation of the West-to-East macroeconomic trend. And while terminology such as the Internet of Everything and smart and connected cities were not yet in vogue, it could easily be demonstrated that KSA's economic plans, once completed, would represent an enormous opportunity for Cisco and other companies to sell products— routers, switches, and data hubs—and services. Yet there were many reasonable questions that needed to be answered.

First, how to find the data points that justified an ongoing role in KAEC's development? SAGIA and the kingdom's political structure seemed poised to commit a vast fortune to building, but even inside KSA's business community there was skepticism. Partnerships had been formed for years with the West, but to embrace an American-led multinational corporation as a partner in a project of national importance was quite another level of exchange.

Yet even at the outset, there was an argument to be made that city building was the beginning of an industry, one in which an ICT provider could—perhaps even should—play a vital role. The exponential rise in connection between machines and people had yet to arrive, but even in 2006–2007, its inevitability was the subject of endless strategic consideration. A brand-new twenty-first-century city simply would not be viable without an IT infrastructure running beneath and between all its components, much as water and gas lines snaked underneath city dwellings and businesses a century before. Of course, there was a new layer of complexity regarding IT, which also created some uncertainty. While Ethernet cables and wireless land area networks bring predictability to the development and proliferation of machines and devices, it is harder to foresee how those devices will interact with their human owners or which of the machines' functions humans will prefer.

So while there was an argument for jumping into Saudi Arabia simply on the strength of the revenue projections and requirements of their building projects, a tactical approach, based on forming many contacts within the budding KAEC ecosystem, seemed to be the most prudent approach. The Cisco team began forming relationships within SAGIA, Emaar, and other KAEC stakeholders.

At first, these connections were informal and not meant to be remunerative. It was important to discover if the decision-makers within SAGIA, in particular, recognized the potential in a symbiotic relationship with Cisco. As work began with Saudi officials on their vision for KAEC, it was important to establish certain benchmarks. On Cisco's side, it was essential to know that its counterparts looked at its business approach and products as an industry standard. But how to establish this trust? Would the Saudis see ICT as an essential element of their productivity and competitiveness in years to come? For the Saudi side, it was important to discover whether Cisco was committed not just to the KAEC project but the greater plan of economic diversity and growth that remained at the root of every building opportunity. Could the company help a kingdom's organizations become innovative, even as the demand for accomplishment and expansion would meet every bold announcement? The corporation and the kingdom both labored under the pressure of expectations for growth and profit: It was a fine point of commonality, but without a long-standing history of partnership, the initial discussions could not begin on a quid pro quo footing.

Throughout 2006 and 2007, emissaries from both sides met and talked about the vision for real estate that was "smart": connected, characterized by quick transfers of Machine to Machine (M2M), People to Machine (P2M), and People to People data (P2P), with pro-business initiatives and development with stakeholders acting in a spirit of mutual benefit. The promise of IoE was beginning to unfold, and a partnership between Cisco and KSA developers was contingent on those developers being eager to embrace the vision and possibilities the company conveyed. Fortunately for both parties, the enthusiasm for the technology was mutual, as was the awareness that it would be essential to any new city's operability.

It soon became evident that leaders such as Amr al-Dabbagh indeed recognized the potential value of partnership with Cisco. And yet, ICT architecture on a citywide scale was a step beyond the company profile. Cisco had the tools, talent, and resources to execute such an enormous project, but there was little precedent, and certainly no urban zone Cisco could showcase for Saudi developers. It was a curious combination of factors that precipitated Cisco's working arrangement, but even at this juncture the company saw evidence of a long-term trend. Whether or not the Saudis could manage to build six new economic cities in rapid succession was somewhat beside the point (although not so much for those in the ranks of tech companies who were tasked with selling and installing their products). Considering what the Saudis felt required to do as a means to enfranchise a large new generation, Cisco could extrapolate similar needs in other emerging markets of the East. Building the ICT network for cities was an industry. It was still in seed form, but the firm believed it was well worth the investment of corporate resources.

A first step was to write a business plan and forecast for smart and connected cities in Saudi Arabia. KAEC was the primary motivation for a long-term commitment to KSA's modernization/diversification gambit. While it was far too early to secure any contracts, or even memoranda of understanding from KAEC authorities, a convincing case for an investment not just of corporate resources, advisory services, and educational initiatives was made. Cisco was in a position to bid for the drafting of ICT architecture for KAEC, the actual building of the network, and subsidiary systems within the urban ecosystem, as well as advisory services.

The business plan made its ascent up the management chain while simultaneously Cisco's team continued to build relationships inside the kingdom. Through hard work, patience, and good faith negotiation, the climate shifted in favor of a commitment on both sides. The economic forecasts were sufficiently bullish for the negotiations to take a giant step forward. Executives liked what they saw in Saudi Arabia, and soon Cisco's most public faces were being seen often in KSA.

A SMART OFFICE AND HIGH EXPECTATIONS

In early 2008, Cisco opened up a "smart office" in SAGIA's Riyadh headquarters. This was a tactical development; with the pace of work intensifying, the company needed office space that contained all of the best ICT features, running off a converged IP network. But the optics of the event were not to be lost on the public: Cisco's then-CEO John Chambers and Governor Amr al-Dabbagh were both on hand for the ribbon-cutting ceremony.

As stated earlier, this spike in high-level meetings in KSA did not make Cisco exceptional. By 2008, it was evident to the technology industry at large that KAEC and other initiatives provided opportunities not just for tremendous business revenue, but also for showcases. No one wanted to be left out.

The Saudis, too, recognized how valuable partnerships could be to the multinationals. They in turn required commitment to their strategic goals as a requisite to a business agreement. A great deal of time was spent discussing the challenges of defining the kingdom as an economic and commercial force that could compete with Dubai for primacy in Middle East business strategy.

It is important to remember that Cisco has earned its fortune as a purveyor of technological skill and development capability. Cisco's engineers were the best of their kind, but they were not *social* engineers. Connected real estate was a natural progression of the firm's services as IoE infrastructure first took root, but it had brought the company to a much more challenging and socially vital role. Cisco was not just discussing how to bring forth cutting-edge technology; now the team was helping Cisco's clients push forward initiatives that promoted national growth and competitiveness. At the same time, this was also the company's first chance to partner on a level that could reasonably be described as social engineering. While the Saudi government was open about its intention to stay out of the way of business, its influence, through SAGIA and other channels, was still enormous as KAEC moved toward the execution stage. Cisco's architects and engineers collaborated with representatives from private companies on the underpinning IT networks, but its work had an extra dimension of connectivity with far-reaching implications. IoE would multiply the channels through which people linked with people. Machines do what people wish (when they are programmed successfully), but people adopt and use technology in unpredictable ways. The IT infrastructure was agnostic, but as a business partner, Cisco could not be so neutral. The firm had to demonstrate its support for the very strategic goals that had given rise to KAEC and the Knowledge City in the first place.

It should be noted, however, that from the point of business calculation, Saudi Arabia looked like an increasingly solid partner. Standard & Poor elevated the kingdom's credit rating in July 2007 on the basis of continued oil revenues and the strong rollout of the 10 x 10 plan.[7] IPOs had yet to be issued for either KAEC or the Knowledge Economic City, but Saudi nationals were eager to buy shares of real estate before building had even commenced. This was still an oil and gas economy, but by 2006, the non-oil private sector demonstrated the fastest growth in the kingdom at 6.3 percent.[8] Cisco's analysis ranked Saudi Arabia as the fastest-growing market in 2006.

When memoranda of understanding were signed between Cisco and Emaar, the Economic City (an Emaar subsidiary formed in 2006, with 30 percent equity offered as public stock), it became official that Cisco had been tasked with the creation of IT network infrastructure and the operational systems to create smart city services throughout KAEC. Cisco's team would act as consultants and advisors to the architectural process; the actual building of the network was a separate offering that would be offered later in 2008. Substantial work had been logged on the architecture prior to the agreement, but now the pressure to create an outstanding blueprint for smart IT connectivity was elevated. Technical and business expertise was the primary part of the package, but Cisco had already pledged $265 million worth of investment in KSA over five years. The company had increased its staffing in the kingdom by tenfold and pledged to roll out 100 educational academies in an aggressive push to prepare young Saudis for IT careers.

Leaders on both sides informed the international business press that mutual respect had made negotiations smooth and a long, mutually beneficial future likely.

THE CREATION OF A NEW ARCHITECTURE

C isco's business had improved the intelligence and function of real estate in other cities prior to KAEC, but the opportunity presented by this greenfield was astounding to contemplate. It is a designer's dream to start with a blank slate, and no slate was "cleaner" than the one provided by this desert bordered by the Red Sea. By 2008, KAEC announced itself with a gate and palm trees lining what would become the major thoroughfare to the city's heart. But around the road was a seemingly endless expanse of sand until it reached the shore and the first buildings could be seen. Standing on the site of what was to become a metropolis, the entire concept could seem hubristic, but it was much less so if one were fortunate enough to watch the designers at their work.

This is not to say that the Cisco team had all the answers or that its client had formulated all the necessary questions. The build out of the IP network architecture was very much the work of a joint team, which was helpful when the work overran the initial time estimate. The concepts of intelligent infrastructure were imported from Cisco's existing smart real estate initiatives, but to deliver bandwidth up to one gigabit per second throughout a city three times the size of Manhattan took the engineering to another level. Consider that the architecture Emaar, the Economic City expected would extend to all public spaces, all commercial and industrial sites, all residences and resorts, and the essential transport hubs. Fiber-optic arteries would be threaded together in a network that would be logical, accessible, and, hopefully, reproducible. It was too soon to consider how this success might translate to other markets, but in those first, heady months on the technological frontier, a great deal seemed possible. If one were able to create an industry best-practice, agnostic network on this great a scale, why should one not be able to offer, in the coming years, a package of IT services to other aspiring cities and nations? Although Cisco's team members did not have the time for the level of experimentation they might have liked, they had the confidence of Emaar and SAGIA, sufficient resources, and a widening network of capable partners. As the architecture progressed, thinking moved to securing contracts for implementing what had been designed. There seemed no reason why Cisco should not begin to generate substantial revenue within one or two years on the KAEC project. This, like so many of the projections, was overly optimistic, and it also missed the value of accomplishments that would be more difficult to evaluate in terms of revenue.

The components of smart city building are staggering in number. Residential and commercial buildings need to be outfitted with "smart" lighting, power, elevators, and security features. The sea and airports require Radio Frequency Identification (RFID) inventory systems, automated transport, and ruggedized connections. Reliable wireless connectivity is a given and must be available everywhere. Above the infrastructure, communications must be state of the art at inception but open to the upgrades and changes typical of technology subject to constant development.

Not only must this infrastructure function, it must generate revenue and be cost-effective as well.

The Cisco consultants drew on their prior experience for a great deal of business planning and researched the gaps. The company also supplied SAGIA and Emaar, the Economic City with business modeling, cost trees, operations models, and analysis of revenue drivers. During the work on KAEC, they initiated a system of city analysis in addition to designing a comprehensive network architecture.

The extent of the labor would suggest that the contract for building the ICT architecture was the most important Middle East objective for Cisco in 2008. While that may be true, it was not the only consideration. The work made sense from a long-term perspective as well. It had become apparent to many in the tech sector that smart and connected cities would be part of their business foundation in the years to come. Saudi Arabia's growth and national challenges were distinct, but there were many other countries reckoning with population explosions and a massive shift toward urban concentrations. Meanwhile, IoE technology, the natural by-product of smart and connected city building, is predicated on the goal of connecting everything and every person. Where is this more important than in cities? The work on the KAEC network architecture was helping to position Cisco ahead of its competition. The potential of these new designs was palpable.

A PRESENTATION FOR THE KING

On June 11, 2008, the grand opening of King Abdullah Economic City took place with its namesake in attendance. For the event, Cisco flew in a team of designers to engineer a demonstration of their TelePresence technology, which is notable for its "lifelike" transmission, but the use of hologram, 3-D imagery would complete the effect in such a way that might impress even a king.[9] Governor al-Dabbagh and Dr. Ahmed al-Yamani, SAGIA's ICT director general, were on hand to demonstrate key features of KAEC technology. The Cisco executive team had no idea whether and how King Abdullah might convey his blessing and approval of the work so far completed; for that matter, its partners at SAGIA and Emaar, the Economic City shared in this anticipation and curiosity. The event had generated intense excitement in Riyadh and Jeddah, and invitations were prized possessions. KAEC, which at this stage still counted for little more than the noise of construction equipment, was alive with activity.

Governor al-Dabbagh welcomed the king to the special tent erected for the presentation. When King Abdullah and his advisors were seated, Dr. al-Yamani appeared on stage to describe the extent of KAEC's technological infrastructure and the promise it contained. He then invited a ten-year-old student onto the stage with him; once the boy had respectfully acknowledged the king's presence, Dr. al-Yamani invited him to cross the stage. The boy, representing the generation that would most benefit from the development of this city, confidently walked up to and through Dr. al-Yamani, and then turned and walked through him a second time.

This was a flourish designed especially for a Saudi audience. Dr. al-Yamani, transmitting from another location in KAEC, made the point that technology, industry, and the will of the kingdom had made such marvels not just possible, but repeatable in the everyday.

King Abdullah thanked SAGIA and Cisco for its efforts and left the tent immediately after the conclusion of the presentation. The kingdom's business-friendly environment notwithstanding, the royal family's influence is still pervasive, and the king's reaction to the presentation was critical to Cisco's standing. From a technical standpoint, it had been a success; there were no glitches, and the power and reliability of the company's IP connectivity was ably demonstrated. Although they had not expected effusiveness, it was difficult for Cisco's team to evade the suspicion that all was not well.

The plan for the KAEC ICT network was near completion. The bid to build the very system Cisco had created was submitted. Opinion was mixed. Some, considering the corporation's reputation, the strength of its plans, and the extent of its commitment to KSA, rendered the selection process a fait accompli. The team had knowledge that other bids were being considered, but most were confident that the quality of the Cisco offer would be the deciding factor. This visit from the king took on a curious indecipherability. Cisco's team of analysts, business operations experts, and engineers, so used to quantifying data and determining potential in terms of energy saved or revenues created, found there was no means for quantifying a king's approval. And so they waited.

It was not a long wait. On the way back to Jeddah, later that day, word came that Cisco had lost the bid to build KAEC's Internet and phone systems. Worth tens of millions of dollars, the contract had gone to the Swedish tech company Ericsson. Despite the prevailing internal opinion and the relationships cultivated and sustained, when it came to actually building out ICT, Cisco would cede ground to another company. As anyone who has ever battled for business and not succeeded can attest, the blow was numbing, and it temporarily obscured all the positive indicators in the firm's Middle East strategy.

Many were surprised by the outcome. In November 2008, Dr. al-Yamani confessed to *Bloomberg Businessweek* that he had been "shocked" by the decision. "But," he concluded, "sometimes dollars talk."[10]

That the quality of Cisco's work was still highly regarded was only cold comfort. KAEC was the most important development in the kingdom. The economic downturn, which would prove cataclysmic in just a few months, had ground down development of the five other cities. Some, such as a development on the Yemeni border, were being reconsidered due to security factors. The implications of losing the contract were grave.

LESSONS LEARNED

No one likes to come up short after meticulous planning, but it was hardly the end. Cisco's relationships with SAGIA and Emaar, the Economic City still were strong, and its status as a trusted, confidential advisor was untarnished. And yet, the team had lost an important bid, one that would have legitimized the Cisco smart and connected strategy, especially for those who had been watching revenue drivers impatiently. The planning had been excellent, the work tireless, the overtures to Saudi partners sincere and informed. Was it possible to monetize a smart and connected city development after all? Had all this work generated a blueprint that could win universal admiration but no revenue? These questions were too complex to evaluate within all the potential markets, but the wrong answer in KSA could have rendered them moot on the global level.

As it happened, the "first generation" referred to in this chapter's epigraph had come and gone with astonishing speed. The 2008 financial crisis proved devastating, but the economic cities in Saudi Arabia were moving forward. They were essential to the goals of a nation.

Within those cities, a synthesis had taken place. More than six years later, they are slowly but inexorably moving toward their occupancy and building targets with smart city value propositions at the core of their growth strategies. While two parties never see a city in the exact same way, Cisco and Saudi Arabia did manage considerable overlap in their vision of urban function and technological underpinnings. Today that vision is driving the growth of both existing and new cities in the kingdom. Real estate development districts have smart city value propositions at their core and will continue to offer opportunities to network architects as KSA's economic cities expand and prosper.

One short-term benefit was Cisco's ability to bid for more architectural contracts. Whether or not the company built the smart and connected network, their mark was all over the blueprints, which was a marketable commodity in every negotiation for smart and connected city building that followed. What Cisco put into those first models and plans, it extracts years later as cities and their services react to increases in population and stretched natural resources.

Regarding the business strategy used, there was room for improvement. Months on a technological frontier had taught several key lessons:

- **Smart and connected city building requires a diversified client portfolio.** The technology required to connect cities was not the only step up in complexity. It also was imperative to deepen the analysis of the macroeconomic trends affecting the plans of those clients. This would help provide better advisory services, as well as alert the firm to subtler market indicators.

    But even with more detailed analysis, there could be problems with the forecasts of developers. Funds committed to large-scale building projects may trickle into a quarterly budget or never materialize.

- **Creating smart architecture does not guarantee the creator will build it.** The team did not turn their backs on their Saudi partners after Ericsson won the bid, because Cisco had committed its resources and industry to their goals. In the best case, the firm advises, plans, drafts, and then builds the ICT network architecture. But this is not a given.

    Cisco's John Chambers told *Bloomberg Businessweek* that Internet architecture is not just a key to Cisco's future success. As more cities and nations adopt it, the pathway to a more connected, affluent, and influential existence is created for large population segments. "It's about raising standards of living and creating large middle classes." This indeed is corporate influence "on a much bigger scale."

- **Do not let initial setbacks cloud judgment.** While the bid loss to Ericsson did necessitate a thorough review of the methods employed, the team had to push beyond the sense that a large loss is an absolute indicator of error. Fortunately, neither the team nor the company leadership inferred a strategic failure from a tactical setback. The needs of Saudi Arabia and many other nations were too pressing for Cisco to pull the plug on a bold play for the future.

Far from being a disaster, the loss of the building contract in KAEC was a particularly sharp growing pain. It would not be the last, but it was the most instructive. Fortunately, the "first generation" of effort did not end in the death of an essential idea.

[1] "Oil Rents (% GDP)," The World Bank Data, data.worldbank.org/indicator/NY.GDP.PETR.RT.ZS?page=1 (2016).

[2] "al-Saud" literally translates as "the House of Saud." Saudi nationals do not use the latter phrase, even when conversing with English speakers.

[3] Dr. Mona AlMunajjed, "Women's Employment in Saudi Arabia: A Major Challenge," Booz & Co., 2012, https://ncys.ksu.edu.sa/sites/ncys.ksu.edu.sa/files/Women002_5.pdf.

[4] Ulf Laessing and Asma Alsharif, "In Saudi Arabia, a Clamor for Education," Reuters Special Report, February 10, 2011, www.reuters.com/article/us-saudi-education-idUSTRE7190MJ20110210.

[5] "Saudi Arabia's Economic Cities," Economic Cities Agency, SAGIA, www.oecd.org/mena/competitiveness/38906206.pdf.

[6] Nicolai Ouroussoff, "Saudi Urban Projects Are a Window to Modernity," New York Times, December 12, 2010, http://www.nytimes.com/2010/12/13/arts/design/13desert.html?pagewanted=all.

[7] "Saudi Arabia's Financial Rating Raised to 'AA-/A-1+'," U.S.–Saudi Arabian Business Council, press release, July 16, 2007, www.us-sabc.org/i4a/headlines/headlinedetails.cfm?id=138&archive=1#.VBxtVGRdU7s.

[8] "Saudi Arabia Industrial Ambitions," Businessweek, 2007, https://www.yumpu.com/en/document/view/4892364/saudi-arabia-businessweek.

[9] American writer Dave Eggers, in his 2012 novel A Hologram for the King, invents a team of one salesman and three young computer engineers sent to KAEC to stage a presentation for an unnamed multinational technology corporation. Ignored by local officials, forced to play cards and sleep for lack of purpose, they wait for the king as if for Beckett's Godot. With due respect to fictional license, Cisco's team was always at center stage, working far too closely with their partners to sleep on the job. As for the hologram presentation, you can watch it today on YouTube: www.youtube.com/watch?v=FI2kqt3KNxA.

[10] Peter Burrows, "Cisco's Emerging-Markets Gambit," Bloomburg Businessweek: November 12, 2008, www.bloomberg.com/news/articles/2008-11-12/ciscos-emerging-markets-gambit.

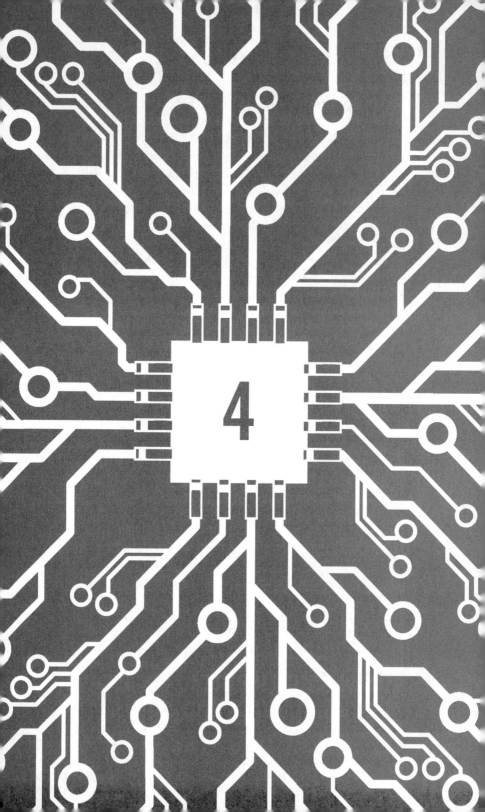

SECOND CHANCE: SONGDO, KOREA, AND THE CITY LAB OF TOMORROW

T HE LATTER MONTHS OF 2008 WERE NOT, to say the least, encouraging for Cisco's smart and connected city strategy. The world's financial crisis seemed to intensify with each passing week; capital for building was drying up, and ambitious plans from past business quarters toppled one after another. The loss of the KAEC contract, in this context, did nothing to alleviate the gloom.

Yet it was precisely at this point that Cisco received a much-needed endorsement and jolt of energy. The company's corporate leadership strongly supported the smart city vision and was ready to give it another try, in Saudi Arabia or elsewhere.

Wim Elfrink, then chief globalization officer and head of Cisco services, had participated in many of the company's meetings in Saudi Arabia and had remained supportive of the team's efforts until the Ericsson bid was announced. As most veterans of the corporate world can attest, that was no guarantee he would continue to acknowledge the team or stay supportive. It is certainly not atypical for senior executives to distance themselves from campaigns that are perceived as failures. Not so in this case. It was clear that Wim and the rest of the senior executive team at Cisco believed the work on citywide network architecture was not only sound but essential to the company's growth.

Simultaneously, the work was endorsed and the team was encouraged to push even harder into new markets. Saudi Arabia would remain a chief concern, but Cisco would expand its reach to other countries and municipalities.

As it turned out, Saudi Arabia was the source of their next important connection. The smart city team had interacted with representatives from SK Telecom, a South Korea–based conglomerate that had won a contract to create an end-to-end telecom network for the sixth of KSA's economic cities, planned for the Eastern Province. This city was an early casualty of the financial crisis, left in a raw planning stage for want of capital expense funds. But SK had also done advance work in the Incheon Free Economic Zone (IFEZ) of South Korea, a development rolled out in 2003 that was still in its technological infancy.

Cisco had been aware of developments in IFEZ for several years. Gale International, the multinational real estate developer tasked with the construction of greenfield projects within IFEZ, had made overtures to top executives at Cisco, Microsoft, and other technology leaders. By 2008, KAEC's development was slowed but not stifled by the economic downturn, and city building had moved beyond the concept phase. The timing was much more propitious.

South Korea had made remarkable progress as a regional economy since the war-ravaged decades in the middle of the twentieth century. In 2006, its GDP was among the top fifteen in the world; brands such as LG and Samsung had established global profiles, and manufacturing had become a national juggernaut. When the financial crisis of 2008 hit, the Koreans felt the shock but stabilized quickly through a combination of stimulus and smart monetary policy. The nation avoided a textbook recession, since it experienced but a single quarter of losses before recovering from the crisis in a manner most nations would envy.

Nonetheless, the country needed to adopt a new strategy to maintain its position and relevance. Its neighbors Japan and China supplied relentless economic pressure. Japan, with a population two and half times greater, enjoyed a reputation for unmatched innovation and vigor, while China's enormous size meant it had more than enough manpower to compete as a technology provider and close the gap created by Korea's hard push toward excellence during the last century. The Koreans had relied on manufacturing for their gains, but that formula would no longer create success in a world that rewarded information and service providers. Whether analysts were focused on Korea's advancement or maintenance of a position, the economic drivers that had brought prosperity would have to be changed out for a new design.

Some observers believed that in a world where marketing is an ever-expanding concept, applying to nations as much as private citizens and companies, Korea, despite its success and affluence, had not established an indelible reputation. As a McKinsey analysis concluded in 2010: "South Korea lacks a cohesive, differentiated brand in the minds of those outside the country. There is no touchstone that brings to mind an idea, or a feeling, about the country."[1]

This tells only a fragment of the Korean story and reflects a Western bias common to many consultants. While it may be true that many Americans or Europeans still might struggle to say what South Korea is about, its brand was (and is) well established in Asia. South Korean culture had established a coolness that easily united the nation's technological sophistication with the arts and less tangible elements of its Korean identity. Japan, China, and other neighbors had no trouble identifying Korean sophistication, savvy, and business acumen, and often followed in the wake of its cultural trends.

Nonetheless, in the coming fight for multinational anchor tenants, the Koreans realized they would have to fight to distinguish themselves from those same neighbors. While the success of attempts to export Korean identity across the Pacific are debatable, it is also true that the country needed to increase its information exchange with the West. Historically, Korea's regulations had complicated foreign investment, leaving a great deal of capital and brainpower outside of its borders. With the flow of information and growth of corporations erasing national borders, Korea needed both a reason why multinationals should come and incentives to keep them there, spending and investing.

Geography alone was a selling point. Most of the cities in Japan, China, and Southern Asia were along short flight paths from Seoul. Incheon International Airport (ICN) opened in 2001 as a replacement for Seoul's outdated international hub, Gimpo. Already regarded as one of the world's best, ICN was just under three and a half hours away from a quarter of the world's population. Of course, its two primary economic rivals were also neighbors. Promoted in the right way, Korea could become a hub, the launching pad from which the expanses of the other Asian Tigers could be accessed. More than that, it might become the entity that drew together rivals into a mutually advantageous position. Without the equivalent of NAFTA or any other trade alliance, the Asian powers still operated mostly as rivals. If South Korea could not realistically keep apace of China, which had more than twenty times its population, perhaps it could exploit its position as a midrange power: dealmaker, haven for foreign corporations, all while remaining a technology leader. But its status as a technological leader required constant management, adaptation, and boldness, even as the economic crisis continued to wither other nations' balance sheets.

To attract foreign direct investment (FDI), South Korea launched a plan to develop new free economic zones. The first, the Incheon Free Economic Zone (IFEZ), was among the first on the continent and perhaps the most essential of nine planned within the country. Regulations would be loosened for multinational anchor tenants, who would also find a nation with the world's highest bandwidth penetration per capita (it retained that ranking as of 2014) and Internet connectivity speed far above the global average.[2] These factors were essential technology enablers, the foundation for the last element, which was to build a new city made to run on information.

Yet despite the importance of modeling a free economic zone, there was little time to spare; work had already begun on Korea's version of the city of the future. Located just thirty-five miles west of Seoul and organized around a new airport, IFEZ would have to become a test tube of sorts.

The free economic zones were multifaceted appeals to business from around the globe. Promising a combination of tax advantages, a business-conducive environment, ample and comfortable accommodation for travelers and tourists, and a seaport, in addition to the Incheon International Airport, IFEZ was an open invitation to work luxuriously and well. The question remained how many businesses would accept the overture, especially since the economic heart of the zone had been, until recently, a tidal basin where commerce extended barely beyond fishing. Incheon was a large, growing city, but it was not a budding international presence.

When the 1997 Asian financial crisis hit, influential analysis described South Korea's situation as akin to a nut in the nutcracker, competing as it did with a savvier technological power in Japan and far greater resources in China.[3] Increasing the national profile as a knowledge economy was a direct response to this evaluation; additionally, the Incheon authorities embraced the primacy of airports as a central concept in their strategy. John Kasarda, director of the Center for Air Commerce at the University of North Carolina's Kenan-Flagler Business School, neatly defined this idea when he coined the term "aerotropolis"; in his view, the airport (which he contends will only increase in importance in coming decades, as cities become more powerful than some of the nations containing them) should be a hub that connects and centralizes all city traffic. The IFEZ planning commission did not take this concept to its literal end. The airport was located northwest of the zone's center on landfill that connected two islands in the shallow sea. Thanks to high-speed airport railroad, travel to downtown Seoul reliably took less than an hour, but the airport itself offered abundant amenities, including a golf driving range. Success for Kasarda's aerotropoli is predicated on ease of getting in and out and proximity to other destinations.

Critical though this airport was, the nerve center of the economic zone was located several miles to the south, and it too had sprung out of shallow water. This was to become the city within a city: a technological marvel and international destination named Songdo International Business District. Songdo (meaning "island of pine trees") would be a retreat for South Koreans feeling choked and overwhelmed by the density of Seoul, but this was to be no mere suburban landscape. The IFEZ designers were intent on building a business destination to rival Hong Kong or Singapore from the ground up, much like KAEC. However, the urgent need for Songdo to become an actual destination was even greater than Cisco had seen in Saudi Arabia.

Gale International had won a prize of astonishing size and complication. Although it had just begun to look outside the United States for business opportunities, it nonetheless landed a contract to lead the planning and construction of a brand-new city in an economic zone that also was barely out of the planning stage. Gale needed top partners to fulfill a grand vision of a new city: architects, municipal authorities, construction firms, and, of course, telecommunications and technological infrastructure experts. The company realized that a city of the future needed to incorporate the best practices of the day; the goal was for Songdo to achieve citywide LEED certification (Leadership in Energy and Environmental Design, a rating system developed by the American Green Building Council), lightning-fast connectivity, and wide-reaching access for residents and visitors alike. From the beginning, the ambition of the plan was on display. Even more so than at KAEC, the entire world was invited to participate in its execution. This would be an easy, advantageous process for multinational corporations because Songdo City was to be smart and fast. Unlike the historical example of a budding city, which grew richer and larger based on economic trends too big to manipulate, Songdo would anticipate its traffic and growth patterns and put in place the necessary infrastructure before a single resident arrived.

Naturally, the promise of such foresight and functionality appeared grandiose to some. Others saw a dangerous precedent. Anthony Townsend, author of *Smart Cities*, remarked that Songdo's architects apparently wanted "to engineer serendipity out of the [urban] equation."[4] Conservative business analysts are never swayed by grand revenue projections, even when they are supported by cutting-edge data and case studies. Combining the enormous price tag, grand plans, and relative inexperience of Songdo's primary stakeholders, the doubters would have abundant fuel for their arguments over the coming years.

In 2008, it looked as if Microsoft would design Songdo's ICT infrastructure. A memorandum of understanding (MoU) was signed in early May, and Bill Gates expressed his satisfaction with this opportunity "to create an ideal technological infrastructure in which access to digital capabilities experiences is an inherent part of the living and working environment across people's lives."[5] Meanwhile, the team was learning more about the plans for Songdo's International Business District (IBD), and talks with Gale and other project stakeholders were intensifying.

As often happens with partnerships, Microsoft and Songdo could not find a way to build on the promise they saw in collaboration. *Fast Company* writer and *Aerotropolis* coauthor Greg Lindsay reported that Gale "threw over" Microsoft for Cisco.[6] Microsoft had not made any missteps, nor had Gale somehow poisoned the wine Microsoft and the South Koreans had shared. Lindsay's *Fast Company* article suggested that Gale, as the project leader, felt a "plumber" like Cisco was a better fit for the enormous task of building out Songdo's ICT infrastructure. Whatever the explanation, Cisco's approach was infrastructure up, not application down. In that respect, its perspective was similar to how a developer would approach this subject.

The firm's initial stake in Songdo was modest. Gale International engaged Cisco in a consulting contract focused on a technological business park in Songdo's IBD. Gale and POSCO E&C, a Korean construction firm, were the primary stakeholders in Songdo, but they were working closely with political leaders to ensure that the national economic strategies were baked into the city's design. It was a curious consortium of partners, but it was evident to all that what was needed to make Songdo a smart city was not just the right software but the ICT infrastructure, the "plumbing" that had become Cisco's trademark over the previous two decades. Now the company had the opportunity to apply that trademark infrastructure to a services-led, smart city model. It was new territory for the Cisco team, as it was for all technology companies.

The concept of a smart and connected city was so new that even innovative companies such as KT and LG CNS were hard-pressed to develop practical applications and service-orientated infrastructure. Tomorrow City, a museum-cum-showcase in Songdo, is an excellent compendium of trial ideas; many are thought-provoking, but monetization is another matter. There are examples of sound engineering and innovation within this futuristic, six-story structure, but some of these prototypes of the South Koreans' "U-Life" concept (short for "ubiquitous life") struggled to gain traction in Songdo and the greater market. For a price tag of $82 million, Tomorrow City is stocked with automated waiters, health scans that recommend exercises, and even robot dogs that dance in unison.[7] It is an enjoyable visit, but much of Tomorrow City does not speak to the underlying mechanics of a smart and connected city. There is little evidence here of a network, the complex but essential mesh connecting urban functions that are traditionally siloed and managed independently. This futuristic museum was in fact too futuristic; on display was imagination running free, leaving one with the impression that there was no business case or quantitative analysis tethered to design. There was no evidence that customers—citizens, FDI, or the municipal or central governments—would generate any demand for Tomorrow City's possibilities. And there was no evidence at all of how these applications and machines might connect to people and to each other.

This was why Songdo needed a plumber who understood and was able to design smart city services that addressed real urban needs and functionality. It also needed another source of investment capital. Fortunately, Cisco met both criteria.

FROM PLUMBING TO NETWORK ARCHITECTURE AND IOE

By the time Cisco stepped into a much larger role in Songdo's development, it was clear that market trends were shaping their mission even as they negotiated their role with the other partners. Songdo would need a tremendous ICT network to function at its forecast capacity. Tomorrow City, fine for the imagination, was not tethered to the problem of how technology could be monetized for providers. Gale needed Cisco to help build the city's nervous system and central brain. Cisco, meanwhile, realized that in a difficult global financial climate, Songdo was the best opportunity for the smart and connected city concept to take root. Working hard to recover from their setbacks at KAEC, the company still needed to construct a smart city pilot that could be examined and evaluated by potential customers. When those clients were governments and municipalities, however, the "infrastructure up" perspective of a plumber would not be sufficient to implement a network that interfaced with residents and workers on so many levels. Cisco would have to create metrics for measuring not only the likely popularity of the network's features, but also how the city might pay for and profit from them. Plumbers may help build cities, but they cannot plan them without direct participation in the process.

Cisco's vision for implementing the Internet of Everything at the root of a city would become the most important product in their inventory. At this stage, the team held out hope that one size would fit all, and that a single network infrastructure could underpin the dozens of cities slated for building in Asia and emerging markets in the next few decades.

Ultimately, Cisco would pledge millions in Songdo investment. Cisco's then-CEO John Chambers met publicly in 2009 with Korea's president at the time, President Lee Myung-bak, to announce the company's intent to commit its capital to research and investment in Korean ventures. The company's investment also lent legitimacy to the government's efforts to create an economic powerhouse and travel hub; this, hopefully, would contribute to increased FDI and a virtuous cycle of foreign engagement. President Lee was correct that an investment this large was "a difficult decision" against the backdrop of global recession, but there was another angle to the partnership that was advantageous to all parties and, in fact, to the rest of the world. Songdo was to be a prototype for sustainable urban life, an example of how a city could reduce its carbon footprint and resource usage in a world with ever-increasing population and climate-related problems. Korea's willingness to "go green" was noted by Chambers as a deciding factor behind Cisco's commitment. Moreover, other companies were expected to endorse the vision. Incheon's mayor also went on record with a projection of three hundred companies that would choose IFEZ as a headquarters for their Northeast Asian operations.

The world business press took note of the photos of President Lee and CEO Chambers shaking hands, pledging to work together. But the big news was assigned dollar signs. The *Korea Times* pegged Cisco's investment in Songdo and the nation at large at $2 billion USD over five years. At this level, numbers became somewhat symbolic for both parties; each was eager to demonstrate the depth of its commitment to the other and to the smart and connected Songdo IBD. While the headlines were splashy, the details were at once more nuanced and provisional. There was no blank check or huge line item in Cisco's accounting. The company's investment in Korea would be gradual and contingent on the success of early ventures. Should the market prove to be as responsive and favorable to investment, it would continue.

The designated recipient of Cisco's investment was the Korean technology. As an opener, the firm pledged $32 million USD to a Korean venture capital fund. This was a tactic the company had used in other countries as a means to assess the viability of future investment. Should the signals be green, more and diverse investments would follow. Although Songdo IBD was not named, Chambers favorably referenced Korea's commitment to "green growth" as a primary reason for his confidence in the partnership.[8] Songdo IBD was mentioned, but only in the greater context of national investment. Yet a fusion of the investment quotes and the ambitious project was inevitable.

With this news coverage, Cisco's brand was undergoing a fusion with South Korea's. The focal point was the city rising on land that was recently reclaimed from the Yellow Sea. For the first time, a smart and connected city plan had the attention of the world. There were no complaints about the headlines: By announcing the projected investment figures, Cisco was putting its money where its mouth was and spotlighting its determination to set new trends in smart city development.

These were bold maneuvers, especially since words used to describe Songdo's IBD and the entire IFEZ region included "test bed," "test tube," "laboratory," "petri dish," and "showroom." While accurate to a certain extent, the fact remained that their work in the Saudi Arabian economic cities meant Cisco's team was not starting from a blank slate. The deep reservoir of knowledge collected during the design of the Economic City's network infrastructure was directly applicable to the tasks the team faced in Songdo.

Despite Cisco's confidence in the network its design team planned to create, there were many implementation challenges distinct to this market (as would be the case in all subsequent market plays for the smart and connected city solution). Primary among these was that Cisco was just a little late to the party. Gale International had been on board with Songdo for five years, and the first buildings were already up and would need to be retrofitted with Cisco's network capabilities. These buildings did not have uniform technological features, and it would take time to retrofit them.

To better describe the enormity of the planning, it should be noted that Cisco's task was to create a network for Songdo's International Business District; there were eight other developers working on other aspects of the city. Perhaps it is still inevitable that so many companies will be involved when the business and residences of entire cities are being planned. Nonetheless, so many plans being created simultaneously is an excellent example of smart and connected city development in its variegated, early form. The technology was developing rapidly, but the population numbers were still well beyond the faculties of any one firm, international or local.

The pool of stakeholders was also heterogeneous, especially compared to KAEC. Gale's U.S. office had brought Cisco on board, but this did not ensure a smooth integration with the company's new arm operating in Songdo, which was staffed mostly by South Koreans. POSCO E&C and representatives from U-Life LLC were more established and had their own sets of protocols in place. Cisco's team soon discovered the need for a technological lingua franca, a set of operational standards and practices that would apply throughout the new city.

As to Songdo's visual affect in 2009, it was hardly polished. There were more tire treads, mud banks, and remnants of seashells than people and buildings—testament to the massive engineering effort required simply to put down dry land here.

Known as Inchon until 2000, Incheon had been an independent city for less than thirty years when IFEZ was created. The site of the landing for United Nations troops, mostly U.S. Marines, commanded by General Douglas MacArthur during the Korean conflict in 1950 and a turning point in that war, Incheon now had nearly three million residents. The only means by which a brand-new city within a city could arise was through land reclamation, and 1,500 acres (approximately 2.34 square miles) of tidal basin had been filled in. When Cisco's advisory team first arrived in this development-to-be, it was not difficult to imagine a time when water covered the entire Songdo footprint.

ESTABLISHING A TECHNOLOGICAL LINGUA FRANCA IN SONGDO IBD

Building smart cities brought a new layer of analysis to the work of Cisco teams. Real estate developers such as Gale must consider the cost of a development first. So not only did the team have to map out the design of network infrastructure, the cost of raw equipment, and its installation, Cisco's partners needed these figures to be interpreted in terms of square-foot costs, real estate services, IT services, and capital recovery models. Not all the services Cisco could provide would make money. Some would not even generate customer revenue. Given this, which services would be used to build the Songdo (and South Korean) brand, and which could be depended on to recover capital expense outlays? Cost trees, detailing where revenue would flow between the various government agencies and service providers, were drawn up for stakeholders to address the question.

With Gale International owning more than 60 percent of the stake (POSCO E&C held 30 percent, while Morgan Stanley Real Estate held the remainder, just below 10 percent), Songdo was, by definition, the largest private real estate development ever seen. However, there were strings attached. The substantial loans required for construction came from Korean banks, and the Korean government did exercise oversight of the project's planning and implementation.[10] The relationship between the investing companies, invested private sector players, and Korean officials would prove complicated at times. For Cisco, diplomatic relationships with both public and private representatives were requisite, since even Gale International founder Stan Gale would, in 2013, describe working with the Korean government as "a process that has evolved and improved year after year."[11] It would take some time for the Cisco team to come up to speed on the existing relationships between partners. The business models created proved helpful in this effort. Gale International, very much the leader of the project, relied on Cisco team members, and was pleased with the amount of time they made for customers and stakeholders alike.

But Gale's Korea office had its independent concerns and reactions to Cisco's proposals for the ICT network. The design team quickly discovered that deliverables agreed on with the U.S. division were not necessarily what Gale Korea expected or even wanted. Meetings between representatives of all the different stakeholders were required simply to smooth out the planning sessions and expectations. If bringing a subsidiary and its parent company into accord was difficult, Cisco's initial engagements with POSCO E&C and U-Life were yet more complex. "We needed drawings of existing buildings for review in order to integrate them into our IP-enabled, converged network plan. As we discovered, however, cooperation with the national partners had to be earned," said one of the consultants involved in the project. Eventually, with another assist from Gale U.S., the design team was given the data and materials it needed, but this was further indication that some South Koreans were less than enthusiastic about the participation of internationals in the creation of this glittering technological jewel. Already the nation was a leader in connectivity and technology, and it had a deep, well-trained workforce. As an American-based company, would Cisco be so hubristic as to see its contribution to Songdo as the second coming of MacArthur?

Had Cisco's top management not seen that the world was changing, the situation might have remained tense. As it was, the Cisco ship was turning to stay within a shifting current of business practices. Smart and connected city development was not going to be a simple, colossal windfall of orders for routers, switches, and other elements of the ICT infrastructure, as originally envisaged by some of the company's sales leaders. The Cisco team had to understand the ecosystem these cities and their multiprocessor developers would be plugging into and anticipate how customers and partners would want to adapt to a smarter, interconnected world. They also had to perceive opportunities for ROI and sustainability. Naturally, this took a great deal of time, patience, and negotiating, even as the team began to undertake the enormous task of bringing the Songdo IBD to life.

Simultaneously, Cisco business analysts, engineers, and network experts began the process of putting the entire IT ecosystem, from end to end, down on paper. This created a conflict in the modeling. IT projects typically project ROI within one to three years. With a project of Songdo's magnitude, such forecasts were hopelessly unrealistic; ROI expectations of seven years or more created some internal disagreement, while public officials were advised some smart city services would require the government to provide suppliers with incentives. Fortunately, Gale International, as a real estate developer, was used to long ROI projections and did not require a hard sell.

With the world economy still a bleak picture, the analysts were worried about the effects of ten-year cost recovery models, which were further complicated by considerations of technical refreshment cycles. The team conducted market research into consumer-facing services in other Korean cities and extrapolated costs relative to brand-new development in Songdo. Since the same team had engaged in this type of analysis in Saudi Arabia, they trusted their methods, but as yet were not wholly confident in their conclusions. Songdo was a place where three-quarters mastery was typical. If indeed the development was a test tube, all the partners took turns adding to the mix and recording the result. This was not random experimentation: analysis was undertaken within the context of operational models and extended business-use cases. Once the work was ready to interface with actual Songdo residents, however, they would have to take time to listen and respond to feedback.

It was with a measure of relief that the Cisco team embarked on the development of the ICT network. Although this, too, was being taken to a new level in Songdo IBD, at least the team was back in its wheelhouse.

To execute, a set of guidelines was developed that covered all ICT and telecom building specifications in the business district. Addressing the differences in the existing buildings was the logical place to begin. One might not have enabled its video connectivity; another, perhaps, did not have integrated utility services. This was an opportunity for Cisco to present not just standards but a roadmap for ever-expanding connection throughout the district and greater Songdo.

Cisco's Korean partners were convinced of the company's technical bona fides, but throughout the meetings it became clear that full trust between both sides hinged on understanding the conditions of this new ecosystem and addressing them through solutions that could be monetized. The teams could not succeed solely on the basis of product excellence and Cisco's reputation as the best plumbers. They had to address, anticipate, and finesse political negotiations. Private or public, Songdo IBD was to be a locus of national pride and empowerment. While the network was agnostic, as enablers of the U-Life vision, Cisco could not be.

To encourage a synthesis between the Korean and international partners and reassure the watchful business and technology press that Songdo would happen, even in a terrible economic climate, Cisco invested in new joint ventures. Gale International and POSCO E&C had formed New Songdo International City Development (NSIC), and the IFEZ authority had governance over their venture. By 2011, Cisco had invested in Songdo U-Life LLC as a minority partner; U-Life LLC was an entity created by NSIC and LG CNS.[12] Later in 2011, Cisco announced collaboration with KT Corporation, South Korea's largest telecom interest, which was named kcss (Cisco took a minority stake). Having understood the opportunity, Cisco now partnered with another Korean entity to go to market jointly in the smart city space across Asia and emerging markets. All the while, the press received regular assurances that Cisco's investment in Songdo IBD was rich, assured, and directed at the development of Korean technology and improved quality of life.

If these announcements seemed boastful, the entire concept of a free economic zone was predicated on a delicate balance between the comforts and perks offered to international visitors and the needs of a local populace. While South Korea's leaders declared IFEZ and the other zones essential to the nation's future, it did not mean everyone who lived in these zones would be happy with the arrangement. The firm found that immersing its teams within the IFEZ ecosystem was a means to make contributions that were both smart and meaningful to anchor tenants and the local population alike.

BUILDING THE CITY OF THE FUTURE TODAY

Cisco's contribution to the Songdo IBD experiment was to converge all city systems and services on a single network. Utilities, water recycling, security, telecommunications, and key resident-facing verticals, such as medicine and education, were top objectives. Songdo, however, was not to be just fast and smart. The capable development team and master plan architects at Kohn Pedersen Fox were attempting to build a livable city, friendly to pedestrians and bikers, free of excessive traffic congestion and exhaust, with ample green spaces and waterways.

Serious planners do not use the word "utopia." In a twenty-first century context, however, the ideal city experience would seamlessly mix and support business and high living standards, while providing ample green spaces and cutting the carbon footprint down to a manageable size. Some of the most excitable commentators could not resist outlandish projections of an ideal life for citizens and businesses in Songdo. That, of course, created both great expectations and skepticism. The city builders could hardly complain, since Songdo's great promise was highlighted in a great deal of promotional material.

Although residents were already moving in by 2009, Cisco had barely begun to lay down the crucial IP-enabled network that would create the structure for delivering and processing a city's worth of sensor data. Before the team had unpacked its bags, observers were looking to it for quick wins. Although Cisco felt the pressure, the team's tasks weren't headline-ready. As with many technological endeavors, what worked well and quietly often made less news than unfulfilled projections or the steady downward indicators from the world economic stage.

As opposed to brownfield smart and connected projects, which endeavor to tear down silos to integrate services, Songdo was to be silo-free from the outset. Every building, every function relevant to citizens and business tenants, would connect to a central locus. As the human body's vascular and neurological systems receive and transmit information, so too would each occupied cell in Songdo IBD.

Cisco's primary concern was functionality. The applications and secondary tools plugging into the network—tomorrow or twenty years from now—would make Songdo distinctive, but they would only be as useful as the supporting network was reliable.

Nonetheless, Cisco brought game-changing technology to the table. A key component of Songdo's connectivity would be Cisco's TelePresence. Initially marketed to corporations that could afford its heavy price tag, this multicamera, state-of-the-art transmission unit creates facsimiles of people that can fool the eye and ear. Marketed as an ideal means to reduce travel costs, NSIC and Cisco took the considerable risk of outfitting all homes in the IBD with a telepresence (TP) screen. Rather than just another appliance (although as ubiquitous as microwave ovens), the TP units hopefully would play a key role in reducing traffic in Songdo. Consultations with medical professionals, government employees, and educators could be anchored in the home, removing the need to travel for office visits and meetings, much as TP did for employees and consultants in private enterprise. Children, even those sick at home, could join classrooms remotely. For professional services, office visits could become personalized "house calls." The benefits of virtual, two-way communication seemed endless, but all were predicated on an assumption: that Songdo residents would share the developers' enthusiasm. The enthusiasm seemed to be a foregone conclusion in this technologically progressive nation.

Touchscreen wall pads would bring control of each apartment's environment—including lighting, heating, air conditioning, and power usage monitoring—to an intuitive locus point inside the home. Remote access to the wall pad controls could be sequenced through smartphones and tablets and computers. Not only could a pocket-size device access the controls of a home from outside, but the sensors within the home could be programmed to help residents remember small tasks and set climate controls before they returned home from work. Songdo was meant to run on information; in the process, it would create a new layer of information exchange and enhancement, which in time would become known as the Internet of Things.

Political conversation had advanced to the point where a smart city would de facto be green, and Songdo was to be a leader in shrinking the urban carbon footprint. At Gale's insistence, development within the IBD was designed with Leadership in Energy and Environmental Design (LEED) certification in mind. A product of the U.S. Green Building Council, LEED ratings had become a seal of approval for new development around the globe. LEED certification applied to nine different categories of building of residential, commercial, and public spaces. By mid-2012, 13.7 million square feet of Songdo's IBD had achieved some version of LEED certification.[13] The sensor systems connected to climate control features throughout the buildings could slash energy waste across the district. Other environmental engineering feats, such as the pneumatic system that literally sucked household garbage down to a subterranean processing and recycling center, storm water capture, and grey water recycling for agriculture, could deliver residual benefits such as reduced traffic noise (there are no garbage trucks) and potable water saved for drinking rather than irrigation. Plus, the city was literally green: 40 percent of the IBD was open space, and its Central Park, located almost dead center of the district, may not have been the busy travel hub that defines an aerotropolis, but to Seoul residents, it was a welcome respite from relentless urban sprawl. Additionally, 40 percent of rooftops would become green space. In all, 75 percent of Songdo's waste was to be recycled in some shape or form—it was a city that put pedestrians and cyclists before drivers and electric and high-occupancy cars in better parking spaces than standard gas-powered transport. RFID technology could read license plates and detect traffic clusters before they became traffic jams.

At its best, Songdo would anticipate the behavior and preferences of residents and visitors alike, staying a step or two ahead of the action and keeping everything clean and under control. At last, a city could serve its masters efficiently.

As smart and efficient as these plans were, their promise would be locked down until some primary questions were answered. How would they be paid for, and how would services and their delivery generate revenue? This was the hard reality factored out by some of the airier descriptions of Songdo's great promise. With fiber-optic broadband creating the mechanism for the district, the team drew on yet more consulting skills that conventional wisdom would not assign to Cisco: They began thinking like real estate developers and builders to solve problems.

THE PRICE OF CONNECTED REAL ESTATE

C isco's smart and connected city building team had grown out of an earlier connected real estate division. Several of its most important members were accustomed to approaching problems from a real estate development vantage point: How much would it actually cost to put Cisco technology in apartments, buildings, and streetscapes? What was the cost per square foot, and how did the price affect real estate and IT services? Gale International was accustomed to performing this analysis, but Cisco's consultants had to incorporate it secondarily into their work on the IBD development. City planning required that they not just see the IP-based platform, but how it interacted with other building features and, most importantly, could add value to the development. To do this, the team needed the calculations for cost per square foot in its business models as much as Gale or POSCO did. While they could bring the expertise to the table, for Cisco at large, this was a new way of calculating business.

The services that would overlay the network were trickier. Which would recover costs in Cisco's models? Which could be charged for? Which were suited to building the U-Life brand and might be revenue negatives? The team's business models needed to provide answers to these questions, all of which were vital to a city that, in 2009, was still, to the untrained eye, a construction site.

Still, the question of occupancy was always relevant. Revenue would increase as more commercial and residential tenants moved in, but by how much, and how quickly would Songdo be filled? Capital expenses, operating expenses, pricing, and occupancy rates had to mesh in a complicated matrix. The partners on the ground expected such intricacy, but this was all new to the sales teams and others in Cisco's command chain who expected favorable and quick return on investment.

As the business model's timelines stretched and grew more complex, the team saw the way to explain how Songdo could work, even with recovery of costs projections that pushed a decade-long limit. They looked to real estate models for guidance; if Cisco aspired to building citywide network infrastructure, the firm needed to model on a citywide scale as well.

Real-estate-orientated, long-ROI models needed to be packaged in different ways for different stakeholders. When meeting with government officials, it was important to highlight the services the team did not expect to be profitable and suggest government incentives. For internal review, they had to manage and defend the long ROI projections. Answering to so many stakeholders and partners, each cleaving to a distinct perspective, was back-breaking work. But there simply was no other way for the team to maintain Cisco's position in Songdo's command capsule.

Cisco compiled long lists of services that could function off their IP-based platform. Some already existed in the catalogue; others, such as widespread telepresence, were as new to the design team as to anyone else. This illustrates how quickly the Songdo project changed the perspective of everyone who worked there. Cities had been designed from scratch in the past, but never with so much technological capability embedded.

The services had to be divided into subscription-based and entitlement categories. For instance, it was unreasonable to expect Songdo's residents to pay for intelligent, sensor-based streetlight management; urban citizens the world over expect it for free. Could these services be paid for with price increases on real estate square footage or land sales? Cost reductions made possible through Cisco's technology were other considerations. Safety and security are citizen entitlements, but could Songdo reduce the size of its police force if it increased the number of cameras at street level? The answers were not always apparent, but these are the sorts of questions that were formulated in meetings, while back at the office, business analysts modeled a realistic fee uplift generated by the technology's convenience and superior logistics. Songdo was being sold as a city with ready-made infrastructure; tenants need only move in to plug in. That meant there were convenience fees to be extracted by the city planners and governors. To provide benchmarks, the team canvassed the South Korean cable industry and tangential concerns to determine how much Songdo could reasonably charge to provide its consumer-facing subscription services.

Every day, there seemed to be new threads of data to pursue. The logistical underpinnings of the work were not new, since many of the business analysts and technical architects had engaged in similar number-crunching exercises in Saudi Arabia. But the Korean market, its demands, and the array of partners were unique; it was unrealistic to expect every meeting would be a success. While the descriptions of Songdo as a laboratory were becoming mundane, they were never inaccurate.

Though more demanding than it had ever been, the work generated an exciting sense of possibility. Interlocking security, telecommunications, energy, and utility maintenance into a single infrastructure contained myriad implications for improved urban life and smarter, more efficient usage of resources. The better Cisco understood this new ecosystem, the more value it could derive from its IT infrastructure and the applications and services it supported. Of course, this is precisely the function an intelligent network is meant to feature; the relationship between users and a network by its nature is symbiotic.

SERVICES ON TOP OF INFRASTRUCTURE, FOR TODAY AND TOMORROW

Naturally, services and applications command the first word in any urban development. Machine-to-people interfacing sparks our curiosity as well as concern. The ubiquity of sensors in Songdo's plan was a major selling point for its designers and the IFEZ governors, but there were less enthusiastic reactions. Some pointed out that sensors on meters and streets that monitored usage patterns could already be found in some European cities, but this is where the ubiquitous nature of U-Life was driven home. This was technology so deeply embedded in a resident's environment as to be literally everywhere. As early as 2005, the press had been invited to marvel at Songdo's services. Radio-frequency identification (RFID) technology on cars that transmitted geo-location information or home-automation options that could open a front door or select music by way of a smartphone were touted as natural outgrowths of South Korea's vibrant technological awareness. Many of Songdo's features (such as RFID cards) had been prototyped by LG CNS in Seoul and other cities; from this perspective, Songdo was the next evolutionary step for a nation on the front line of IT innovation.

But while U-Life was South Korean in origin, Cisco had a stake in making it successful. The company needed approval of the people who would actually live with and use these services. Try as they might to model success in this realm, as with any scientist, there came a time for the IP architects to stand back and observe the reaction to their work.

When they did, a social component to technology usage emerged; in a nation as capable and proud as South Korea, the work of a foreign multinational like Cisco does not automatically win plaudits. In fact, its participation in Songdo's creation stirred some resentment (occasionally, a "Cisco Go Home" banner would take flight from one of the new apartment buildings). While this was troubling—the IP architects shared a genuine desire to see that Songdo *worked*—they knew the partnership with Gale International, POSCO E&C, and Incheon authorities was the true test bed of their ability to work toward South Korean interests. The more they proved that they could understand their practical and strategic concerns, the firmer those relationships became.

But these positive developments were also behind the scenes. The South Korean press generally had been supportive of Songdo and willing to accept that it would not be perfected overnight. Western commentators, however, voiced concerns early. Well before Cisco became a partner in Songdo, concerns about privacy were voiced; "ubiquitous life" sometimes took on a less benevolent connotation in translation. Of greater concern was the uncertain public response to services. Offerings were one thing—adaptation and popular usage were quite another. As early as 2005, B.J. Fogg, an expert in human behavior and persuasive technology at Stanford University, was pushing back against some of the U-Life publicity. While acknowledging that South Korea derived a "competitive advantage" from this opportunity to test services in the open market, he was less sanguine about the near future: "I foresee that many services will fail . . . that's the nature of experimentation. They should be prepared for the frailties of human nature to emerge."[14]

Once reviews from early residents began to roll in, there were obvious indicators that some service verticals were not performing as the developers hoped. Telepresence, the key to improved medical and educational services (as well as a concurrent decrease in travel), did not take off. A large percentage of Koreans were skeptical of this expansion of their virtual home and less willing to invite "guests" to observe them in private than hoped. RFID technology, still at the cutting edge of innovation when Songdo's developers broke ground, was being supplanted by newer technologies. The people were moving in, and real estate prices were high, but Songdo's new residents clearly were intent on experiencing the city in ways the business and service analysts could not predict.

More troubling were the larger economic indicators. The anchor tenants who were targeted by the advantages of the economic zone were not coming quickly enough. Construction on the Northeast Asia Trade Tower (NEATT) was suspended. The nation's tallest building, the NEATT was to be the jewel in NSIC's crown, a mixed-use, state-of-the-art activity hub that displayed the best of Songdo's smart features. While the building structure was complete by 2011, it was not open for business, and many interiors were left unfinished as the expected economic uplift failed to arrive. The economic climate was still too bearish, and the future too uncertain, to prompt many multinationals to invest in Songdo. Until 2014, the NEATT stood out as a sore reminder of Songdo's unfulfilled expectations.[15]

The slow growth was not testament to the effort of the developers. There was no question about the quality of work that had gone into the IBD and surrounding areas. The South Koreans had been aggressive in the array of services they offered. Excellent schools had sprung up that were connected to top-ranked universities in the West; regulations were favorable to investment; the nation had a deep reservoir of well-trained workers to take on; the city boasted an exceptional subway system; and there was no lack of luxury features and accommodations, even a golf course designed by Jack Nicklaus. No one knew the answer, but those with real estate backgrounds, such as Gale International, could fall back on the expectation that Rome would not be revenue-positive in a year, or even five. That mattered little, however, when the streets of Songdo remained quiet and a single data control center was sufficient to monitor all the services and sensors Cisco had embedded throughout the city. Some went so far as to wonder if the South Korean government would pull the plug on the entire development, or if it had no choice but to press forward to preserve the national reputation. But as we will see later when revisiting Songdo, these skeptics were wrong and a successful smart city did indeed materialize.

THE SUCCESS OF CONNECTION VS. SUCCESS OF A CITY

Here, the story of Cisco diverges from the story of the city it helped create. The company's name was indelibly tied to Songdo: Cisco had invested heavily; John Chambers had signed MoUs and met publicly with President Lee Myung-bak; the company had pledged to build a Global Center for Smart & Connected Communities in Songdo IBD to help define innovation in Korea as well as propose smart and connected solutions for other cities.

The Cisco team had come to Songdo to help its partners execute a bold design for a modern city and had accomplished its goal. They had gained invaluable experience while working with those partners and understanding the perspectives they inhabited.

The essential idea that gave rise to the Internet of Everything was pushed to its logical ends. Cisco's connected real estate teams had been working for some years to replace the multiple networks in building construction with a single IP protocol. Still a cutting-edge idea at the turn of the twenty-first century, converged networks were now standard, and Songdo IBD proved to be an exceptional showcase of the concept. Some of the ablest members of the team were not experts in Cisco products; their value derived from their knowledge of non-IT systems and devices that could benefit from the Internet of Everything's convergence hallmark. Cisco's smart and connected city consulting was no longer a simple vehicle for Cisco products. The team now understood how to derive value from a full-on embrace of IoE principles. This, as it turns out, would prove to be an exceptionally marketable asset. More importantly, members of the team had developed a language of progress they could speak with stakeholders in many other markets. They would continue to seek solutions, but these solutions would always be presented within a context that conveyed value and would be future-ready.

Advance teams had begun to host city planners from other nations in Songdo. Cisco's networks, data analysis, and nuanced understanding of Songdo's infrastructure sent a clear message: *We can do this for you.* Critics looked at the IBD's housing complexes and green spaces and saw artificiality. But many of the decision-makers who visited saw the possibility. Those from China, who likely had viewed the decade-old "ghost cities" at their emptiest, could see in Songdo's clean lines and gradual progress a positive developmental vector. Partnered with Gale, the team began to believe its success in Songdo could be replayed, as ground was broken for new cities across Asia. The Global Center in Songdo would be an idea factory and showcase for development models worldwide.

LESSONS LEARNED

Songdo taught the team—and indeed, the industry—key lessons about the feasibility of intelligent urbanization. Each lesson had broad implications for the developments Cisco's business developers were exploring even as the work in Songdo continued.

- **There are many variables to predict the ongoing health of a metropolis.** Smart developments bring convenience, better function, and sustainability, but they do not, intrinsically, hold the extra factor that makes a city grow in sudden spurts. The popularity of a city may always be greater than the sum of its parts.

However, in the twenty-first century, it may well be that a successful city will be de facto smart and connected. Songdo, like so many other cities, is making a play for the best and brightest: the most dynamic corporations, the top talent in innovation. It defies logic to believe that this population, which is making a tremendous amount of its gains in markets related to or directly tied to IT, would settle for anything less than best-practice connectivity between its devices, homes, workspaces, and security apparatus.

• **Smart and connected city building is a long game.** Like most of the stakeholders at Songdo, the team underestimated the development and revenue time frames. The magnitude of the project was such that large numbers were thrown about and the push for contracts was overly aggressive. When the economic realities began to set in, the executives realized that they were in danger of becoming overextended. They had correctly perceived the business potential presented by Songdo IBD, but failed at first to see that not all could be realized as short-term gains.

•**Smart and connected city developers must anticipate problems, even before clients do.** The timing for Cisco's involvement in Songdo IBD was fortuitous: An innovative, ambitious nation was in a transformational stage and seeking a multinational corporation to help execute its vision.

Some of the team's complex array of skills came by design; the rest came out of a need to better serve the concerns of the firm's partners. ICT technology may indeed be the most important utility in the modern city, but the supplier of that technology must understand the intersection points with other services and critical city functions. To transcend the "master plumber" role, Cisco has had to anticipate the problems, cost trees, and revenue analysis of its partners' business and provide solutions that speak to the relevant context.

Songdo was an essential finishing school for Cisco's Smart+Connected consulting services. While each new project and market would entail a new round of research, modeling, and consensus building, the company now had a blueprint for that multistage process.

• **Smart and connected Songdo was a critical test bed for the Internet of Everything.** The terminology changed as Songdo rose above its landfill, but the critical developments were far more than semantic. In South Korea, the team began to see how an intelligent network could be executed, refined, upgraded, and replicated. Life around the control centers, sensors, cameras, and IP networks would maintain its varied, accidental nature, but the Internet of Everything would continue to function as a symbiotic nervous system. In greenfield developments, it would take root as the concrete was being poured and the roads were blacktopped; in brownfields, it would thread through isolated structures, service verticals, or districts and, eventually, link up with another connected entity. The struggle would not be to find opportunities to enable IoE. For Cisco, the challenge lay in finding motivated partners who had need for smart development and a willingness to search for the elusive solution to economic sustainability.

Cisco's executives believed they had found a viable partner in Gale International. Both companies made it known that Songdo appeared to be the beginning of a collaboration of great potential. As more civic leaders were invited to tour Songdo and discuss building opportunities, it became evident that the next market was just across the Korean border. China's growth was not as robust as it had been before the crisis of 2008, but it was still the envy of most other nations on the planet. The urbanization needs were great, and the vacancy rates of the "ghost cities" were beginning to shrink.

China had economic muscle, great need, and the open space on which to build dozens of cities from scratch. Cisco had maintained a presence in the country for years, but the borders of their engagement were about to be extended. Although the sun indeed was rising in the east, Cisco looked to China's "wild" west.

---

[1] "South Korea: Finding its place on the world stage," McKinsey & Company, April 2010, http://www.mckinsey.com/global-themes/asia-pacific/south-korea-finding-its-place-on-the-world-stage.

[2] Akamai's State of the Internet report, Second Quarter 2014, https://www.akamai.com/us/en/about/news/press/2014-press/akamai-releases-second-quarter-2014-state-of-the-internet-report.jsp.

[3] Alexey Volynets, "Case Study: Korea's Transition Towards Knowledge Economy," World Bank, 2016, http://go.worldbank.org/2KQGBF91M0.

[4] Anthony Townsend, *Smart Cities: Big Data, Civic Hackers and the Quest for a New Utopia* (W.W. Norton, 2013), p. 28.

[5] Microsoft Named Preferred Technology Partner in "City of the Future" Project, Microsoft press release, May 9, 2008, http://news.microsoft.com/2008/05/09/microsoft-named-preferred-technology-partner-in-city-of-the-future-project/#sm.0000sejqhlx73ddjydb1lilqjfiiy#7vXsTmeBmQGoO2ky.97.

[6] Greg Lindsay, "Cisco's Big Bet on New Songdo: Creating Cities From Scratch," *Fast Company*, February 2010, https://www.fastcompany.com/1514547/ciscos-big-bet-new-songdo-creating-cities-scratch.

[7] See YouTube: www.youtube.com/watch?v=IrxKIRIp3nw for a demonstration of the digitalized dogs at work.

[8] Gale International LLC, Songdo IBD press release (2015), http://songdoibd.com/.

[9] U-Life LLC was a joint 2006 creation of LG CNS and Songdo International City Development LLC (NSIC). Its mandate was to bring the "ubiquitous city" concept into functionality and apply it to essential city services.

[10] Oversight in such a massive project is necessarily complicated, and sometimes hard to define. It could be argued that POSCO, in its role as contractor for NSIC LLC, had certain control mechanisms in place, including guarantee obligations in connection with NSIC's loan financing.

[11] In-Soo Nam, "South Korea's $35 Billion Labor of Love," *Wall Street Journal* online, December 6, 2013, www.wsj.com/news/articles/SB10001424052702304579404579236150341041182.

[12] Gale International LLC, Songdo IBD press release, July 4, 2011, http://songdoibd.com/.

[13] "Korea's Songdo International Business District—One of Asia's Largest Green Developments—Surpasses Milestone of 13 Million Square Feet of LEED Certified Space," USGBC press release, June 26, 2012, www.usgbc.org/Docs/News/LEED%20Release%20Final.pdf. Estimates for 2015 put the total square footage at 19 million.

[14] Pamela Licalzi O'Connell, "Korea's High-Tech Utopia, Where Everything Is Observed," *New York Times*, October 5, 2005, www.nytimes.com/2005/10/05/technology/techspecial/koreas-hightech-utopia-where-everything-is-observed.html.

[15] In-Soo Nam, "For Rent: South Korea's Biggest Skyscraper," *Wall Street Journal* online, July 10, 2014, http://blogs.wsj.com/korearealtime/2014/07/10/for-rent-south-koreas-biggest-skyscraper/. The NEATT opened for business in July 2014. A representative of Daewoo International, which co-owned the tower with POSCO, admitted that the new task of finding tenants would be a "headache," as "prospects aren't rosy."

ENTER THE DRAGON: CHINA'S CITIES OF THE FUTURE, TODAY

THE SMART CITY BEACON IN SONGDO AND AN EXPO

A s the lights in Songdo's International Business District proliferated, the frontiers of China were illuminated in the glow. Due to the late twentieth-century rush for business touched off by China's steady growth, numerous tech companies had longstanding involvement there. Cisco, for example, was a trusted supplier of IT equipment and technology, and the company's hardware was in demand in many of the most important new developments. While the 2008 financial crisis took its toll, there was a strong case for Cisco's increased involvement, particularly as it related to consulting and IT master planning services.

With IoE generating attention and the engagement with the real estate developer Gale productive, the Cisco team saw an opportunity that scaled far beyond the reach of Songdo. China's population of 1.3 billion was nearing the brink of a 50-50 division between urban and rural inhabitants (it would tip over into urban majority by 2011)[1], and there simply were not enough building units to keep pace with the growing trend toward city life. To the south, there was India, also with a ten-figure population and ambitious plans for modernization and growth, and the burgeoning economies of Southeast Asia. From a technological perspective, Songdo was a success of unparalleled complexity and opportunity, and the news of its intelligence spread quickly.

Moreover, the company's executives didn't need to travel to China to gauge that nation's interest. Chinese municipal leaders were visiting Songdo regularly to check on its progress and generate ideas. The need for intelligent urban infrastructure was much on the minds of governments and urban planners.

In fact, when China hosted the World Expo in 2010, the months-long event worked around the theme "Better City—Better Life." The implication behind this theme was clear: China, which would be tasked with housing hundreds of millions more city dwellers in the coming decades, had a vital interest in efficient solutions to urban population density. But rather than be classified as the world's biggest urban problem, the nation instead would promote solutions. China was determined to attain a mark of distinction in the ongoing attempt to refine the world's sense of city life.

The future has been on display at World Expos around the world since 1851. China was determined to set new benchmarks in 2010: more participating countries, more corporate displays, and most important, more visitors than any prior Expo. The BBC reported that nearly £38 billion (nearly $59 billion USD by 2010 exchange) had been spent on the event's production, while 189 nations and dozens of corporations and other entities contributed displays for the six-month-long event.[2] As to the visitors, Chinese authorities set weekly quotas in the hundreds of thousands to keep the nation's residents coming, paying admission, and adding to the final total. In the end, the nation reported that 73 million Expo visitors had witnessed this massive display of new, efficient urban living.

The *New York Times* somewhat skeptically noted that just 5.8 percent of those visitors were from other countries,[3] but China had made its point. It would provide test labs for solutions to assuage its own overpopulation problems. Indeed, the following year Shanghai's government collaborated with the United Nations and the Bureau International de Exhibitions to produce *Shanghai Manual: A Guide for Sustainable Urban Development in the Twenty-First Century*. A declaration within the document laid out propositions for future urban life; among these was a pledge "to build a smart and accessible information society." IT network infrastructure was established as a goal on the same plane as an "ecological civilization," "balanced growth," and "sharing multicultural society."[4] Smart and connected features were no longer luxuries; China recognized how vital they were to attaining a stable future of cities that could withstand the pressure of rapid growth.

If Cisco could not pick up its accomplishment in Songdo and carry it to Shanghai, the company's pavilion at the Expo was the next best thing. As the sole global purveyor of IT technology to set up shop, Cisco also spared little expense when it came to demonstrating the future (which in this case was called "Smart + Connected Life" to strike harmony with the Expo's primary theme). But the Expo's organizers expected no less; Cisco's participation was sealed by formal agreement in November 2009. It was an arrangement of mutual benefit and affirmation of the standing Cisco had attained in China. In 2008, John Chambers and other top Cisco leaders officiated over memoranda of understanding with Chinese officials that formalized the company's role in advancing IT technology and development in government and business spheres. As in Korea, there were pledges of investment, including $20 million for a new leadership institute associated with Peking University.

The symbiotic nature of these plans was an excellent example of investing in both the long-term benefit to the company and the social good of a business partner. Chinese municipal planners would have direct access to Cisco's expertise, while the company would benefit both from business contracts and a deep source of well-trained technicians and business leaders.

When it came to smart and connected city building, Cisco wanted to align its business strategy with China's development strategy.

Despite this alignment of priorities, business deals still had to be struck. The pavilion included private areas where government leaders could review building plans and technology demonstrations. Planners of many nations toured during the Expo, but of special importance were the Chinese delegations, any of which could follow up a pavilion visit with a short flight to Incheon. This, in fact, is what many Chinese leaders did. Songdo's ability to pull in Foreign Direct Investment and anchor tenants was still being tested, but the IoE infrastructure that knit together the IBD quickly proved to be a powerful draw. It was, perhaps, inevitable that a smart city infrastructure would come to be seen as an exportable product.

As will be discussed later in this chapter, the export process for Smart + Connected China had already begun when the Expo began.

But the Cisco team that had designed and deployed technology in Songdo saw no reason why this brand-new city should not be exported and reproduced across a market that had undeniable need for intelligent urbanization. China's ambitious plans, by one projection, could add 3.28 million square feet of floor space to its nation by 2025.[5] Songdo's builders saw greenfield projects by the dozen, provided China's economic growth could maintain its juggernaut pace.

China is too vast and complicated a country to be considered through the prism of a single marketing gambit, but the goal of covering this market with a smart and connected city campaign was logical on its face. Songdo's functionality, coupled with the abundant interest from the Chinese, seemed like an excellent export in a nation with such a need and determination to urbanize. As happens in particularly bullish markets, the language describing Cisco's intentions was in tune with the spirit of the time. Analysts, considering the urbanization plans of China, India, and other Asian nations, regularly numbered the cities to be built over the next few decades in the hundreds. Once the success of Songdo's IT infrastructure made news, there was a rush to describe the future of city building. As a consequence, all sorts of new terminology rolled out to accompany the media hype.

"City in a box" was perhaps the catchiest phrase, but it was inaccurate. No one at Cisco who had been studying the markets expected to create a city assembly. The needs and preferences of each municipality vary and are influenced by myriad conditions, including leadership, economic climate, embedded industry, and prevalence of national trends. In the aftermath of the 2008 financial crisis, governments were announcing enormous projections of financial stimulus to prop up desperate economies. China was a prominent example, pledging an estimated four trillion yuan ($186 billion) over two years to public works, including housing and infrastructure.[6] In a country attempting to align its identity with better urban life, this meant municipal works, the smarter the better.

Furthermore, Chinese visitors to Songdo were happy to encourage the idea that city building could become a reproducible, modular process. Many said that the stakeholders in Songdo simply needed to move the model over to the Chinese mainland. The Communist

Party's Politburo Standing Committee would have the last word, but municipal leaders were enjoying modest gains in autonomy. If they could facilitate the flow of PRC capital, hope for a series of Chinese Songdos could prove sustainable.

It may well prove that smart and connected city life becomes a tipping point for IoE, but Cisco believed that the Internet of Everything would also be the Internet of *Everywhere*. Its ascendancy is not necessarily predicated on the success of smart cities, especially since so few of the Western metropolises have the room for new, greenfield projects.

Since China had determined that 8 percent GDP growth was the minimum required to sustain the projected growth of urban population and building, it was reasonable to assume that stimulus and government investment would continue far beyond 2010. As Cisco's team reckoned with the sheer size and depth of the financial crisis, the mood was somber. Would Chinese municipal leaders look to build smart and connected developments as complex and large as Songdo? Could Cisco include any of these new cities-to-be in future marketing plans? A measure of conservative skepticism colored the team's thinking about the future of smart and connected cities in China.

Nonetheless, its partnership with Gale had produced enough success that the two companies began open exploration of new projects. One of the first prospects, found by Gale, was a development in the Meixi Lake region of Changsha, an ancient city and the capital of the Hunan Province. From the start, many of the players were direct from Songdo, including Cisco, Gale, and architectural and engineering firms Arup and Kohn Pederson Fox Associates. Like Songdo, the Meixi Lake development was a ground-up, greenfield project meant to be, in Stan Gale's words, "smart, sustainable, and technically ambitious."[7] Rather than contribute to urban Changsha's densely packed 3.6 million people, Meixi Lake would provide brand-new housing for up to 180,000 residents and offer a more spacious and environmentally friendly lifestyle. In many ways, this seemed to be the ideal first installment on the road from Songdo.

Yet Cisco's involvement in the Meixi Lake development did not last beyond a feasibility study. It turned out that its relationship with

Gale could not gain traction in the Chinese market. This speaks to the particular challenges of doing business in China rather than any shortcoming on Gale's part. The developer was able to push forward (along with the architects) at Meixi Lake; meanwhile, Cisco's position in China was still strong. So why did such a sensible partnership not blossom?

For one, a foreign real estate developer in China faces an entirely different set of challenges than a technology purveyor such as Cisco. After constructing a team with the requisite language and cultural knowledge, there are daunting regulatory and legal demands that real estate developers quickly run up against. And even a seasoned foreign developer will fight uphill against local competitors on the inside track. Simply put, Chinese officials may have liked what they saw in the Cisco Expo pavilion, and in Songdo if they traveled that far. They may well have desired similar developments within their own municipalities. But that did not mean they were so convinced of their value as to invest. And even if they accepted the wisdom of consultants and moved to exploit the new technology, they would not necessarily want a foreign company to assemble and maintain it. Landownership rights were another matter that was not resolved.

As for Cisco, the company was welcome in many Chinese municipalities eager to secure a multinational anchor tenant. Cisco could trade on a reputation for delivering best-practice solutions, which many believed were a cut above its direct Chinese competitors, such as Huawei. So while a Gale-Cisco partnership for China made sense for both companies, the value didn't necessarily translate for the customers they were targeting. Eventually, Gale exited the Meixi Lake project, although the global strategic alliance with Cisco continued.

A CITY OF DREAMS FOR A NEW DECADE

With China standing as the largest consumer of technological products in the world and competition increasing from Huawei and a variety of technical mergers, the pressure to sustain Cisco's profile and earnings in China was immense. The company did have some advantages, however. It had made some beneficial partnerships with Chinese companies, and its knowledge of this tricky, politically sensitive market was unparalleled among foreign multinationals. As an analyst quoted by Reuters put it, "If you want to play in the market, you have to be aware of the finer nuances, which Cisco has been very good at." Another tipped his hat directly at the then-CEO: "You would be surprised how many U.S. companies don't get China. John Chambers gets it, and that's important."[8]

"Getting" China required the Cisco team to be very selective. In a nation of more than thirty provinces and innumerable moving parts, it was imperative that the investment choices make tactical and long-term sense. This was the general principle underlying an array of projects, which on their face might seem unrelated. But each was an important step toward establishing Cisco's position as a leader in smart and connected city building.

One of the first projects was located off the Chinese mainland in Macau, one of two special administrative regions nominally under Beijing's influence, but in reality holding fast to an economic identity forged in the nineteenth century. Along with Hong Kong, Macau has its own currency, passports, and jurisdiction, all holdovers from its status as a Portuguese colony, which terminated in 1999. The city benefits from the military protection of the People's Republic while retaining economic autonomy—a complexity of the Chinese landscape often lost in descriptions of the nation as a hegemonic, centralized power. This is just one example of how a Chinese strategy can never be a "one size fits all" proposition.

Gambling had been the key industry on this island for generations; in the modern day, it accounted for roughly half of the regional GDP and made the island into an attraction even larger than Las Vegas.

In general, the casino hotel industry had been slow to adapt to IT solutions, even though its focus on customer satisfaction and security would seem to be a strong basis for exploring IoE-based solutions. The competition among casinos to provide cutting-edge amenities and amusements is fierce, and as any visitor can attest, the results are often dazzling spectacles. But beneath the display and efficiency, there is great need for the same quickness, data analytics, and IP connectivity that formed the bedrock of Songdo. Macau's gaming and entertainment industry represented an opportunity of somewhat smaller size but no less complexity.

As in Songdo, a massive building push in Macau began with a land reclamation project. Two square miles of a shallow bay had become Zona do Aterro Cotai (Macau, as a former Portuguese colony, retains Portuguese as an official language). The landfill had one objective: to pump more blood into Macau's gaming and tourist industries. The "Cotai Strip" featured three new casinos owned by the Las Vegas Sands Corporation and two by Galaxy Entertainment Group. Up against the apex of competition, Melco Crown Entertainment wanted its contribution to the Cotai Strip to be state of the art in more than one aspect: Not only would it produce one of the most sensational resort hotels and casinos, the network underneath its business would be end-to-end IP, a first for an Asian Pacific casino. Songdo, perhaps, would have greater long-term implications for urban life, but as a cutting-edge testament to the power of a converged network (and residual benefits for both customer and contractor), Melco Crown's City of Dreams (CoD), which opened in June 2009, was hard to surpass.

The ambition of the City of Dreams plan was astounding. Three hotels (Crown Towers, Grand Hyatt, and Hard Rock) account for 1,400 rooms; 420,000 square feet of space house nearly 2,000 gaming tables and machines in the casino; there is a large retail mall that includes twenty restaurants and bars; two theaters deliver entertainment (including a water show, Dancing Water Theatre, and a "Vquarium," featuring seascapes projected onto sixty-foot-high video walls) to rival the gaudiest attractions of Las Vegas. All told, CoD comprises a total of six million square feet. For Cisco, this described a network convergence challenge that in many ways was a smaller-scale replication of Songdo.

The City of Dreams project enjoyed a strong start early in the development's construction cycle. Cisco's engagement began during the construction phase, before Melco Crown had purchased any technical products. This had the dual benefit of assuring the implementation of an end-to-end IP network and assuring that the team formed relationships with the construction teams, partners, and the 130 suppliers who were tapped to outfit the complex.

CoD required 10,000 phones, 5,000 cameras, and 30,000 data ports. Obviously, Cisco was interested in fulfilling the order, but the team also supplied critical program management support, technical assistance, and quality assurance. Melco Crown could effectively cede oversight of CoD's early operations development to Cisco.

Ultimately, it was all about the network. This would be the first end-to-end, IP-enabled network in a South Asian casino. Not only would the network service Melco Crown's assets, Cisco's architecture was designed to integrate the ICT needs of the partners at hotels, high-end retail, and the food industry. CoD was a de facto city and, like any commercial (or residential) area, it needed to be outfitted for expansion. All key features that defined Songdo IBD's network architecture—flexibility, quality assurance, robustness, sustainability, and low environmental impact—applied to CoD.

Melco Crown was crafting a new flagship for its enterprise, and it needed to stand out on the Cotai Strip against formidable rivals. To meet the prescribed schedules, a multifaceted approach was necessary. Cisco's team needed to understand this project from the perspectives of operations, business strategies, client interface, suppliers, and partners. No casino is "too big to fail" in a dog-eat-dog ecosystem.

What assured the Cisco team that it had an optimal partner was Melco Crown's view of the IP network. "We believe technology is a major differentiator for a top-notch resort operator now, and that is why we chose to create the single largest converged infrastructure in Asia Pacific to support our business and development," Melco Crown Entertainment's senior vice president and chief information officer, Roger Seshadri, explained. "We regard the IP network as the fourth utility."

Each network is subject to a distinct list of requirements. A casino resort, like any institution that operates constantly and supports huge numbers of financial transactions and interior communications, requires speed, efficiency, and security of data as a baseline for operations. Security against criminal activities is also critical. Cisco's camera networks and video analytics could fulfill the function of protecting the house and players from criminal activity. No less important was security against unsolicited packets of data embedded deep in the IP network. Cisco was tasked with securing the gates at all layers of this city's function.

City of Dreams, by definition a greenfield smart and connected project, had the option of leapfrogging. Many legacy businesses and institutions are forced to operate both circuit-switching and modern packet-switching networks to conduct daily traffic over phone and computer. Packet switching is the future, but it is a technology in transition, having been essential to the development of the cloud and the Internet in the twenty-first century. Because it requires time and expense to transition entirely to packet-switching networks, many organizations will phase out circuit-switching networks. This usually means that voice and data configurations are kept separate, with voice networks remaining on legacy circuit-switching networks even as packet switching is brought in to handle the massive flood of data (which will increase as the Internet of Everything expands).

In this case, City of Dreams could jump directly to a single packet-switch network with support for voice and data protocol. This meant that CoD's 10,000 phones would all be IP instruments. It was a future-oriented decision, but it was not an obvious one. Many executives and IT departments are conservative with regard to solutions that depart from legacy assets. Melco Crown's leaders had confidence in Cisco's design, as well as the team's ability to work with operations staff and assure a smooth rollout.

The project was a success and was delivered on schedule. Melco Crown's leadership gained better control of its business strategies while Cisco readied the staff to assume the operations of the casino resort. "It was the smoothest opening we ever had," Seshadri said. For Cisco's teams, the City of Dreams was an excellent opportunity to refine their practice of assessment, business and cost modeling, advisory functions, and planning a distinct and difficult network.

JUMPING ON THE WESTERN-BOUND JUGGERNAUT

B eginning in 1999, China began pushing development beyond the coastal provinces and stimulating new industries, particularly in the western provinces.[9] In this context, the government defined three economic zones: Chengdu-Chongqing, Guangxi-Beibu Gulf, and Guanzhong-Tianshui. The urban population of these zones was expected to increase output of high-tech industry and natural resources development.

As China moved west, so would Cisco. To meet its need for high-tech development as well as the goal of 11.7 percent GDP growth for the western regions, China would need standout partners. Cisco argued relentlessly for the best-practice value of its hardware, even as Chinese competitors continued to provide cheaper versions of the same equipment. This was an old story; what was new was the effort on behalf of the tech company to promote its consulting services, which would prove another acute challenge. Maintaining the sales of hardware while nurturing the new consulting and planning services associated with IoE and city building was a formidable task for Cisco.

China's western big inland cities are projected to become among the largest in the nation.[10] While they are long-established and often crowded, the team saw ample opportunities for Cisco to expand on its smart and connected portfolio deep inland. Rather than Beijing and Shanghai, the focus became Chongqing, Chengdu, and other ascendant western cities. Chongqing and Chengdu will likely become "megacities," with populations in excess of twenty million, by 2025; by 2010, their municipal or administrative regions, including rural areas, already far exceeded that number. Here was the future.

At the same time, China was committed to the development of its national technical industry players: the makers of smartphones, telecom networks, and connected real estate solutions. For Cisco, maintaining its position in the market while encouraging overall growth would not be easy given that the pivot of long-term projections was on domestic companies. Chinese tech companies could be profitable even if they catered only to a local client base.[11] And while their products might not match Cisco's in quality, many customers would be swayed by the price differential.

It is a common observation that all business in China is political. Since the government and private sector share so many bloodlines and Beijing is capable of exerting its influence in any transaction, it would be easy to think that a national focus on city building and technical modernization would lead to receptive partners in every province. The problem with this assumption lies in a confusion of what the central government can do and what it *does* do on the local level. Beijing's influence in the affairs of any municipality cannot be counted on; faced with a strong local political leadership, it is important to build trust on that level and trust the instincts and cues of business partners. Many decision-makers in China expect to be underestimated, and they resent foreign nationals who fulfill that expectation.

The economic "megaregion" of Chengdu and Chongqing held particularly high promise, since the Chinese government had effectively made it the epicenter of the western economic push. The eleventh Five Year Plan, the latest set of benchmarks for economic, environmental, and public services, targeted the region as a key to western development by early 2007.[12] The same year, the Sichuan province and the city of Chongqing (which is classified as a municipality directly controlled by the central government) signed an agreement to promote and support the Chengdu-Chongqing economic area.

Long known for heavy industry and agriculture, the Sichuan province, and the city of Chengdu especially, was developing into a tech and information hub. The city had enjoyed strong economic performance and created the backbone for new information technology leadership. Beijing was eager to invest in the city's development, and in 2008, the need for investment became critical: The Sichuan earthquake of May 12 devastated much of this economic region. Downtown Chengdu had, by and large, weathered the shock, but 70,000 people in the region had died, and hundreds of thousands had been injured. Internet capability throughout the region was effectively obliterated. In this climate, the best Cisco, or any other multinational, could do was to apply its capabilities to relief measures. In Cisco's case, this meant deployment of mobile clinics outfitted with networking technology, which could bring assistance to some of the most remote areas. A regional healthcare "cloud"—essentially an enormous wide area network—connected ravaged villages and towns to regional hospitals. In the face of so many lives and homes lost, it was just one effort of many, but the company's efforts nonetheless demonstrated that wireless technology and video capability can be, in the event of emergency, the difference between months of disconnection and suffering and a recovery of normal life.

With commerce upended (some five million in Sichuan were left homeless), the central government was determined to rebuild as quickly as possible. Plans to make this region one of the most vital in the nation had been in development prior to the tragedy; ultimately, the earthquake enabled those plans to move forward with even greater urgency.

In April 2007, Sichuan and the independent city of Chongqing, one hundred miles from Chengdu, had signed an agreement of cooperation in the urban and rural spheres. Chongqing, an unruly powerhouse of industry only recently on the national radar, had some thirty million people living in its orbit and ambitions for modernization that rivaled Sichuan's. This pilot area, perhaps to become one of the first to refine the definitions between city and region with a modern twist, was a vast pool of development potential. As it turned out, however, Cisco's experiences in Chongqing and Chengdu would prove to be quite distinct from each other.

Chengdu's reputation as an IT center dated back at least twenty years; the Chengdu Hi-Tech Zone (CDHT) had been established in 1988, and by 2010 was the fourth largest in China. Multinational anchor tenants, attracted to the zone and its relatively low cost of operation, had congregated in Chengdu. The "Go West" policy virtually assured that this city would become a prime candidate for investment. Although it was mostly spared in the earthquake, Chengdu was still a developing city in need of modern infrastructure. Cisco's engagement, in 2008–2009, reflected both the economic opportunities and desperate needs of the area.

Cooperation with the Chinese government was a straightforward process when it came to relief. The Cisco foundation and individual employees gave more than $2.5 million to the Sichuan region in the form of cash and grants. Soon, an MoU was signed that committed up to $45 million in Cisco investment for a "Connecting Sichuan" program that targeted health and education advancement while the region recovered. Cisco Networking Academy sites were opened across the region to help teachers and students become more adept with ICT technology; universities could make greater use of our wireless networks and hardware to embed the future's technology in recovery efforts of the moment.

While Cisco's leadership led the effort to aid the population of Sichuan, the business development and consulting team continued to work toward partnerships in the burgeoning IT sector of Chengdu. Smart cities were still very much part of the long-term growth strategy. The intention was to create new business models to demonstrate the capacity of S+CC community features. Soon, the team was tying into the Tianfu Smart + Connected City Project, in particular the expansion of the Tianfu Software Park (TSP), the region's hub for ICT and outsourcing companies since 2005.

Chengdu's population was well into the millions, and the city's ICT market was advanced by national standards. Building was ubiquitous. There were modern office towers to attract FDI, but a great deal of the city was distinctly twentieth-century in appearance. Broad new roads were paved by malls and modern office buildings and created an impressive view for visitors. Beyond these, however, a visitor could see block after block of grey, compact, well-weathered housing and storefronts. The modern top layer of the city was thin. Great opportunity or daunting challenge intermingled in this landscape.

The work at Tianfu, like many S+CC developments, was projected to roll out in phases over several years. The city's strategic goal was to promote greater efficiency and interconnectivity among social services and public resources while addressing the ever-present challenge of climate conditions. Cisco's technologies would be applied to the Smart + Connected City pilot project. Unlike Songdo, the first phase was applied to a specific target. The Tianfu High Tech Park was planned out to 3.7 million square meters of construction (1.3

million, over 300 acres, were actually under construction or finished by 2012). Already established as a hub for software development, business process, and IT outsourcing, it was by definition a mix of green- and brownfield development. This was not just another business park. Besides its enormous size, TSP was home to dozens of IT and telecom companies. Anchor tenants included IBM, GE, Dell, Siemens, and many more.

The expansion, as detailed in an MoU released in July 2009, outlined how business and education were meant to intersect. In collaboration with the University of Science and Technology of China, Cisco announced the intention of building a joint green research lab inside TSP.

While the strategic goals were clear and well-considered, the TSP managers the team was dealing with were hazier on the actual deliverables. Smart and connected applications were still new enough that many in Chengdu simply did not know yet what they wanted from the technology. Cisco's consultants had to adjust to the need to give tactical advice about IT development and how advanced service delivery platforms and integration could translate into increased local GDP and revenue for TSP.

Promoting greener, safer quality of life worked well in press releases. In reality, the team needed to show how the Chengdu managers could save and earn money. TSP's size worked to Cisco's advantage: The larger the development, the greater potential return on bringing intelligence to even a single service.

The "city in a box" concept was not based in reality, but the interactive prototype for S+CC service delivery certainly was. By engaging the business community at TSP and regional hospitals and educational initiatives in Connecting Sichuan, the team could demonstrate Cisco technology and solutions within multiple verticals and for a wide array of services. The emphasis had to be on value delivered in the short term.

While this work was going on, there was no indication that Cisco or any other ICT purveyor would be given the chance to reproduce Songdo in China. The task, instead, would be to push forward vertical by vertical. Every existing city has pressing needs in infrastructure, services, or business development that might be alleviated, at least in part, by the adoption of interconnectivity within a sector that was ready to be modernized.

This incremental process would have its advantages and disadvantages. The variety of solutions Cisco could deliver would multiply, as would the business cases they could develop and present to future customers. During the research and visits to new markets, it became more and more obvious that the technology the team had helped to lay down in Songdo was needed just about everywhere. Building new cities in nations such as China, in which existing cities were already straining to share resources and could barely contain pollution and unsustainable energy usage, was more than a sound business case: It was essential to the enfranchisement of millions into the growing middle classes and, quite likely, to the sustainability of national economies.

In Chengdu, the Tianfu Park was a suitable initial public project. Partnering with a motivated municipal government, the interconnectivity the team provided formed a basis for an efficient high-tech zone and smart city management.

By 2011, TSP had undergone four phases of development and created a sustainable environment for multinational outpost offices and R&D facilities. Meanwhile, Chengdu's thousands of ICT graduates and trainees now had a strong local opportunity for employment—a critical addition to a region that had sustained an estimated $130 billion economic loss as a result of the 2008 earthquake.[13] Chengdu and the surrounding areas had come back stronger.

By 2015, development in Chengdu had scaled up, both in terms of volume and quality. Outside the city, thousands of acres were being converted into a mixed-residence community that caters directly to affluent residents looking for higher quality of life outside the east coast cities (and at prices that, while still in the millions for private dwellings, were bargains compared to the overheated eastern markets). A private, local real estate firm has rolled out LuxeLake, a massive, 4,400-acre, mixed-residence development south of the city center. Top U.S. architectural firms had been engaged to create luxury standalone houses, apartment complexes, sculpture gardens, and community service buildings, restaurants, museums, and a golf course around dredged lakes and a matrix of marinas (many houses can be reached only by boat).

Cisco was providing the Internet connectivity platform for the primary buildings of LuxeLake. Most of the development was still underway in 2014, but the implications of smart development are ubiquitous. The developers are depending on the opportunity to provide connected education and concierge services. This is an outright bid to create the same privileged lifestyle and amenities one might find in Silicon Valley. The level of success Chengdu can achieve in business and social metrics remains to be seen. But smart and connected technology is essential in any case.

CHONGQING: THE TRIAL OF POLITICS

While Cisco had been able to have discussions with the mayor and other top officials in Chengdu, most of the team's involvement during the TSP project was with the local managers. This is not insignificant; bureaucracy is the rule in China, and mid-level administrators can, in fact, wield a great amount of power. Nevertheless, the potential for business development increases when multinational companies are able to engage with top leaders. This was what happened in Chongqing, the now infamous, rougher sister city of Chengdu and origin of perhaps Cisco's most unusual and controversial smart and connected project.

The municipality of Chongqing includes more than thirty million inhabitants; the primary city contains about seven million. A gateway city, it was a locus for commerce between the affluent east and the distant western provinces and served as the nation's capital during World War II. Known for heavy industry, cars, motorcycles, and farm equipment and long served by a busy port on the Yangtze River, Chongqing had enough noise, commerce, and criminal activity to feel like a frontier outpost. But it was also growing at an explosive pace and had a powerful, charismatic leader who was determined to make the city not only safe but also modern—yet in a way that glorified China's past. This was Bo Xilai, the party leader of Chongqing, which the journal *Foreign Policy* called—as late as 2010—"the biggest city you've never heard of."[14]

Bo had been given Chongqing's party chairmanship in 2007 after serving in many important positions, including a long tenure as the mayor of Dalian, a city on the northeastern coast, and as governor of Dalian's Liaoning province. The son of one of Mao's most trusted lieutenants, his family had known prestige, persecution, imprisonment, and redemption in the course of the party's tumultuous history. By the time Cisco began to work in Chongqing, Bo was firmly in control of the city's political apparatus and was viewed as one of the most important party representatives in the nation. Certainly he was among the most visible.

Chongqing's growth, even during the devastating 2008 economic crisis, was something of a marvel; its GDP actually *increased* after the financial collapses in the West, and FDI was growing at an impressive rate.[15] Bo Xilai's predecessors had minted the "Chongqing Model," a collection of social reforms, anticrime measures, and economic initiatives, but as the party chief of Chongqing, Bo soon became the public face of the city's growth. Because Chongqing has been one of just four direct-controlled municipalities in China since 1997, connecting it directly to the sources of party power, the party chief was effectively the city boss, especially if the boss was comfortable with power. Bo, like some American mayors and governors of the twentieth century, was more than willing to exercise all the strength he could muster.

Chongqing's leaders were motivated—they wanted everything to come faster, from its trains to better traffic to cleaner, safer streets. They wanted twenty-first century standards of living and community service that could rival those of the West. And in Bo, the city had a "boss" who was determined to work in bold strokes.

In 2009, Cisco signed a memorandum of understanding with Chongqing, the scope of which was strategic and on the full municipal level. The company's Smart + Connected services platforms were to be instituted in support of city logistics, but it was unclear as yet what services would be affected. Chongqing's leadership was eager to create an environment that encouraged outside attention. Like Songdo, the tax rates were advantageous to corporations (15 percent, versus the 25 percent typical of China). And although there were millions of urban residents in the Chongqing area, in 2008, 64 percent of people living in the municipality were still officially described as farmers. Many of these people were destined to become urban dwellers. In the meantime, Chongqing had rolled out the nation's first land exchange agency. Even as he earned a reputation for dealing ruthlessly with the city's criminal element, Bo Xilai was known for his common touch and for working to enfranchise workers as the city modernized.

Like everything else in China, Chongqing was not a paragon for best practices. But it nonetheless was receptive to foreign influence and ideas, even as Bo Xilai championed a Mao-era "red culture" that emphasized party fealty with a distinctly twentieth-century flavor. He was, nonetheless, a shrewd consumer of IT technology who realized that a successful city will be, de facto, smart and connected. Cisco believed it could work with this sort of leadership.

As in Chengdu, a primary step of the collaboration was to build out an existing industrial park that could act both as a model for S+CC services and provide support for city services as built out network infrastructure. In addition, Cisco was expected to facilitate the manufacturing of telecommunications products within Chongqing; considering the city's extensive infrastructure and advantageous trade position, the forecasts for telecom business were bullish. Tapping into the national interest in clean tech, Cisco also pledged to develop a Joint Laboratory for Green Technologies and an Innovation Center. Like the Shanghai Expo to come, these centers were meant to be launching pads for ideas generated both within Cisco and by local partnerships. The objective was to promote the company's technology through example and interaction until the city was committed to implementing the network infrastructure the team was laying down in TSP and Songdo.

Chongqing came to Cisco with specific projects. The "Five Chongqing" initiative was an opportunity to promote smart and connected technology through a broad range of civic goals. The five categories—healthy, green/forest, accessible, livable, and safe—were meant to better the lives of residents while assuring visitors (and anchor tenants) that Chongqing was a pleasant, reliable place of business where opportunities could be pursued in a modern, efficient manner. Given enough time, video capabilities could have positive impacts on healthcare, traffic, and other aspects of urban life complicated by fast development and dense population. Sensor networks could aid parking and downtown congestion (as in Barcelona).

There is no denying that Chongqing wanted surveillance, and a great deal of it. Its infrastructure lacking, the municipality was working with Hangzhou-based Hikvision Digital Technology, the world's largest supplier of video surveillance, to install and connect 500,000 cameras throughout its urban sprawl. This is many times the number of cameras employed by similarly sized cities (New York City, in 2013, doubled the number of surveillance cameras, bringing the city total to 6,000).[16] In the United States, debate and indignation raged after the *Wall Street Journal*, working off interviews with Hikvision executives, reported that Cisco was close to finalizing a deal to help build the camera network. Other multinational tech companies, such as Intergraph in Hewlett Packard, were also in the running for contracts.

The *Wall Street Journal* article raised questions about the difficulties of doing business in China. It quoted Hikvision's president, who pointed out the serious safety concerns in Chongqing. The report also noted that the debate over the use of surveillance equipment was hardly exclusive to China: Civil libertarians in many nations have drawn attention to the potential for camera and sensor networks to be used for repressive purposes.[17]

Bo Xilai was also attempting to root out what he described as metastasized corruption within the city government. "Without help, the disease will become fatal," he announced in December 2009, referring not so much to the criminal underworld as the old way of getting the city's business done. A leaked cable by the U.S. consulate in Chongqing described a wharf culture of organized crime that was similar to Hong Kong's Triads, given Chongqing's centuries-old river harbors that link western China to the sea. In addition, he declared that public morals had become lax. He waged a campaign against the city's red-light districts and emphasized the need for safety in the streets. Always quick to consider the angle of foreign investment, Bo was shrewd enough to realize that business would not take root in a city with a reputation for unsafe streets and neighborhoods. His decision to outfit the city with a great deal of surveillance was informed by a desire for social order, to be sure, but the financial aspect of his thinking was just as important.

Cisco was committed to expanding Internet network infrastructure throughout China's cities. The core function of IoE technology is connectivity: When a strong service delivery platform is in place, multiple services can make use of it. On its own and through partnerships, Cisco was looking for opportunities to develop a single city service or asset for multiple purposes. A surveillance network can generate multiple benefits for a community, including traffic enforcement and control, crime detection, parking enablement, and many more. Once the infrastructure is in place, add-ons, at a fraction of the cost, become possible.

This is why Chongqing's proposed camera network was exactly the sort of smart and connected development the team had been championing. It would illuminate and refine important silos of city function—such as traffic control and citizen safety—while carrying potential for civic revenue. Over time, it could create a mesh for a variety of services, which could share accumulated data and become, collectively, smarter.

It is of critical importance to understand that Cisco was negotiating with Chongqing over the sale of unmodified network infrastructure. Beyond the obvious benefit of winning business, each city deal is an opportunity to create technological infrastructure and advance the concept and execution of Internet network connectivity. By doing business, the benefits of living in a connected city can be demonstrated.

Considering Chongqing's economic position and the determination of its leadership, there seemed to be far more potential benefit to putting down agnostic infrastructure in Chongqing than immediate harm. A common conviction then, as now, was that a modern city, with complex communications, would ultimately be freer and more open than one without. Beyond this, Bo's business deal tactics are also too easily reduced to black and white, especially when they are divorced from his strategic objectives. The abuse of political dissidents and other "undesirables" cannot be separated from the robust economic ties connecting China to the rest of the world (and, indeed, connecting many other countries with definitions of civil liberties not aligned with Western nations'). Multinationals often at least are in a position to lead by enabling education and employment everywhere they do business. This alone will not make a repressive regime tolerant enough to suit all critics. Still, socially responsible companies can deliver much more than products and services by remaining a vital part of the business of these countries.

In Chongqing's case, Bo's reforms created enemies on multiple fronts. In early 2012, his police commissioner and trusted police deputy, Wang Lijun, fled to the American consulate in Chengdu in search of asylum, having received a surprising demotion and expressing fear for his safety. It was the beginning of a strange tale that soon involved a murder accusation against Bo's wife and speculation about Bo's own declining fortunes, the latter of which proved well-founded when Bo lost his party chairmanship and disappeared.[18] The tabloid-ready details were not, to the thinking of many China experts, sufficient explanation for Bo's demise. Soon enough, reports surfaced that Bo's government had taken cyber surveillance to extremes; there was evidence he had used cloud computing and other sophisticated methods to create "a comprehensive package bugging system covering telecommunications to the Internet."[19] Wang Lijun had enabled the surveillance of internal party communications, including those of leaders who outranked Bo and whose favor he courted. Officially charged with embezzlement and bribery, by 2013, Bo's fortunes were irreversible and he received a life imprisonment sentence. The progress of "Peaceful Chongqing" and other technological advancements he had championed slowed down.

But with its strategic location between the Jialing and Yangtze Rivers, Chongqing continues to push aggressively for infrastructure modernization. Recently, a city official told me that Original Equipment Manufacturers (OEM) in Chongqing had produced more than one hundred million smart handsets in 2013 and were looking to produce three million cars in 2015. As an important hub along China's new Silk Road, the massive railway project linking China to Europe, Chongqing is linked directly to the industrial center of Duisburg, Germany. Freight trains, running three times a week, can make the trip between these two cities in thirteen to sixteen days—a significant improvement over the standard of thirty-four days via container ship. Bo's public downfall notwithstanding, massive infrastructure improvements and expansions are a priority under Chongqing's new leadership. This is still a city to watch, and one that can take the lead in smart and connected technology as it deepens its economic ties to the rest of the world.

The irony of one leader's downfall also illustrates a fundamental truth about the neutrality of hardware and software. Surveillance did, in fact, lead to trouble in Chongqing, and it did not spare the very man who had directed it. Technology companies can do only so much to secure against inappropriate use of the products they create and sell. The cautionary element of the Chongqing drama to users and purveyors of Internet of Everything technology may be, simply, that these solutions will be successful only when they benefit the many instead of the few.

A SUCCESSFUL PARTNERSHIP IN HANGZHOU

Cisco continued to push for S+CC initiatives in other provinces and through other means. While the limelight was still on Chongqing, the Cisco China team forged a partnership with Insigma Corporation, an IT services and software outsourcing provider based in the Zhejiang Province. Zhejiang is a prosperous, coastal province, and its capital, Hangzhou, is yet another example of booming Chinese urban economy where the municipality, businesses, and citizenry have all prospered. Insigma, founded in 2001, was the sophisticated counterpart Cisco needed in order to approach the China market from another angle for both hardware and consulting services.

Hangzhou is an old city with a well-established power structure that remains in sync with Beijing and yet maintains an unusual, flexible hold on regional autonomy. To become established here, it is necessary to learn how each step forward might affect existing relationships. The businesses of Hangzhou and Zhejiang take the long view and are famous in China for their business acumen. The effect of every transaction is weighed in relation to its potential impact across the market and social fabric.

Insigma's position was particularly advantageous due to its origins. Yunhe Pan, the company founder and executive vice president, had also served as the president of Zhejiang University, among the most prestigious in the province and nation. The company's 5,000 employees are drawn regularly from the student body and faculty; it is not unusual to meet former professors of economics and engineering in corporate headquarters. Beyond the draw of talent, Insigma benefits from its positioning at the crossroads of the city's elite and best-educated citizens. Since education had long been a primary conduit for Cisco's corporate social responsibility, they had a great deal to discuss with Insigma's leadership from the outset. Beyond that, the company's approach to enabling municipalities was very much in accord with Cisco's.

A key preliminary step was establishing a research and development center in the city in 2011. This signaled both Cisco's commitment to the region and a willingness to work with the very student population that was so essential to Insigma's growth. Soon enough, collaboration followed. With Insigma, Cisco partnered to develop a smart city study and business case for Hangzhou. In this way, Cisco created a forum for their solutions, methods, and products while building relationships with the city's decision-makers. Unlike other cities in China, in Hangzhou, Cisco's team could move forward in the presence of an accepted, established corporate entity. This model required only that Cisco persuade the government to employ their consulting strategies and hardware.

To ensure Cisco had a reliable sales channel for hardware in Hangzhou, the Cisco China team and the global S+CC specialists built a joint company, Connected Cloud International (CCI), with an Insigma subsidiary, Qware Technology. CCI was a vehicle for research, development, and sales of S+CC platforms and cloud computing services in the national and international markets. Cisco was obligated to fund initial rounds on the condition that affiliated companies would purchase agreed amounts of Cisco hardware during the funding years.

Cisco was impressed by Insigma's ability to discuss the concept of smart and connected city services with their end customer. Since that end customer most often was a municipal government, this often required business cases that demonstrated the values that could be added to a city's holdings. Streetlights, for example, make an excellent basis for value adds. Since a municipality in China will likely own all the streetlights within city limits, it will already own a deep network of transmission points: cameras, sensors, and other IoT components can be mounted on the lights and be connected to an existing power source. The potential savings of LED lighting could be mapped out by adopting the technology in Insigma buildings; to test this use case, the company purchased 70 percent ownership in an LED factory and simply charted the substantial drop in its energy unit usage. These are general concepts that have informed many projects for Insigma and CCI; the applications spread across the network of urban function, including power supply, transportation, smart building, food and drug safety, and citizen services. Some of the best S+CC use cases have arrived in these forms. Although China often is described as a nation transitioning to a modern lifestyle, it has, in fact, implemented many IoE prototypes that compete against solutions deployed in the West.

Insigma was a presenting partner of Cisco at the Shanghai Expo of 2010, focusing on the "Green Intelligent City" as a counterpart to Cisco's "Smart Connected Life" theme. Since then, the company has branched out into IoE services far beyond the traditionally green, energy efficiency services.

China can take the lead in the collection of civic data since there are fewer legal impediments to breaking down silos. Insigma has been able to propose and implement e-government and real estate data sharing solutions that can stand as models, at least from the technological point of view. Because there are fewer immediate concerns and protests about the use of private data for administrative purposes, China can aspire to deep, interactive databases that can allow data collected by one to be utilized by others. A successful example was created for the General Office of the Henan Provincial Party Committee. Insigma helped to build out a matrix of independent electronic systems and Internet portals to allow electronic documents created by various offices to be shared with other internal party business. It is precisely the sort of free information exchange prototype championed by smart city advocates as an antidote to hopeless bureaucratic inefficiency. With an overarching "digital management solution" ready for adaptation, Insigma has helped many Chinese municipalities build internal government service platforms, devise a phase-in strategy, and collect information. This has implications for physical infrastructure maintenance, sanitation vehicle and GPS supervision, waste disposal, sewage treatment, and also connected services, such as food inspection and safety—a vital service, given the sporadically maintained food safety standards in China.

Insigma's success working for city governments has allowed them to refine the delivery and maintenance of IoE technology even as it continues to be refined. CCI will continue to participate in consulting projects and maintain Cisco's alignment with this quiet, steady rollout of smart city services.

China may have a great many services to refine, and delivery of anything—tangible or intangible—to 1.6 billion people will never be simple. But the combination of aggressiveness, high risk tolerance, concentrated power, and key partnerships means that Cisco's work will continue to be innovative, even when the headlines of the day turn bleak. The inevitable signs of economic slowdown began to appear in 2012–2013; by the next year, a wild card news item assured that Cisco's efforts in China would be a rough ride for the next few years.

LESSONS LEARNED

By 2014, the political winds, far stronger than any experienced in Songdo, were buffeting Cisco's business strategy and results in China. As Edward Snowden became famous to some, infamous to others, fresh questions about nations undertaking surveillance—and embroiling IT companies in the efforts—surfaced and consumed the media's attention for weeks. The U.S. National Security Agency, long regarded as aggressive in its tactics against other countries, stood accused of intercepting and modifying IT equipment before it was shipped to China and other nations. China, already sensitive about similar accusations concerning Huawei and ZTE Corporation, was quick to punch back. *China Daily* (English version) called for the punishment of "pawns" that had compromised national cyber security at the behest of the American government. Economic trends predicted a difficult fiscal year for Cisco; the effect of Beijing's stance was impossible to quantify, but the drop in the company's sales was bruising in any event.

The circumstances were so unusual and grave that Cisco's then-CEO John Chambers was compelled, in May 2014, to write a letter to the White House. He addressed the alleged interception of IT products and stated, "We simply cannot operate this way; our customers trust us to deliver to their doorsteps products that meet the highest standards of integrity and security." Along with a request for Washington to help restore confidence in U.S. industry, Cisco sent a clear signal to Beijing, to say nothing of existing Cisco customers, that the company acknowledged the gravity of their concerns and saw no benefit in leaving any "back doors" open in the networks they constructed.[20]

China is not a market for the fainthearted. Beijing is determined to spur innovation until the nation has reclaimed its dominant position as an innovator, a position it held through much of recorded history but lost during the nineteenth and early twentieth centuries, when Western nations succeeded in wresting control of territory and markets. To make the gauntlet yet more difficult to run, the Chinese are intent on becoming leaders in ICT. The call to "punish" Microsoft, IBM, Cisco, and other Western-based internationals did not start the fire, although it certainly fanned the flames. Supplanting these companies with their national competitors would not be a simple reaction to Snowden's revelations: It would be the fulfillment of a greater strategy.

Of course, these challenges are not exclusive to ICT companies. China's productivity is so impressive, its sophistication as a competitor and a creator so daunting, it would be a surprise to few if the level of nationwide FDI dropped considerably in the years to come. The money to be earned fueling this nation's growth has brought uncounted businesses to China's borders, but not all will be able to cross. Fewer still will be able to persevere once on the other side.

Despite these challenges, I remain optimistic about China, and Cisco's position within it. Numbers do not lie, and conditions for investment and revenue will remain challenging for several years. But the lessons derived from years spent working with the leaders of this nation hold a great deal of value.

- **Corporate responsibility is community responsibility.** Cisco's response to the Sichuan earthquake was not simply an attempt to maintain good public relations. The company's work in China has continued long enough to recognize and respect the nuances of its position in the country. No Chinese business leader will begrudge a Western company for trying to make money in his or her country. But that leader will be, in all likelihood, alert to the tendency of foreign companies to focus on short-term sales. In this market, such awareness almost guarantees that the company in question will be in for an uphill climb for market share. Indeed, why should a Chinese official work with an American company, for example, that does not evince a genuine interest in and commitment to his city or province, especially when there may well be a Chinese company bidding for the same project and offering products or services of equal value?

In contrast, when Cisco contributed solutions for new schools and Internet infrastructure, in addition to relief funds, they demonstrated both a desire to boost the local economy and to contribute to a better quality of life. Those that claim Cisco's cash reserves enable the company to "help" more lavishly miss the point. The best investments are a function of resources and time. Business plans that take the future—the customers and the providers—are good bets to gain traction. But they need to be more than investments in the company; the investment in the community at large must also bring measurable results and better opportunities.

- **Look for motivated government.** Bo Xilai in many ways was an anomaly in Chinese political circles, but his unusually flamboyant style was not what mattered most to Cisco. The key was his boldness. Bo was willing to take risks and think about his city in the grandest terms. It is precisely this boldness that will underpin any greenfield smart and connected city of the future; it also will characterize the actions of any leader who is willing to break with past methods and embrace IoE solutions with shorter success trails but extensive potential to make a city work better for more people.

Those who believe such imagination and risk tolerance are rare finds in China likely have given the market only a cursory glance. This is a nation of ambition on many levels; the ambition runs deep enough for opportunity to exist for motivated outsiders as well as the burgeoning national suppliers. But sales and consulting arms will have to be aggressive in courting them.

- **Seek co-creation partnerships.** The Insigma partnership continues to provide Cisco with legitimacy, business opportunity, and productive, collaborative competition. Any one of these elements would justify Cisco's investment in CCI; together they represent a form of insurance against market downturns that is hard to overvalue. There is no doubt that forming such partnerships is a tricky business; companies such as Cisco, with intellectual property and source code to protect, need to find a way to make the collaboration balanced. But when it happens, a company can exploit the advantage of engaging what might be competition on neutral terms. Both companies benefit from the proximity and exchange of ideas. Meanwhile, the host partner's reputation acts as an endorsement and opportunity for the visiting partner.

What is common to all these lessons is the importance of time. Investments in China necessarily are long term. This can be frustrating to companies or teams in need of quick wins, but Cisco's experience in this nation suggests no alternative. When observers discuss why Cisco representatives "get" China, the critical piece of the puzzle may well be that the subjects of inquiry have spent the time on the ground that turns business relationships into something of more lasting and complex value. China's modern business culture is evolving at a blinding pace, but the historical antecedents that shaped the country's fragile relationship with Western nations inform a great deal of decision-making. Perhaps there is no lesson beyond the one that helps foreign investors engage China as the shrewd, aggressive equal it has become.

---

[1] "Urban population (percentage of total)," The World Bank, http://data.worldbank.org/indicator/SP.URB.TOTL. IN.ZS.

[2] "China Opens World Expo 2010 in Shanghai," BBC News, April 30, 2010, http://news.bbc.co.uk/2/hi/asia-pacific/8653426.stm.

[3] David Barboza, "Shanghai Expo Sets Record with 73 Million Viewers," New York Times, November 2, 2010, www.nytimes.com/2010/11/03/world/asia/03shanghai.html?pagewanted=all&_r=0.

[4] Shanghai Manual, November 2011, released via United Nations website, http://www.un.org/esa/dsd/susdevtopics/sdt_pdfs/shanghaimanual/Introduction.pdf.

[5] Richard Dobbs and Shirish Sankhe, "Comparing Urbanization in China and India," McKinsey & Company, July 2010, www.mckinsey.com/global-themes/urbanization/comparing-urbanization-in-china-and-india.

[6] Andrew Batson, "China Sets Big Stimulus Plan in Bid to Jump-Start Growth," Wall Street Journal, November 10, 2008, http://www.wsj.com/articles/SB122623724868611327.

[7] Elizabeth Woyke, "Very Smart Cities," Forbes online, September 3, 2009, www.forbes.com/forbes/welcome/?toURL=http://www.forbes.com/2009/09/03/korea-gale-meixi-technology-21-century-cities-09-songdo.html&refURL=https://www.google.com/&referrer=https://www.google.com/.

[8] Ritsuko Ando, "Cisco takes aim at China despite trade tensions," Reuters, U.S. edition, April 15, 2010, http://fr.reuters.com/article/idUKTRE63E4RN20100415.

[9] It is testament to China's enormity that the "western" regions targeted by this economic plan are, of course, not the westernmost of the nation. Tibet, Xianxing, and Qinghai are three of the largest regions, bordering eight nations. They are also among the most sparsely populated; only Qinghai is not officially autonomous. Western expansion also meant a continuing attempt at decentralization.

[10] Janamitra Devan, Stefano Negri, and Jonathan R. Woetzel, "Meeting the Challenge of China's Growing Cities," McKinsey Quarterly, July 2008, http://www.mckinsey.com/global-themes/urbanization/meeting-the-challenges-of-growing-cities-in-china.

ENTER THE DRAGON: CHINA'S CITIES OF THE FUTURE, TODAY

[11] Steve Lohr, "In 2015, Technology Shifts Accelerate and China Rules, IDC Predicts," *New York Times*: Bits blog, December 2, 2014, http://bits.blogs.nytimes.com/2014/12/02/in-2015-technology-shifts-accelerate-and-china-rules-idc-predicts/. The IDC projects that 500 million smartphones will be sold to Chinese customers, and 680 million Chinese will be online, in 2015: these numbers are 3 and 2.5 times the corresponding numbers in the United States, respectively. Of greater concern to multinationals, IDC estimates that 85 percent of those smartphones will be products of domestic manufacturers.

[12] Significantly, the eleventh Five Year Plan goals included an increase in urban population, from 43 percent to 47 percent, and the creation of 45 million new urban jobs (a figure that mirrored the number of rural workers to be moved out of the agricultural sector). For key details, visit China Daily and China.org.cn.

[13] Vivian Argueta Bernal, "Four Years On: What China got right when rebuilding after the Sichuan earthquake," World Bank blog, May 12, 2012, http://blogs.worldbank.org/eastasiapacific/four-years-on-what-china-got-right-when-rebuilding-after-the-sichuan-earthquake.

[14] Christina Larson, "Chicago on the Yangtze," *Foreign Policy*, August 6, 2010, http://foreignpolicy.com/2010/08/06/chicago-on-the-yangtze/. The article also helped to establish Chongqing as "Chicago on the Yangtze," and compared Bo Xilai to Chicago's Democratic mayor, Richard J. Daley (1954–1976), who also built public works at a frantic pace, was quick to unleash his police units on those he considered undesirable, and was comfortable with both centralized power and corruption that favored his administration. On many levels it is a valid comparison, and instructive when it comes to understanding the modern power structures of Chongqing.

[15] Bo Zhiyue and Chen Gang, "Bo Xilai and the Chongqing Model," East Asia Institute, World Bank GDP data, http://www.eai.nus.edu.sg/publications/files/Vol1No3_BoZhiyueChenGang.pdf. In 2008, Chongqing's 14.3 percent growth rate was well above the national 9.6 percent. As late as 2013, the city was still comfortably above 10 percent growth, while 225 of the world's Fortune 500 companies had outposts in the city, up from 93 in 2008.

[16] Chris Francescani, "NYPD expands surveillance net to fight crime as well as terrorism," Reuters, June 21, 2013, http://www.reuters.com/article/usa-ny-surveillance-idUSL2N0EV0D220130621.

[17] Loretta Chou and Don Clark, "Cisco Poised to Help China Keep an Eye on Its Citizens," Wall Street Journal, July 5, 2011, http://www.wsj.com/news/articles/SB10001424052702304778304576377141077267316?mg=reno64-wsj&url=http%3A%2F%2Fonline.wsj.com%2Farticle%2FSB10001424052702304778304576377141077267316.html. The article also noted that while the Chinese market for surveillance was growing faster than any other, it still was not the biggest. The United States and Europe both represented healthy growth for surveillance hardware and network suppliers.

[18] Bo Xilai's rise in Chongqing made the world news; his fall kept Chongqing in the headlines for months. See the *New York Times* and the BBC website for timelines and examples of contemporaneous reporting. For a comprehensive treatment of the scandal, see John Garnaut, *The Rise and Fall of the House of Bo*, Penguin, 2012.

[19] Jonathan Ansfield and Ian Johnson, "Ousted Chinese Leader Is Said to Have Spied On Other Top Officials," *New York Times*, April 25, 2012, http://www.nytimes.com/2012/04/26/world/asia/bo-xilai-said-to-have-spied-on-top-china-officials.html.

[20] The vociferous tone of China's response likely could be attributed, at least in part, to a 2012 U.S. Congressional report that singled out Huawei and ZTE as security threats to U.S. interests: "Investigative Report on the U.S. National Security Issues Posed by Chinese Telecommunications Companies Huawei and ZTE," U.S. House of Representatives, October 8, 2012, https://intelligence.house.gov/sites/intelligence.house.gov/files/documents/huawei-zte%20investigative%20report%20(final).pdf. For photos and report on NSA interception referred to in Chambers's letter: Sean Gallagher, "Photos of an NSA 'upgrade' factory show Cisco router getting an implant," arstechnica, May 14, 2014, http://arstechnica.com/tech-policy/2014/05/photos-of-an-nsa-upgrade-factory-show-cisco-router-getting-implant/. The Chambers letter can be viewed at Wall Street Journal online, http://online.wsj.com/public/resources/documents/WSJ-20140519-CiscoLetter.pdf. A synopsis of the People's Daily's comment on the NSA revelations is digested at "China state media calls for 'severe punishment' for Google, Apple, U.S. tech firms," Reuters, Technology News, June 4, 2014, http://www.reuters.com/article/us-china-usa-tech-idUSKBN0EF0CA20140604.

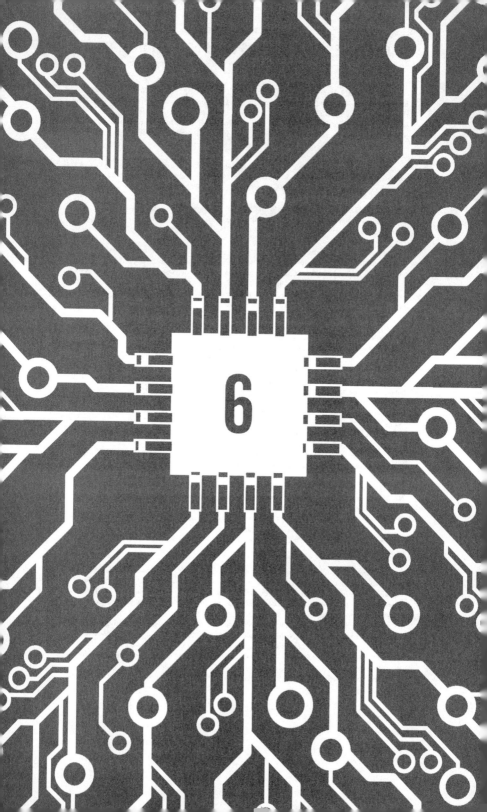

TRANSFORMING INDIA INTO A DIGITAL NATION, THE DEMOCRATIC WAY

T HE YEAR 2014 WAS REMARKABLE for India's politics and its urban ambitions. The Bharatiya Janata Party (BJP) won a clear majority of parliamentary seats and became the first political party since 1984 to gain sufficient strength to govern without coalitions with competing parties. Narendra Modi, after thirteen years as chief minister of the Gujarat state, was elected prime minister. His platform was considered reformist: pro-development, business-friendly, and intent on achieving higher status in the global economy. The nation's urban growth projections and economic competitiveness were paramount discussion points.

Modi's Gujurati record was trumpeted by his campaign. Gujarat is one of the most economically powerful and diverse states in India, and its friendliness to private-sector investment has earned it favorable international press. While there were controversial elements to Modi's management style, India, with his ascendance, had captured the world's attention. A potential turning point seemed apparent to most, although observers inside and out of the nation were split on the likelihood of potential converting to reality. "His challenge as prime minister is to prove that he can get decisive and efficient government out of a political system long unable to get things done," *The Economist* opined in the election's aftermath.[1]

A country with a population in excess of one billion has an inexhaustible list of things to get done, many of them critical to national prosperity and security. India's leadership structure, long notorious for inefficiency, corruption, and disinterest in much beyond the status quo, would not bend to the vision of a single leader. Many believed that entrenched interests would overwhelm the Prime Minister's reformist zeal, that the cult of personality surrounding one man or even a political party could not make a nation more functional. Nevertheless, the BJP majority, and its determination to get things done, fostered a sense that things *could* be different in this new era, and that the change could be for the better.

CISCO JUMPS TO A NEW HEMISPHERE

C isco also made news in 2014 by declaring that it would bet heavily on India in the near future. Noting India's youth, 600,000 new engineers educated each year (compared with 60,000 in the United States), and an internally driven economy, the firm argued the country had the tools to succeed. Of course, a bet's notoriety is a product of the risk involved. "They have all the problems of the world's largest democracy," noted Cisco's then-CEO John Chambers, in addition to a history of "self-inflicted" economic woes.[2]

Cisco knew more about the Indian landscape than many Western countries; eight years before, it had made its first big bet in India. It was 2006 when the company opened Cisco East in Bangalore, a campus that would become a hub for the frenetic activity in the Eastern emerging markets over the next several years. Cisco's chief globalization officer Wim Elfrink was tapped to lead the new center, and since 2006, the firm has bid for—and won—contracts to provide ICT planning for several urban landscapes on the top of the DMIC docket.

Bangalore was to become more than a regional headquarters. The campus was to be a state-of-the-art smart city in miniature, a step beyond standard business park functionality. In many ways, it demonstrated the advent of the Internet of Things: If Internet connectivity was the way of the future, and Cisco was ready to play a vital part in its development, why not show regional partners and customers how the technology benefited the company's own operations? The Bangalore campus would become a test bed for telepresence and other aspects of modern communication technology. This wasn't innovation for its own sake. If the underpinning technology proved unreliable, Cisco risked more than a professional loss of face. Basic internal communications and operations would be compromised.

Global communications went beyond operations; they informed a strategic shift. Cisco was essentially dividing into Eastern and Western hemispheres. San Jose, California, would remain the epicenter, but over time Bangalore was expected to develop into a command center of equal size, strength, and importance. As the Internet of Everything and its citywide implementation began to take shape in Southeast Asia, China, and the Middle East, the company would need a central command on the same side of the Pacific.

Bangalore in many ways was the ideal location for Cisco's home away from home. It has a long history of innovation and engineering skill. India's innovative energy has a strong pulse in this city, although visitors quickly learn that Bangalore is no exception when it comes to the general problems of India: decayed infrastructure, overcrowding, pollution, and poverty are all in evidence on the long drive between the airport and the Cisco campus, which is located in the city's eastern suburbs. Stretches of modern highway soon give way to roughly paved roads with no discernible lanes, insufficient traffic lights, and large groups of young men who congregate at all hours of the day and night with nothing much to do. Delivered blindfolded into Cisco East's business park, a visitor might think they were anywhere in the world. Yet even in 2015, just outside the walls of the park, visible to hotel guests on higher floors, are vacant lots dotted with tin-roofed shacks and cows. Bangalore's modernity exists in pockets surrounded by blankets of twentieth-century congestion and sprawl. San Jose is 8,700 miles away, but it may as well be a million.

"Cisco chose India as the location from which to expand its globalization vision because India has a highly skilled workforce, supportive government, innovative customers, and world-class partners that already have global capabilities," Chambers explained in December 2006. With 2,000 employees already embedded in India and an investment north of $1 billion announced in 2005, the company was poised to expand its presence in the Indian market. Even at that early date, it was clear that the primary goal would be to facilitate the planning and development of the Delhi-Mumbai Industrial Corridor.

Still, taking a wide view of Asia in 2005–2006 will help illustrate the importance of a bona fide Eastern command hub. South Korea, China, and Saudi Arabia were showing signs of tremendous development in the coming decades. Malaysia was gearing up to modernize much as its autonomous neighbor, Singapore, had done through the nineties. New airports and aerotropoli were springing up across the continent. Countries with hot climates, large populations, escalating urban trends, and a need to jump in front of the West in terms of city modernization and growth presented myriad opportunities to address some of the century's most fundamental problems and establish Cisco's brand on a global scale. Seen from this perspective, the plans for the Bangalore campus needed to be ambitious.

ESTABLISHING THE IT IDENTITY—AND PROTOTYPE—IN BANGALORE

Although not a smart and connected city per se, Bangalore for many is the vanguard of modern India. Not only is it Cisco's "second home," it is a city that has managed to define itself within a global market and become a destination both for IT talent and the companies that thrive on talent. Many people hope it is a forecast for how India will do business within its urban centers in the future.

When Cisco announced the build out of the Globalization East Center in December 2006, it was both an announcement to India's leadership and a challenge to the company at large to up its technological game. Like other multinational IT companies, Cisco's path toward a real-time, IP-based interconnectivity may seem short in hindsight, but those engaged in the effort have worked hard to adapt Cisco's internal operations even as they propose solutions to their clients. In many ways, the Bangalore campus became first a test case, then an operational standard for the firm's facilities worldwide. Simultaneously, the Center has become a real-time, breathing demonstration of S+CC capability, which can be observed, analyzed, and adapted for use in urban developments.

For Cisco, the center became a hallmark of new standard, scalable solutions as well as an S+CC prototype that could rival Songdo, in functionality if not in scope. This would be more than a business campus; it was a legitimate proof of concept for the nascent Internet of Everything.

Like many Cisco projects that began before the beginning of this decade, the Bangalore campus predates IoE-specific terminology. But the case studies that gave rise to the technology were (and are) embedded in this campus. Just as Cisco routers had led the first wave of Internet development in the nineties, new technologies showcased in Bangalore would help usher in the next generation of connectivity and speed. The best Cisco developments are symbiotic and generate value for its partners and host countries as well as for the company. Think back to the 600,000 Indian engineers graduating into the global market each year; it is in the company's and nation's fundamental interest to provide them with in-country work opportunities that are attractive, cutting-edge, and applicable to the extensive S+CC real estate initiatives represented by the DMIC and other connectivity infrastructure opportunities.

Bangalore's campus includes eight buildings, parking for two thousand cars, and more than two million square feet of open working space. It is "smart" in that it presently stands as the most successful, interactive S+CC business case in India. But its significance goes deeper: The campus is a scalable model for urban infrastructure, a condensed version of India's technological ambition. And it has youth on its side: 60 percent of Cisco's Gen Y employees work in Bangalore. These workers are changing not just the face of Cisco's India operation, but also its methodology. They have brought preferences and innovation to Cisco, and the workspace has adapted accordingly. The company believes that this, too, is the future writ small—for the time being.

In a perfect world, technology companies such as Cisco could build worksites and offices to suit their particular preferences, without the need to "translate" interior functions to the outside world. On Planet Earth, there will always be variations in energy delivery, telecommunications, ingress and egress roads, utility scarcity, and a host of potential complications within each operational silo. This reality explains the essential function of a service delivery platform that can "talk" through the lines of connectivity that attach each of a building's functions to its environment. The last mile of delivery usually is the source of many distinctive features, which means many possibilities to plan for, and next to no uniformity of process. The service delivery platform that works best is multifaceted and able to find a common language at the intersection points. As these intersection points proliferate with the explosion of IoE technology, the platform works as a linchpin for the entire smart assembly.

This platform is the source of the "seamless" IT experience and function. Seamless is a word common to promotional literature, but what does it mean? It depends on one's orientation. Facing toward the majority of a company's employees and their guests, the end users, it means they can achieve reliable connectivity for the applications and programs they use. Building managers are able to realize cost savings because they spend less time and energy maintaining optimal working conditions. For the engineers concerned with security and IP-enabled integration into existing power sources, it means the S+CC facility has clear paths for data transmission to other company and/or security sites without creating new, exploitable breaches in the IT infrastructure network.

Just as Paris and other cities once demonstrated ingenious and efficient methods of water delivery and usage for the last "modern" age, the Bangalore campus demonstrates the potential of data transmission. Unlike water, which must be contained, data encourages the breakdown of silos within a building, office tower, or business complex. Rather than chaos, this seamless dissemination of data encourages sophisticated and efficient function. This is the clear advantage of greenfield S+CC building: When there are no legacy assets to incorporate, a new building complex can operate off a single, uniform design.[3]

Bangalore assumed great importance because controlling global strategy and interaction from a single hub in San Jose was no longer practical. It was a multinational corporation's version of the lesson Rome learned when it created a new Eastern capital. That done, Bangalore needed to develop a platform onto which Cisco's campuses in Singapore, Macau, Malaysia, and elsewhere could share information, assume control in emergencies, and participate in meetings. The company needed a solution that was standardized and scalable.

Bangalore's IP infrastructure not only increased the efficiency of its internal operations; it also made the campus one of five to support a Security and Facilities Operating Center (SFOC). The SFOC is a command consul from which the security apparatus of any Cisco campus can be monitored in real time. In the event of an emergency, the buttons and codes needed to prevent access or keep operating systems running can be enabled at another SFOC. IP telephones, another standard feature, further enable a solid, seamless connection to the rest of the Cisco network.

Given several years to monitor the benefits of S+CC technology, the Bangalore campus has demonstrated a number of key value adds to the technological implications. Among the most prominent:

- **Maintenance in minutes.** With systems such as HVAC, lighting, waste disposal, and utilities working off a single redundant IP platform, routine checks can be completed in a fraction of the time required to review a segmented building apparatus. The IP platform also makes it much easier to identify the areas of a building not in use and reduce the energy output to the minimum needed.

- **Greater security inside and out.** Company buses are a popular mode of transport; each is equipped with GPS and RFID tags. If any vehicle deviates from its established route, the Bangalore security receives an alert.

- **Triage through the cloud.** Bangalore's medical center relies on telepresence to communicate with hospitals; paramedics can load relevant medical data via the cloud and expedite diagnosis and treatment options.

- **Finding the elusive parking spot.** In a feature that has had tremendous implications in city environments, Bangalore parking lots are equipped with sensors indicating where there are vacancies. Less driving means more time for workers to safely check their phones and other devices.

- **Bringing the command consul to the conference room.** The lighting and temperature conditions of meeting places can be set in advance and adjusted via IP phones. The IP network also allows for more current messaging and signage, leading to fewer disruptions. It has become much easier to handle technological disruptions right in the conference room without calling tech support. In addition to better conditions and efficiency, this allows workers in Bangalore to feel the buildings work for them.

Any of these features, isolated from the rest, could seem insignificant or even unnecessary to better living standards. But the difference in operating cost is incontrovertible. The Bangalore campus estimates that these and other features save a single facility some $150,000 annually. On the scale of a city, with the consequent addition of transit, education, and tourist verticals, the efficiency of IoE technology comes into stark relief.

BUILDING AND INVESTING FOR EMERGING GENERATIONS AND BEYOND

Beyond its infrastructure, Cisco believes that the Bangalore campus and its operations represent a fundamental shift in its approach to business. Established multinational corporations are often slower to adapt to the preferences of younger workers who enter their ranks. As the startup world demonstrates on a regular basis, it is much easier for lean organizations with smaller balance sheets and fewer investors to create new, innovative approaches to work that can attract fresh talent. Yet Cisco and other multinationals cannot cede initiative to smaller concerns. The Bangalore campus is an aggressive bid to attract young talent with the same sort of work approach and environment that might be found in a Silicon Valley or New York startup.

As of 2015, the bid seemed to pay dividends. Bangalore's workforce of 8,500 is young indeed, the single greatest concentration of Generation Y and Millennials in the global company. The "seamless" experience of IT applies here in a quality of work/life balance. The campus is open; workstations can be assigned by an employee's preference for a particular day (as well as monitored for light, temperature, and other features) via personal devices and QR codes. Rather than unyielding forests of cubicles, employees can choose to work in gardens or conduct meetings in gaming centers or telepresence rooms. With an intramural system keeping track of the "reservations" for workspace, the campus is able to maximize space usage (it stands at approximately 58 percent as of late 2014).[4]

Bangalore's promise lies in its combination of fluidity and density. The best of S+CC communities will contain their functions and sprawl to create tight, kinetic environments that are fluid and interactive. India's population, which will continue to grow younger in the coming decade (as China's and Japan's age)[5] and generate huge, raw numbers of educated workers, will need dynamic cities to keep the best of its talent at home. Much emphasis is placed on India's need to educate and train its upcoming generations, but also of great importance is building centers of industry and intellectual capital to mine the best of their talent and energy. As Cisco and other multinationals invest in India, the objectives of building smart work and life spaces and education institutions are inseparable.

WHY INDIA: THE BIGGEST PROBLEMS, THE BIGGEST OPPORTUNITIES

As it relates to the larger story of smart and connected city development, India exhibits many of the economic drivers endemic to its neighbor, China. Up to 2008, India had added 230 million people to its urban environments in less than forty years; it is expected to add 250 million more by 2030. With a population of 1.252 billion in 2013, there remains a large underclass both in rural areas and in hastily constructed extensions of already overpopulated cities. A population explosion in the robust middle class is expected over the next two decades; as in China, this class's earnings are expected to fuel national growth projections.

Meanwhile, India is putting its institutional muscle behind a construction blueprint of staggering size, much as China did with its Go West policy. This is the Delhi-Mumbai Industrial Corridor, a plan to develop a wide swath of the country's interior into a manufacturing powerhouse that encompasses transport, expansion of existing cities and towns, and greenfield, streamlined cities with Internet of Everything capabilities and ICT network overlays. A public-private partnership (PPP), DMIC's initial price tag is close to $100 billion, but realistically, the project will require much more money, considering the number of markers on the futuristic maps. Twenty-four new cities, in addition to three ports, updated freight lines, and expanding connectivity into hundreds of smaller brownfield developments have been proposed. Along with seven new manufacturing enclaves, skill zones and vocational training facilities have been blueprinted as the need for skilled technicians, highly anticipated by planners and workers alike, mushrooms.

After the 2014 elections, the spotlight on these proposals for India's transformation was sharpened and quickly became intense. DMIC had been in the planning stage for years; meanwhile, Narendra Modi had been a relentless advocate for smart building in Gujarat throughout his tenure as chief minister. Modi is a conduit for national ambitions; he did not create them. To handle the pressure created by its population, India has long recognized the need to grow smarter, as well as richer and more influential. Meanwhile, the nation's bright but unsecured future was a powerful influence on Cisco when the company decided to go east.

The work inside China proved to be harder, with trickier politics. Songdo stood out as an anomalous greenfield in a fully developed nation. India, meanwhile, had the potential to become a breadbasket for international technology companies. Although GDP growth had slowed in recent years, the 2014 elections did seem to be like a bellwether. Notorious for its dysfunctional business climate, India seemed intent on untying its own hands. After years spent trying to lay necessary groundwork, Cisco was ready to aid the push toward a modern India. The potential for growth was rivaled only by China, which by 2014 had become more challenging for many multinationals.

JAPAN AND INDIA: AN UNUSUAL PAIR OF ECONOMIC ALLIES

In terms of smart and connected cities, perhaps no nation better encapsulates both the urgent need for modern city planning and the tremendous possibilities for improved quality of life. India is an amalgam of problems created by poor city planning, or a complete lack of it. The number of people living in slum conditions reached sixty-five million in 2011, according to Indian census data, a 25 percent increase over 2001 figures.[6]

Urbanization is an irreversible trend. With the consumption of the new middle class becoming ever more conspicuous and opportunities to do more than subsist in rural regions dwindling, the cities will continue to be filled, with corresponding stress on natural resources and environmental factors. There are innumerable accounts of bad roads (no country has more traffic fatalities), overcrowding (Mumbai's population density stands at ten times New York City's), an unreliable power grid (outages are common and can last for days, with resulting millions lost in productivity and health threats, not to mention pummeled quality of life metrics), and a shrinking reserve of potable water.[7] Perhaps nowhere else is the collision course between population growth and resource management more acute than in India. Smart urban planning and necessary infrastructure, in this context, takes us far beyond the context of quality of life. Technological solutions are part of a race against the clock, while a nation's progress can lead to either prosperity or ever-growing problems and shortages.

Although industry levies an enormous tax on natural resources, India has long seen it as the key to its upward mobility. What's more, the country is diverse enough to create large pockets of great improvement. Gujarat, for example, actually saw a decrease in the number of slums over a ten-year period as it continued to stand out as one of the most prosperous regions.[8] Meanwhile, national plans for the Delhi-Mumbai Industrial Corridor (DMIC) came into being and created an interesting array of partnerships.

Political will is worth little without investment capital. In 2005, it found an international investment partner with Japan. By 2006, Japan and India announced that work on DMIC would be underwritten by rupees and yen. The Japanese government was eager to extend its manufacturing base within India's expanse, particularly for automotive companies. This economic driver also supplied the impetus for modernizing the nation's rail as well as its industrial capacity. Freight does not move quickly through India. Today, it can take a load from the land-locked states several days to travel to the ports. DMIC was conceived as a means to build and move the national product as well as those of anchor tenants.

Stakeholders and potential partners viewed the project with reserve. The difficulties stem to a large degree from competing vested interests and corruption at local and state levels. For example, review processes for new buildings were abundant, and too often an opportunity to deplete a project's resources while slowing it down. The cycle was well-known to anyone who did business in India through the nineties and the aughts.

Nevertheless, the reasoning behind the DMIC was sound. With improved manufacturing and supply chain infrastructure, India could extend its global reach. The prospect of creating more jobs in the new and galvanized urban landscapes along the corridor was the best hope of stemming the tide of unemployment as the rural-to-urban transition continued. As India burnished its credentials as a hub for engineering excellence, with Japan it gained a partner skilled in the development of transportation and shipping infrastructure. Few commentators could find arguments against the DMIC in theory; the reasonable position of doubt focused on the practical matter of doing what had not been done before.

Japan, of course, had strategic reasons for investing in a nation with which it historically had maintained only a cool relationship. In

India, it found a partner with the geography, inexpensive manpower, and incentive to grow on a scale almost as impressive as that of their common rival, China. When Japan's Prime Minister Shinzo Abe first visited in 2007, it was a clear signal that his nation was poised to become a highly engaged investor in India. The DMIC was the salient project; Japanese funds were expected to account for a third of its financing. Funding from the two nations would be blended through public-private partnerships and the establishment of various corporate and financial entities, but much of this work was far enough in the future to render Abe's visit mostly a symbolic gesture. Still, it was a beginning. Over the next several years, investment capital would indeed materialize, but not in lump sums that would allow for a rush toward engineering and construction planning. Even without bureaucratic difficulties, the DMIC would require years before physical evidence of the work appeared.

This helps explain some of the criticism that smart and connected city building has endured. Goals as ambitious as DMIC or Songdo inevitably breed high expectations, and the time frame for deliverables can be projected into years that barely impress on public consciousness. To be fair, the architects of smart cities must accept impatience as a function of human nature; skepticism and criticism are often rooted in deferred hopes. It also is quite fair for observers to account for the wide array of possible accidents and delays that accompany large-scale plans.

In the case of India, there were many hurdles: vast tracks of land would be needed to build out new cities; some environmental and engineering challenges along the corridor had no immediate solutions; financing from the Japanese, while much needed, did not come without obligations, and some in India worried about favoritism being shown to one nation in a manufacturing basin that was, in theory, open to all. From the real estate angle, there was the likelihood of cost overruns, delayed approvals, and missed completion deadlines. Above all these logistics was the ever-present question of economics: Would these new cities and connected infrastructure attract investors and tenants? Would they demonstrate value to the people who would call them home?

Even so, critics of DMIC and other Indian mega projects could not deny the utter, irreversible fact of the nation's exploding population and demand for resources. Established methods of urban planning clearly did not apply in a nation of great potential for both success and terrible problems. The old way of working had yielded too many half measures and continuing cycles of poverty and shoddy building practices.

With a strong financial partner that expected results, India found yet more incentive to break from its historical track. But this still was not enough for many global corporations to take a fresh look. For most, India's risk could not be leveraged. Cisco, however, was willing to bet heavily on India, representing the company's need to stay ahead of cycles and anticipate the next opportunity in advance of an investment rush.

DHOLERA: ANOTHER CITY PLANNED ON SALTWATER FLATS

As in Chongqing, a key objective for the DMIC was to design master ICT network infrastructure. In India, however, it remained an open question as to which city's plans would mature first. The DMIC stretches across six states; the encouragement a project might receive from the regional authorities and the resources available would vary widely. As in the United States, where a multinational corporation can expect very different treatment from one state to another, India's states can encourage or hinder business depending on their laws, economic vitality, and the level of pro- or antibusiness organization among the population. Because of this, the business strategy Cisco's team followed promised to be a much more complicated affair than the model created for other ambitious projects, such as Songdo, in which there were many partners but only one overarching authority, the Incheon Free Economic Zone Authority (IFEZA). In India, not only did the team have to reckon with ministers from the central government, the DMIC Development Corporation, and local authorities, but the influence of each of these entities might vary with geography and project to project. And while DMICDC could be seen

as a monolithic corporation, in fact it exhibited the multifaceted nature of this project's vested interests. India's Department of Industrial
Policy and Promotion, along with the Ministry of Commerce and
Industry, represented the government at large and held a 49 percent
share in the company's stake. Japan's Bank of International Cooperation (JBIC) held 26 percent, with the remainder being split between
three private Indian corporations.[9] This was a PPP juggernaut with
many channels for funding—or objections to plans in the making.

When the Cisco team first arrived in Songdo, there was visible
development: hotels for team members to stay in, roads connecting
to Seoul—sufficient indicators, that is, to show that a city was in the
works. By contrast, the Dholera Special Investment Region (SIR),
part of the DMIC project, seemed almost as unlikely a place for a
new city as the Saudi Arabian desert. It did, however, sustain a local
population of approximately 40,000, most of them living in small villages as subsistence farmers. It was hard to believe that DMIC officials
anticipated a metropolis of 349 square miles (903 square kilometers),
a footprint larger than Mumbai's. Yet the plan Cisco was engaged to
create was intended to enable the many stages of development.

It is important to remember that Songdo's planning stages
stretched back to 2001; approximately seven years had passed before
Cisco was brought in to consider ICT overlays to the city's master
plan. By 2014, Dholera was still not a business destination, but it
has been on the drawing boards only since 2007. Laying out urban
planning, trunk architecture, securing approval on state and local
levels and committed financing requires years of labor. In this case,
the team was able to provide much more than its technical expertise.
It was also able to influence the city planning through a five-year
contract with DMIC Development Corporation (DMICDC) for program management.

The first phase of development began in early 2009, when Dholera's special investment region status was enacted. This meant establishing the administrative infrastructure, the official definitions of
industrial areas and investment regions, a methodology for dispute
resolution, and official channels through which private investment
could be channeled into the DSIR utilizing existing local laws. Thus

the state government established its interactive process with national regulatory administration as well as DMICDC. The result was a complex matrix of authorities, which would prove to be far more difficult to negotiate than the regulatory bodies in Songdo or China.

Cisco consultants now were tasked with yet more challenges beyond understanding the role of their technology in the city master plans. The team also had to understand how this matrix of money, authority, and influence worked, and when to engage different elements within it. The concerns and mandates of local, state, and central overseers had to be considered at many junctures, and the solutions had to strike a balance between the needs and concerns of each party. In India, this requires an enormous amount of preparation. Once ICT technology has become a connecting thread through a city's many verticals, it is essential that its potential and requirements can be explained in detail to a great variety of unrelated managers and overseers. Furthermore, since technology is the key to high-quality services and lifestyles in these new urban landscapes, its advocates also need to make contact with the people who will call them home.

Mapping Dholera's master plan was the next phase, which lasted until late 2010. The state government, which came closest to the definition of Cisco's "client," was the most involved collaborator, but these officials often requested the team attend meetings on the municipal level as well. The details of the plan showed exactly how the trunk ICT infrastructure would interweave with civic infrastructure. The water, utilities, fiber networks, lighting, and security features and their centralized monitoring centers were laid out from the underground up; the cost benefits of efficient water and electricity delivery were emphasized and contrasted with local standards (which were far better than India at large, Gujarat's delivery system being more reliable than most states').

Rail and road infrastructure, effectively the raison d'être of the entire economic strategy, were crucial to the city plans. No matter how populous Dholera might become in decades to come, it was conceived as a key node on the dedicated 921-mile (1,483-kilometer) freight corridor between Delhi and Mumbai.[10] The industrial corridor encasing the rail lines in time will extend 93 miles (150 kilometers) on both sides of the track. The DMICDC selected Cisco's S+CC Advisory Services to develop the first two city master plans in the corridor in 2012.

The build out of healthcare and educational verticals were also covered by the master plan and brought to the municipal level for input and review. This was a natural segue into the Development Plan, which took up the next fourteen months and was declared complete in December 2011. During this time, the methods for citizen interaction and services, including public grievance redress and land record management, were proposed and explained regularly in meetings with local officials.

The master plans delivered in India may be well served by Cisco's software and hardware solutions, but the purchase of the company's phones, routers, cameras, and IP links remained an ancillary benefit. Remember that smart and connected cities are projects measured in decades, not annual sales cycles. The news and tenor of one year, or even several, will not reveal the full extent of the company's investment in these ambitious plans. The S+CC advocates within Cisco are confident not only of continued investment in smart urban solutions, but also the indispensable nature of the Internet of Everything. In the long run, though its competition will expand and become more sophisticated, one should expect that Cisco will remain vital both to the planning of S+CC initiatives and to the construction of the technological nervous systems and command centers. In India, with four of five existing DMIC master plans bearing its imprint, the team delivered on the planning.

S+CC TRIALS BY LAND AND WATER

As with all other greenfield projects, Dholera's plans faced numerous challenges through 2014, although ground had yet to be broken for a single building. Here again, India pays a price for holding fast to its democratic values. Much of what is planned to be a 355-square-mile (920-square-kilometer) footprint (larger than Mumbai) is today farmland. Owners of the land have raised the alarm about potential hostile acquisitions of the land; instead, the negotiation for land values and rights has been factored into the planning process. This is hardly surprising in a nation that has a long history of fealty to the notion of self-sustaining small communities, as crystallized by Gandhi's proclamation that the nation's best future would be realized in "70,000 villages." Compensation for land and the continuation of farming within urban zones proved to be difficult issues. Dholera SIR officials have struggled to find an equitable arrangement with landowners. Cisco consultants have attended many meetings to help explain the virtue of technological development in a region with many strong traditions but also an established history of poverty and meager opportunity for new generations. Prior to Narendra Modi's election, national law placed severe restriction on land purchases, including the buy-in of at least 80 percent of the landowners with holdings in question. This meant an uphill climb not just for S+CC development, but for infrastructure projects associated with energy, housing, and other essential uses.[11]

Representatives for farmers in villages affected by the development of the Dholera Special Investment Region (SIR) arrived in Gandhanager with a list of concerns for then-Minister Modi in 2013. There was concern that land could be acquired by force or that the terms of sale would be disadvantageous to landowners, some of whom preferred to deal with Dholera's future tenants rather than a governmental authority. There was also a question of how much land would be ceded to urban or industrial development. Gujarat state officials encouraged the plan to buy only portions of landowners' holdings, leaving them in possession of parcels that would, over time, greatly increase in value.

The state had land to sell to developers as well, and there have been instances in which the companies offered early allotments have not come through with their down payments and then seen those offers rescinded. Reports (which have been contested by government officials) indicated that several car companies had been on the ground floor of Dholera SIR investment, but these industrial tenants voiced concern over the region's tendency to flood in monsoon season. Whenever investors experienced cold feet, it became evident that the DMICDC would have to conduct engineering studies and implement solutions before investment would come to fruition.

Dholera SIR responded to the land acquisition debate by reducing the size of the special investment region by nearly 80 percent. This does not mean that the vision of Dholera has shrunk in accord; rather, the focus now is on land owned by villages more inclined to sell. The idea is to break the project down into stages, and therefore spare the entirety of development from red-tape strangulation.

The land acquisition difficulties highlight both India's interest in the Chinese model of city building and the limits of applying that in India. The Central Party of China has been able to relocate agrarian populations and set the terms for land sales more or less by edict. The Indian government and PPPs must instead contend with the varied and often contentious workings of democracy.

Meanwhile, the engineering challenge of reducing flooding in the Dholera SIR—which is located in a delta—will have to be tackled with straightforward planning and execution that is time-consuming and expensive. The flooding problem is in great part due to a buildup of silt in the five rivers that converge on the SIR; during monsoon season, there simply is not enough cubic space in these channels to contain the water flow. Rivers will be dredged, the problem rectified. But until then, Indian citizens will be free to ask how long the development will take and how much it has cost so far.

Those questions, while understandable, attempt to shrink the time frame of greenfield development to the point where skeptics may miss the forest for the trees. While it is true that some city development forecasts are unrealistically optimistic, the potential embedded in these plans is made of much more than wishful thinking. It has taken years for DMICDC to prepare for the groundbreaking ceremonies, but here again there are significant differences between the growth of a planned twenty-first century city and the organic growth of cities in the nineteenth and twentieth centuries. Modern development requires strict accounting of resources used, pollutants created, and productivity lost to congestion, to say nothing of the human misery created in thrown-up slums and barrios. The city planners

Cisco worked with in India realize that to avoid catastrophic levels of emissions and a poor response to the population pressure bearing down on the nation, an entire generation of city building must be skipped. The model of a city surrounded by expansive suburbs and dominated by car culture, the norm for twentieth-century America, is simply untenable in this century's India. But without methodical infrastructure plans and strategies for relevance, these cities will fulfill the worst-case scenarios evoked by skeptics of greenfield cities.[12]

Nonetheless, a plan for surmounting legal and practical barriers to building out India's smart cities must strike a balance between meticulousness and inspiring public confidence. Cisco believes that their partners in DMICDC and the layers of government have been consistent about making themselves available to the media and affected populations, and explaining both the challenges and benefits of S+CC futures. There are many forces outside the control of the city development agencies, and Narendra Modi and his allies, in vowing to streamline the approval and oversight process, are embroiled in a daunting task. The success of the DMIC and smart cities strategy may well turn on the success of a handful of initial projects. To that end, Cisco's engagement has certainly generated optimism within company ranks.

Innovation will be a requirement on all fronts. In terms of financing these projects, Indian S+CC players are even referring to old playbooks. The municipal bond market in India was nonexistent until 1998 (Ahmedabad issued the first municipal bond), and barely two dozen offerings had been made in the intervening eighteen years. Looking favorably at markets such as the United States, Canada, and South Africa, where muni bonds bring in billions USD for building projects, it is easy to see an untapped source of revenue. Some have estimated that over 10 percent of the DMIC project cost may be covered by muni bonds.

The challenge? It is tied to the root problem of India: archaic systems and a history of corruption. Municipal bonds have been a tough sell in India, since traditionally, the cities have depended on the state for financing and thus could not issue their own guarantees. Municipal systems, often served by outmoded accounting processes and unnecessarily complex bureaucracies, have rarely been able to vouch for their own credit worthiness. But in service of their ambitious plans, DMICDC and city-level planners are lobbying for the opportunity to wrest control from established authorities and control their own destinies.

Vast as India is, the cities will never eradicate the rural system that has existed for centuries.[13] But city building is not the alpha and omega of IoE's potential. The verticals of health and education present tremendous possibility for innovations such as telepresence, provided the political will and infrastructure spending can come into alignment. Can smart cities coexist with Gandhi's vision of 70,000 villages? It is a question that is years away from an answer. Nevertheless, we see the potential for astonishing advances in India, potential that justifies both Cisco's financial investment and application of the best of the firm's technological abilities.

It has been said that India "missed" the industrial revolution. This helps explain the tremendous shortcomings in the nation's infrastructure and political structure. If growth is predicated on examples from Western nations, it would seem time and resource scarcity would be aligned to keep India's growth rates down. Cisco's bid, however, is predicted on the belief that many of the growing pains experienced in twentieth-century economies can be avoided if India moves aggressively toward solutions based on IoE technology. The bet is risky for all involved; like Saudi Arabia, India could win handsomely if it creates opportunity for its young population or crumble underneath its weight.

It was almost ten years ago when Elfrink stated that India's IT presence and expertise could define it, just as "Saudi Arabia is now known for oil."[14] The subsequent rise of the DMIC and other S+CC initiatives seems to be bearing this out. But will one hundred new cities be under construction by 2022? That prediction, like so many informed by the vast potential of IoE technology, seems far-fetched. If the five city master plans can be implemented in the next decade, and the new cities can in turn affect commerce and demographic patterns, the way can open for more investment and more cities along the DMIC and elsewhere. Simply put, a nation beset by daunting demographic and resource scarcity problems needs a great deal of talent and drive, qualities India has in abundance. As the nation adopts the vision of the smart city and IoE, it will continue to harness those qualities. The work itself will be a bumpy ride, as most smart city projects tend to be. Nonetheless, it may well be that 2014's optimism was not misplaced. It is difficult to say which market ultimately will contain the tipping point for S+CC technology. But for the good of the nation as well as the world, India would be an excellent candidate.

As to the gamble of moving critical command and operations to the Far East, the game will keep playing out for years. Embedded in Bangalore, a short flight away from one of the world's most ambitious engineering projects—to say nothing of new cities in Saudi Arabia, Malaysia, and China—Cisco will remain relevant. But success can't be measured solely by the company's stock value or the ebb and flow of its sales. The Internet of Everything is going to be a vital part of future prosperity in India and the rest of Southeast Asia; it will help enfranchise and secure a growing middle class and promote cleaner, less congested cities. A secure digitized future will be the ultimate indicator of Cisco's success.

---

[1] "Promising Good Times," *The Economist*, May 24, 2014, http://www.economist.com/news/briefing/21602710-overwhelming-election-victory-promises-reshape-indian-politics-promising-good-times.

[2] *Wall Street Journal* video, September 24, 2014, http://www.wsj.com/video/cisco-chambers-why-im-betting-on-india/BF716B7F-4C94-4E0C-880D-36DB35AE51F5.html.

[3] On a citywide scale, the feasibility of one IT provider outfitting the entire urban landscape is questionable. Songdo is an excellent test case. The IBD, which was outfitted with Cisco's IT network, is but one of eight districts within the new city. Before Cisco came to the project, some buildings within the IBD had already been outfitted with IT assets that did not match Cisco's specifications (or even those of each other). Cities are immense undertakings, beyond the abilities of any one company to design and build. Even greenfield environments inevitably will require extra work to integrate the IT features of developments separated by time of construction and the standards of their architects.

[4] Moinak Mitra, "Cisco's Campus in Bangalore: Lessons for PM Modi's Smart Cities," *The Economic Times*, November 12, 2014, http://economictimes.indiatimes.com/magazines/corporate-dossier/lessons-for-pm-narendra-modis-smart-cities-from-ciscos-smart-campus-in-bangalore/articleshow/45058047.cms.

[5] By 2020, the average Indian national will be twenty-nine, versus thirty-seven years in China and forty-five in Japan: "India's Demographic Dividend: Asset or Liability?" Wharton University of Pennsylvania, January 9, 2013, http://knowledge.wharton.upenn.edu/article/indias-demographic-dividend-asset-or-liability/.

[6] Rukmini S, "65 million people live in slums in India, says census data", *The Hindu*, October 1, 2013 http://www.thehindu.com/todays-paper/tp-national/tp-newdelhi/65-million-people-live-in-slums-in-india-says-census-data/article5188234.ece. By the government's reckoning, an Indian slum must be notified, recognized, or identified as such. Only "identified" slums are unofficially designated, but even these must conform to the definition of "a compact area of at least 300 population or about 60–70 households of poorly built congested tenements, in unhygienic environment usually with inadequate infrastructure and lacking in proper sanitary and drinking water facilities." See Census of India 2011, "Primary Census Abstract for Slum," http://www.censusindia.gov.in/2011-Documents/Slum-26-09-13.pdf.

[7] In 2007, the nation's water supply-demand gap stood at 27 billion liters per day. That number is forecast to grow to 94 billion liters by 2030. In 2009, McKinsey measured India's water supply at 740 billion meters cubed; by 2030, the *demand* was projected to hit 1500 bmc. See Water Resources Group, "Charting Our Water Future," McKinsey & Company, 2009, http://www.mckinsey.com/business-functions/sustainability-and-resource-productivity/our-insights/charting-our-water-future.

[8] Census of India 2011, "Primary Census Abstract for Slum," http://www.censusindia.gov.in/2011-Documents/Slum-26-09-13.pdf.

[9] See DMICDC website: http://www.dmicdc.com/cpage.aspx?pgid=5.

[10] With 38 percent of the total length of the DMIC located in Gujarat, the state's importance to the health and future of the project cannot be understated. See Dholera Special Investment Region website: http://dholerasir.com/dfcprojectdetails.aspx.

[11] At the end of 2014, the government passed an executive order intended to ease land-purchasing restrictions. DMIC projects were not mentioned specifically, but in 2015, planners in Dholera and other S+CC developments will be eager to see if this order is in fact a key element of Modi's strategy to spur business investment by removing long-standing bureaucratic impediments to the building approval process. While the move was certain to be controversial, it should be noted that landowners' compensation rates were to remain stable: at four times the current market price. See Nigam Prusty and Krishna N. Das, "India clears order to ease land acquisitions in reform push," Reuters, December 29, 2014, http://in.reuters.com/article/india-reform-idINKBN0K70I920141229.

[12] Ayona Datta, "India's Smart City Craze: Big, Green and Doomed from the Start?" *The Guardian*, April 17, 2014, https://www.theguardian.com/cities/2014/apr/17/india-smart-city-dholera-flood-farmers-investors. Detailing a raft of arguments against Dholera, the article concludes by stating, "For some Indians, the only way Dholera can be a smart city is if it never gets built at all." While the author notes the relentless urbanization trend, the article stands mute on a key corollary to the author's point of view: namely, how else might India reckon with the inevitable pressures of people, pollution, and strained resources.

[13] There are excellent arguments supporting the limits on affluence and rising living standards in India and other populous nations. For more extended discussion, see Chapter 9.

[14] Steve Hamm, "Inside Cisco's Bangalore Play," *Bloomberg Businessweek*, December 12, 2006, http://www.bloomberg.com/news/articles/2006-12-12/inside-ciscos-bangalore-play.

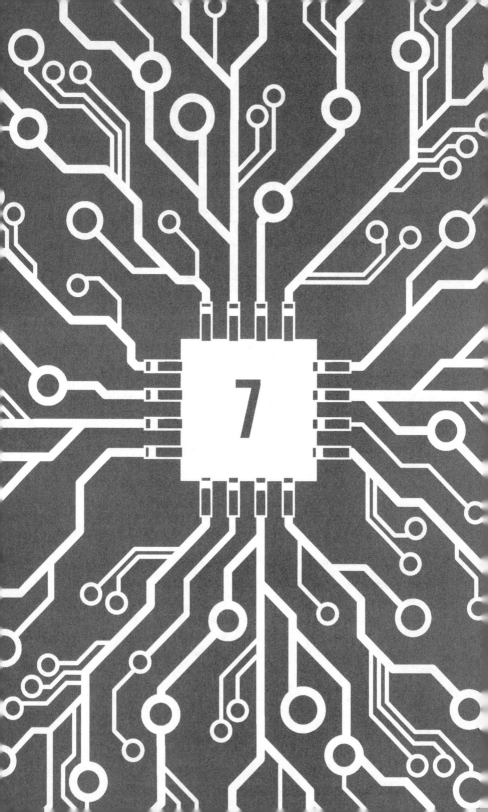

THE INTERNET OF EVERYTHING TRANSFORMS BROWNFIELDS AND BEYOND

I F THE SUCCESS OF A TECH COMPANY's IoE growth depended solely on the progress of huge projects, such as India's DMIC, it would take either great courage or foolishness to keep at the game of building smart cities. But important breakthroughs have occurred in many markets through a wide array of technological advancements. As Asia has considered the impact of brand-new cities for millions of new residents, communities in Europe, Africa, Australia, and the Americas have seen a great deal of progress, measured in improvements to a single service or perhaps two at a time. The Internet, given twenty years to infiltrate business and private living practices, could transform Kansas City as well as KAEC, should the funding and political incentive come into play.

This chapter will explore how multinational tech firm Cisco's smart cities business strategy expanded in two metrics. One is geographic, the other of project scope. Both will help to illustrate how Cisco's teams approach their work today.

The green shoots of IoE are ubiquitous. Often they are a city's first foray into IoE technological solutions; in other cases, a region needs to harness the cumulative power of shared services and is ready to take the next step toward true interactivity between neighboring districts or different service verticals. Some of the business cases go deep into the details of industry or government. Because there are so many challenges—and opportunities—connected to the implementation of digital services, innovation must be relentless. Smart city technology may well be prototyped far away from any residence, avenue, or business park, but assuredly it will find a way back to the zones where citizens are working and living. Many important strides will be taken with a minimum of disruption: a new kiosk system in

Guayaquil, improved signage and parking systems in Barcelona—these are changes that might be perceived as the "overnight" variety. Others, the most challenging, will accompany large infrastructure improvements that require many partners, billions spent on manpower, building materials, and potential service disruptions. Taxpayer dollars will underwrite the cost of these projects; governments will need political will and foresight to justify the improvements. Cisco's future as a technology creator and purveyor will depend on the quality of the businesses cases that demonstrate the economic potential of smart city projects. Fortunately, there are many leaders who are eager to stay at the forefront of digital connectivity. Greater connectivity is a goal everyone wants in some variation. In turn, the advisory team has to create the most penetrating service catalogue and the most innovative and cost-effective patch-ins with old analogue systems.

ENVISIONING THE TREES AMID THE FOREST: NUSAJAYA

The success of modern cities such as Singapore and Dubai is infectious. Many building projects straddle the divide between green- and brownfield developments as other nations and cities seek the means to jump to the front rank of modern life and services. Expos such as Beijing 2010 and new smart city forums, which are held annually, are well-attended departure points for many city executives who are eager to reach for new possibilities. These are excellent beginnings, but to follow up on a demonstration of new technology is to introduce a host of pragmatic considerations. Before money or political capital can be weighed, there is often a reckoning with the most fundamental question of all: Where to start?

Developers and civic leaders who ask this question often are the most committed to finding effective solutions. City managers and planners are tasked with gauging how far money can go and how much return they can expect once smart technology is in place. Most are well aware how much rides on their initial choices. Since there is no one formula for city building, consultative analysis must balance out as many competing factors as possible. There are the practical considerations of the master plan, in which the trajectory of a city's improvement is charted over time. Cost trees, gap analysis, and return on investment diagrams may satisfy administrators who see to the project's funding; they may not, however, address political considerations or the greater objectives of city identity.

Malaysia, with the development of Nusajaya, on the southwestern tip of the nation's peninsula, is competing with Singapore for the title of an ASEAN (Association of Southeast Asian Nations) destination that works so well foreigners will come to avail themselves of its services. There has been a particularly strong push in healthcare and education. The plans for the Afiat "Healthpark" are city-like in size and scope of objective. Afiat is a play for status as the Mayo Clinic of the East, attracting talent and a strong client base through a reputation for efficiency and cutting-edge treatment. And many will not need to fly: Singapore, like China, has an aging population with more needs than the nation-state will be able to manage. EduCity Iskandar is set to offer a wealth of higher education and R&D facilities via original development and partnerships with foreign universities. Malaysian students are expected to comprise the majority of participating students, but the EduCity model is determinedly international, catering directly to students from other Asian nations but also to Africa and the Americas. The focus, global in the best sense, is predicated on the theory that for a growing number of people, national borders will be less important than finding a residence that attracts the like-minded and ambitious. If the city or campus is dynamic enough, it can be found anywhere.

Nusajaya is the core of a Malaysia 2.0 grand strategy that emphasizes open access and new standards for connectivity in all city functions. Like the Delhi-Mumbai Industrial Corridor, which it rivals in size and ambition, Nusajaya will grow in fits and starts as pieces of the master plans are built out and mature. In scope, it dwarfs even Songdo in geography—at 24,000 contiguous acres, it is part of the Iskandar special economic zone in Johor—and as a component of national strategy, it rivals India's DMIC in importance. In 2011,

Cisco signed agreements with two of Nusajaya's largest developers to create the smart and connected master plan. The company was convinced that the developers saw the potential of combining services from the outset of this enormous building plan, making use of existing infrastructure and building a new, greenfield one. The Johor region had a solid foundation for development, thanks to solid infrastructure and proximity to Singapore (about thirty minutes' journey by car, although this likely will change once a new coastal highway is completed). The potential for success has created a rush of investment. Most of the funding has come from Malaysia,[1] but Singapore is also investing heavily, as are businesses from the United States, Europe, and China. Singapore's engagement is of particular note, since its proximity to a new, ambitious urban zone brings up new possibilities for economic ties and collaboration that could benefit both nations.

Consider the expansion of telepresence as it might be applied to the Afiat Healthpark and Singapore. Close enough for in-person consultations, doctors and patients could follow up and transfer data without leaving their respective countries. As technology implementation consultants, there is likely great potential in analyzing the costs and benefits of developing TP and other IoE components to help Nusajaya establish itself in one critical area of service. Once the health vertical becomes robust and new campuses and infrastructure begin to recoup costs, development companies then have incentive to build on the success, simultaneously aiding the national strategic goals of regional—even global—competitiveness.

If one tries to see the proverbial forest for the trees, Nusajaya is a forest. The Malaysian government and development companies have demonstrated a keen vision of this wide ecosystem, in which they have an opportunity to establish the nation as a purveyor of modern living. Oftentimes, however, the greater challenge is to determine which trees in the forest can grow first, thereby encouraging expansion of the forest at large. But this is precisely the objective Cisco has pursued in the development of their Smart + Connected master plans.

VISION FROM THE TOP: BARCELONA

Barcelona is an ideal city for demonstrating the potential harmony between the old world and the smart, new one and serves as a powerful example of brownfield city engineering. Today, removed from the medieval age of Europe, it's difficult to appreciate the fact that the grandest cathedrals, some built over multiple generations, were in their time fine examples of future-proof innovation. The vision and craftsmanship of Notre Dame's first architects was advanced for its time, but nearly one hundred years after ground was broken, the cathedral required substantial remodeling and new ideas about how the thin, Gothic-style walls could rise to new heights and still retain their structural integrity. For more than six hundred years, visitors to Paris have seen a completed masterpiece. It requires the rare ability to see history in a static environment to appreciate how much thinking—and rethinking—went into the construction.

When one looks up at Antoni Gaudí's Sagrada Família in Barcelona, however, there are still cranes and scaffolding amidst its pinnacles. Construction began in 1882, but less than half of Gaudí's plans had been implemented by the time he died in 1926. Some would argue that this architect's vision was so distinctive that his buildings do not belong to any time; they certainly reflect both the present and the past. Barcelona is the rare place where the earliest Roman ruins seem of a piece with the modern subway system. This has long been a place of abundant (and, in Gaudí's case, often startling) innovation.

So it was not surprising that Barcelona jumped to the front rank of cities working with digital architecture. Leaders and citizens here have received acclaim not only for embracing IoE technology but also their careful selection of services and effective deployment. Barcelona was an early adopter of fiber-optic cabling, and its network has grown to more than 310 miles (500 kilometers) worth of cable over the past thirty years. The push for IoE connectivity received a huge boost when Mayor Xavier Trias was elected in 2011. Like Narendra Modi in India, Trias bet aggressively on the technology and sought partnerships with Cisco and other purveyors. Barcelona has embraced the concept of innovation, and by so doing it has captured the essential concept of converged networks. There are twelve verticals affected by IoE innovation, comprising no less than eighty-three separate projects. From the outset, the "Smart City Barcelona" initiative (launched in 2012) aimed at breaking down silos. City agencies historically working in isolation would begin to share data.

An open-source sensor network, named Sentilo, is a data aggregator that contributes to monitoring of water, energy, and lighting, but this is only a beginning. All the data collected by the city's sensor will be funneled into Sentilo, and it will be made available for all departments that can benefit from it. Today, Sentilo can be downloaded on Github, and it can support many technologies across its platform. For instance, a new application program interface (API) connecting software that gathers data from city infrastructure—such as elevators, escalators, and fountains—was connected to Sentilo in spring 2015.

Focus for a moment on fountain data. Barcelona has experienced dire water shortages—it was receiving tankers full of fresh water during a 2008 drought. Aridity will almost certainly lead to future shortages. It is in the municipal interest to maintain a data-rich network that monitors water usage, leakage, irrigation systems, and illegally opened pipes. With a strong, interactive network and open-sourced interfaces, the job will not only become easier, it will be more transparent.

Payoffs have already been realized. In 2014, the city announced a savings of $58 million from its smart water technology and another $50 million from its high-profile parking technology. Barcelona, a compact city of 1.6 million, has struggled with traffic congestion. Wireless sensor technology, created in partnership between Cisco and Streetline, helps drivers find parking more quickly and transportation managers see the entire street network.[2]

While Barcelona's planners recognize the need for a muscular, top-down approach to these infrastructure projects, they are leaving the door wide open for bottom-up innovation. Another aspect of smart Barcelona is the "Open Government" initiative, which supports a network of forty-four kiosks and an "Open Data" portal available to citizens and businesses. Applications and APIs can be created and plugged in by interested parties, allowing for the transparency and adaptability that befit a truly interactive city. This also acknowledges the contribution of the taxpayer. An old factory, named @22, will be the epicenter of a new smart and connected campus in Barcelona, which will be shared by Cisco and Schneider Electric. The companies have provided more than $6 million to the renovation of the factory, but Barcelona has put some $230 million toward the project.[3] The high price tag is justified: Barcelona is building out three open-software platforms to transform sensor data into value, savings, and quality-of-life improvements.

The networks are just one part of Barcelona's strategy. It is also investing in smart lighting, low-emission vehicles, urban mobility apps, and renewable energy. Meanwhile, with 14 percent of its economy based in tourism, efforts to preserve its landmarks, history, and distinctive urban experience will need to keep pace. Barcelona's prospects for the future are bright in large part because its people recognize that modern thinking need not erase history. Like the Sagrada Família, technology exists on a continuum that can include the best ideas of many generations.

THE POWER OF COLLECTIVE DATA AND ACTION: SOUTH EAST QUEENSLAND

Barcelona has also maintained a strong position on the IoE vanguard by perceiving the value of export. As one example, the Sentilo platform has been offered as a solution for other cities; there is little point in restricting the reach of connectivity to a single geographic area. In fact, it is reasonable to aspire to concerted action to attack problems at the regional or even national level. It may be too early to consider the creation of a new, countrywide smart energy grid and delivery system, but there is abundant opportunity for smaller, vitally connected towns and cities to adopt shared smart and connected solutions to common problems.

Traffic congestion, energy inefficiency, and unreliable connectivity are nearly ubiquitous problems. Almost every city in the world is seeking ways to reduce congestion, keep its citizens safer, and do more with less. IoE solutions lend themselves to collaborations between adjacent communities. Rather than adopt a disparate array of solutions, civic leaders are encouraged to think about their problems at a regional level.

South East Queensland (SEQ), on Australia's east coast, is a dense population pocket: Almost 15 percent of the continent's population is concentrated in this administrative region. In many ways, the local governments and cities of SEQ are coalescing through shared economic ties and urban growth. Two agglomerations here, Brisbane and Gold Coast, are among the largest on the continent, but the region's administrators have been focused on collaboration since the 1990s. The problems of congestion and safety require plans that shape this growth without undue restrictions. SEQ's Council of Mayors is focused on building out infrastructure in a green, sustainable way; while there are rural areas interspersed with urban, the council has endeavored to see SEQ in a holistic way. For all intents, this is becoming a single metropolitan region.

In early 2015, Cisco engaged with the council to discuss the digital component of infrastructure projects, to which SEQ has already pledged billions of dollars. The region already affords its residents an abundance of digital technology services, but this is just a beginning. Administrators have learned one of the essential truths about smart technology: The more people experience it, the more they expect it, rely on it, and even demand more of it. With so much innovation afoot worldwide, a well-traveled and educated population will not long be satisfied by a complacent attitude toward digital solutions. Governments of all types must put their resources to work—wisely. Since 81 percent of Australians own a smartphone, and 66 percent shop using their phones, they want to know how to connect and what impediments they might face during the course of a day. They expect wireless technology to provide the answers.[4]

Research done uncovered that the cities of SEQ were not exploiting a partner-based ecosystem. The communities, including Brisbane, Gold Coast, Ipswich, Lockyer Valley, and Sunshine Coast, had similar goals: more smart parking, lighting, public safety, universal

Wi-Fi, and recruiting personnel to monitor the networks. While they may have known that the city next door had the same goals, the administrators had not considered the potential benefits of collaboration and cost sharing among partner communities.

The communities could consider the possibility of sharing in a single service development. If all five parts of SEQ committed to a smart lighting solution and built out a service platform to connect all the sensors in the region, they could introduce economies of scale as well as shared costs and savings. Respecting budget constraints, smart service improvement could be applied to a single vertical—tourism, for example—with the intention of expanding to other verticals—agriculture, perhaps, or government-run utilities—as the business cases are studied and results analyzed.

With $134 billion pledged to infrastructure investment over the next two decades, SEQ is at a key juncture. Should the region's administrators continue to act in concert, the communities within, although classifiably brownfield, could begin to take on attributes of a greenfield project. There are many excellent trials of smart technology being considered, but if SEQ can transcend the piecemeal approach—even in a single vertical, such as smart lighting or parking—these communities can grow in size *and* intelligence. But this will require a growth strategy that blurs the boundaries between areas, rather than defining them. New laws and protocols will accompany the development, adding to the complexity of the projects. Much remains to be decided, but SEQ is an excellent example of how even a large, mixed-use area can begin to think like a single city.

EDUCATING A POPULACE: GUAYAQUIL

If huge price tags, such as $35 billion in Songdo's case, were barriers to entry into modern, connected life, much of the Internet of Everything would remain trapped in white papers and revenue analysis. Few municipalities have anything like that kind of money to lavish on digital technology projects. In times of economic duress, cities are often left to fend for themselves if they want to upgrade their technological services. Innovation and high aspirations are possible on far smaller budgets.

Guayaquil, the second-largest city of Ecuador, with 2.7 million inhabitants, is largely known as a trade and agricultural hub. Internet penetration, as of 2014, was gauged to be 44 percent. City leaders, however, have made digitization of city services a priority. The "Digital Guayaquil" program, inaugurated in 2004, has set 2018 as a target date for providing the entire city with Internet service.

"The mayor wants every citizen converted into a digital citizen," said Xavier Salvador, who has been assisting in this goal as a director of the city's Informatics Department since 2003. Guayaquil's leadership is concerned with how the IoE revolution, like every technological advance, will create winners and losers. Regionally, Guayaquil can compete; there are few South American cities that are far ahead as technology hubs, but there were major impediments to progress. City politics can make too much change at once a losing proposition. Consultants involved in the city projects have often seen the effects of technological overload on potential customers and partners.

By the time the ICT master planning work started in Guayaquil, it was apparent that any agreements struck would have to be justified by a strong socioeconomic argument. Not only would the digital solutions be impressive, they would bring immediate benefit. Tempting though it may be to leapfrog over implementation steps, in many cases a city must first adopt basic services before users grow accustomed to more sophisticated solutions.

A related study that formed the basis from which to learn was a four-month engagement in Sao Paulo with Prodam, the city's technology management service. The technology supporting Sao Paulo's healthcare, education, transportation, security, sports, and entertainment was compared to worldwide best practices. The gap analysis showed Prodam how a mix of tech-enabled services could bring higher standards to each vertical.

Comparison is not, of course, a recommendation to emulate the practices of a city 8,000 miles away and ruled by separate economic conditions. The list of service strategies and implementations has become exhaustive, because most solutions are highly specified to a single municipal problem or upgrade. In Brazil, it was particularly important to demonstrate how the technological solution could move the socioeconomic needle. If Sao Paulo's primary goal is to reduce crime, an analysis of their street security and data collection is paired with an operations model that highlights strengths and weaknesses. The services Cisco and others can provide and facilitate are then promoted as gap-closure solutions.

The work in Sao Paulo gave Cisco's team credibility in Guayaquil. When the city opened its technical consulting contract to international bidders, the company's commitment to solutions that fit the South American economic circumstances carried weight. With no federal funds available, the city had approximately $2.5 million to commit to the upgrade of its digital infrastructure, with a similar amount pledged for each of the subsequent five years. The existing support for the city's CIO was hardworking but small, developing solutions in house but suffering from inevitable bottlenecks created by insufficient support. The allotted funds needed to cover hardware, technicians, consultants, and support staff.

Mayor Jaime Nebot, however, had a clear focus that helped surmount these disadvantages. While he green-lighted a full gap analysis of city services, he was clear in stating that Guayaquil needed digitally based education for students and adults. For a beginning, the city needed complete Internet connectivity. Citizens needed to grow accustomed to relying on the Internet to learn. A first step was to place fifty new free Wi-Fi hotspots throughout the city, with most located at schools and universities. The city also opted to install Internet kiosks to encourage residents to patch into municipal government services to pay fines, apply for permits, and gather information. Students can use the kiosks to access class materials. So far, they have proved to be very popular.

Healthcare also received a boost when Guayaquil connected its hospitals to local clinics. Rather than require patients to undertake separate visits to specialists, they can now take advantage of video conferencing, potentially connecting with a patient they would never have gone to see due to budgetary or time constraints. This might seem to be a modest improvement compared to Songdo's aspiration to have patients interface with medical professionals in their own homes via high-definition screens, but it is not the single step that bears consideration. The goal in Guayaquil was to create a road map of services that can be implemented over three, five, or ten years. This solution fits both the budgetary constraints and the scheme for bringing a city with low digital penetration up to speed.

The proliferation of hotspots and kiosks in Guayaquil has been popular, in large part because the Informatics Department has taken time to work with citizens and help them grow accustomed to navigating the Internet via a new resource. Although they started with less digital awareness than the citizens of SEQ or Barcelona, Guayaquil's people demonstrated the same acquisitive enthusiasm for smart and connected services. This has begun as a one-way opportunity, with the government providing service to the public. The coming challenge will enfranchise the businesses owners and private citizens, who can find ways to conduct business and connect over digital platforms. This next step can "pay later," as one Guayaquil technical officer noted, in the form of tax revenue. The needle needs to keep moving toward productive connectivity.

LESSONS LEARNED

Multiple variations of the projects described here can be found on six continents and in dozens of cities. The cities of tomorrow are, for many people, to be the very same cities they've lived in their entire lives. Young and middle-aged people living today in Chicago, Barcelona, or Brisbane could leave for twenty years and return to a city that is pleasingly familiar. Of course, there will be changes—extensive, fundamental changes—but the continuum between the twentieth-century city and that of the twenty-first is not so hard to navigate as skeptics would suggest.

Brownfield cities still have many difficult choices to make. The innovators and risk-takers who embrace IoE are still on the vanguard. Many are following, but as those communities consider modern, digital platforms as a key factor in future prosperity, there are a few important points to make:

- Be ready to lead the way. Private citizens make excellent second responders and critics. They do not have the institutional muscle or the mandate to create and sustain a well-functioning city. Mayors, planners, CIOs, and private partners have the funds available to take action. They should not be squeamish about doing so, although they should be prepared to keep dialogue with citizen groups and advocates open.

- Consider expanding the city limits. As communities within larger regions become more integrated through commerce and providing services, they should look to the possibility of shared solutions. As more sensor networks connect and feed to data centers and the cloud, there will be an increase in opportunities to expand the reach of many services. Regional leaders should be on the lookout for opportunities to think—and possibly act—in concert.

- Take the time to evaluate connectivity options. Guayaquil's leadership took the time to evaluate complex gap analysis and weigh the conclusions of ICT consultants heavily. But in the end, they did not forget their primary motivations, which had led them to seek bids for IoE services in the first place. Once they circled back to the prime motivation—education—they could make informed choices about where allotted funds were best spent.

- Build for some, but try to connect all. Urban development can be tricky, since there are many people who expect at least a residual benefit from the sacrifice of money, potential displacement, or the loss of an old way of life. Satisfying all who are affected may be impossible, but if more receive a tangible benefit, the political price may not be as grave.

This book's premise is that the best cities of tomorrow will de facto be smart. They will be connected. They will be fast. No community can lose out entirely if any element of IoE connectivity can be delivered. Since IoE will become part of the foundation of commerce, quality of life, and social benefits, it becomes an excellent source of quid pro quo negotiation. New office towers and apartment complexes will not be the lot for every city dweller for generations to come. But state-of-the-art connectivity, smart security, and a digitally enhanced lifestyle are all within the grasp of rich and poor alike. It is up to the decision-makers, for now, to understand that potential.

So what could the smart and connected city approach and master plan do to rescue one of the oldest, largest, most polluted, and poorest megacities in the world? This is a question we will explore in the next chapter.

---

[1] About two-thirds of the capital behind Iskandar is Malaysian, but prominent investors from Singapore and other nations have been tied to development, although the Malaysian government has instituted measures to rein in property speculation, including taxation and permit requirements for bulk sales of housing units. See "Malaysia's 50 Richest, 2014: The Road to Iskandar," Forbes Asia, March 2014, http://www.forbes.com/forbes/welcome/?toURL=http://www.forbes.com/sites/forbesasia/2014/02/26/malaysias-50-richest-2014-the-road-to-iskandar/&refURL=https://www.google.com/&referrer=https://www.google.com/. "The Malaysian Government Has Successfully Slowed the Housing Market," Global Property Guide, November 12, 2014, http://www.global-propertyguide.com/news-The_Malaysian_government_has_successfully_slowed_the_housing_market-2035.

[2] A common estimate puts gas burned while searching for parking at 40 percent of the total burned in congested urban areas. See CC Chin, "Reinventing the Automobile: Personal Urban Mobility for the 21st Century," MIT Media Lab, 2011, http://ilp.mit.edu/media/conferences/2011-vienna/chin.pdf.

[3] Lucas Laurson, "Barcelona's Smart Ecosystem," MIT Technology Review, November 18, 2014, https://www.technologyreview.com/s/532511/barcelonas-smart-city-ecosystem/.

[4] See South East Queensland Regional Plan, 2009–2031; Council of Mayors SEQ, http://www.dilgp.qld.gov.au/resources/plan/seq/regional-plan-2009/seq-regional-plan-2009.pdf.

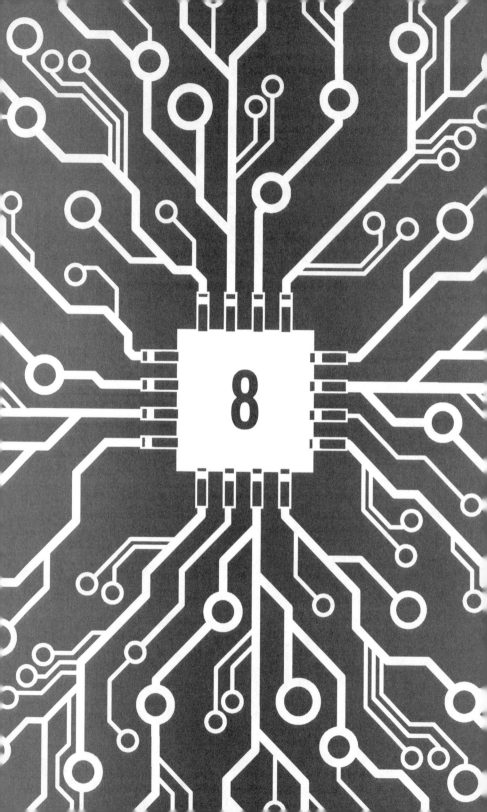

EGYPT, 2015: THE SMART CITY AS A PROMISING PERSPECTIVE

N CAIRO, during the Muslim fasting month of Ramadan, cannons fire from the Mameluk citadel towering over Cairo, announcing the time to break the faithful's fast at dusk. Cairo's city police, sweating in their white summer uniforms, stand at overcrowded intersections and try to manage a flood of cars and increasingly agitated people on foot, on buses, on donkey carts, on bicycles. Everyone is trying to get home before sunset for one of the great celebrations of the Muslim calendar. Tempers fly. The ancient city's infrastructure creaks under the concentrated assault of its human inhabitants. A police general, standing next to his officers under one of the Soviet-style flyovers that dominate the downtown streets, looks exhausted. He tells me the hour before the cannon reports is more grueling for him and his men than any declared state of emergency they've yet handled.

Even drivers experienced in the haphazard ways of Cairo streets can be overwhelmed in the rush. Streetlights, which receive only occasional respect in the city and often do not function at all, effectively disappear. When most everyone working in this metropolitan area of twenty million wants to get home at the same time, for the same celebration, through a choked, decrepit transport network, *emergency* is no hyperbole. Rarely does this city seem closer to bursting at its seams.

The problem of so many millions living in a geographic space that was planned for barely one million residents manifests as snarled traffic, a choking atmosphere, and general chaos (not to mention annual figures of roughly one thousand traffic deaths and $8 billion in lost productivity).[1] This urban uproar that is downtown Cairo stretches the imagination.

But those accustomed to Cairo's hustle and bustle gain an important realization: Opportunity and dysfunction do not cancel each other out. Both reflect the reality of most twentieth-century cities. So how can the smart city concept and the technology master planning approach described and tested in the previous chapters be used to tackle the ultimate brownfield challenge: centuries-old megacities like Cairo, Mexico City, and many more that have tens of millions of inhabitants and are indispensable to their nation's economic growth and social peace. Smart city technology is not just a trillion-dollar industry; it is the key to tackle some of the most pressing challenges of the twenty-first century.

Cairo is the epicenter of a nation that has been counted on as a pillar of relative stability in a volatile region. Among the top-tier crowded megacities, few can match this complex, fascinating place for sheer unpredictability. Cairenes are resilient people who often deal with the strain of living in their crowded city with good humor and plenty of street-level, extemporaneous adjustments. When the power cuts out, as it often can in wealthy and poor sectors alike, residents get by without water, subway transport, fuel for cars, and other essentials. They've had plenty of practice.

Since the removal of Hosni Mubarak, who held power for almost thirty years, troubles in Cairo have spiked. A massive power outage in August 2014 caused citywide blackouts. Even here, where power in the hot summer months is historically sporadic, this was an unprecedented failure. But it's hard to be surprised: Demand has risen, while energy prices and antigovernment sabotage have destabilized supply. Meanwhile, Egypt has demographic challenges we have seen in other emerging nations. People under age twenty-five comprise 50 percent of the population; there is 13 percent unemployment and a growing national deficit as the government struggles to provide the basics. Most of these unemployed live in Cairo.

But there are many positive signs as well. In April 2015, Moody's raised Egypt's primary financial ratings to stable, citing a projected 4.5 percent GDP growth for the short term and 5–6 percent for four subsequent years. Cash reserves are up and primary lenders are recommitting their support. Perhaps most important, Egypt is determined to reform its economic structure and reduce its deficit.[2] While the infrastructure of downtown Cairo is decrepit, new cityscapes such as 6th of October City and New Cairo demonstrate earlier attempts to transcend the constraints of the original, outdated Cairene city plan. The plans are still nascent, but Egyptian leaders have are seeking a return to growth.

Cairo has long been known as a cultural powerhouse. Its music, literature, and television are influential throughout the Middle East and Africa. The city also harbors impressive technological innovation. The deadly traffic patterns have given rise to apps like Bey2ollak that provide traffic information to its users: crowd-powered, the child of a recent startup, and "more essential to traffic than traffic lights" for close to one million users.[3] This isolated example is highly instructive. City dwellers, used to cooking and even driving in the dark, can be expected to manipulate digital technology with enthusiasm.

Much of this human capital has been created by a vibrant middle class, which has existed since the beginning of modern Egyptian society. It has fueled the nation's universities, media, and other cultural indices. The lower strata of the middle class—lower-skilled workers and employees—have been hit hard in the recent national turmoil. These are the people who depend on the health of small and medium-sized businesses (SMB), which, as we are seeing in a globalizing economy, presumes the existence of best-use Internet capability.

So Cairo, innovative though it is, requires even more forward thinking and economic initiative. The city's small businesses require flexible (and dependable) digital technology to grow to scale. A smart and connected platform could electrify and streamline this city's flow, and Egypt at large could increase its influence over the region and set positive trends in culture and technology in the twenty-first century.

Since so much of the nation's commerce runs through Cairo and Alexandria, ICT master plans for both cities, properly outlined and executed, could provide a huge lift to this nation that, like so many, could be defined by either its potential or its troubles.

The fundamentals of a Cairo ICT master plan would be similar to the case studies described in this book. Ultimately, though, every city and region must succeed (or struggle) on its own terms. While some of Cairo's needs are applicable to any urban landscape, the particulars must reflect local conditions and the needs of its people.

The ICT master plan would need to address the following:

- The creation of innovation clusters, which would promote the development and outreach of the city's small and medium businesses.
- Promote remote worksites to decrease traffic and bring more women into the workforce.
- Encourage FDI and the creation of new worksites on the outskirts of Cairo. 6th of October City and New Cairo have not achieved "tipping point" popularity with Cairenes because they are removed from economic centers. Business, digital technology, and teleworking need to be brought into new developments to make them attractive enough to relieve pressure on the downtown.
- Provide the surveillance and safety features to protect the tourist economy, and increase safety and security across all parts of the city, wealthy and poor.

Underpinned by a digital service platform and covering as a first step its new residential and business neighborhoods, Cairo could modernize quickly. Downtown Cairo, with its now famous Tahrir Square, may never quite be a paragon of order and efficient flow. Then again, cities like Rome and Paris are also criticized for their traffic patterns. But if progress is made on all fronts, the pressure that comes from untenable practices and inefficient delivery systems can be brought down to manageable levels.

Remote work locations for women are an example of a concept that can play an important role both in traffic avoidance and in dealing with unemployment. A 13 percent unemployment rate is troublesome enough, but unemployment among Egyptian women stands at 29 percent. This represents a severe drain on the GDP, as even educated women are often discouraged from taking jobs. A Pew study from 2010 found that 54 percent of Egyptians favored segregation between the sexes in the workplace, a higher percentage than in Nigeria, Jordan, or Indonesia.[4] Poor women in agricultural communities often leave school early, although middle and upper-class Egyptian women have more opportunities. Additionally, women from all classes face the threat of sexual harassment in the streets. This is a serious deterrent to women who must travel to work. Digital employment opportunities can play an important role in pulling women into the workforce.

Digital remote work centers could be a useful bridge technology between old and new. Close to schools and residential neighborhoods, they would dramatically reduce working women's commuting needs. A pilot program could consist of a few family-friendly remote work centers—"office space as a service"—with broadband connectivity, IP and video capabilities, and a supervised space for children to play while their mothers work. Even the initial introduction of three or four centers, jointly financed by the government, regional suppliers, and a technology firm, could become a social demographic game-changer. It's a solution that fits the circumstances, and the culture.

With just 5 percent nationwide broadband penetration as of 2015, Egypt needs to increase fixed broadband access. Further components of a smart city plan for Cairo include smart energy management, enhanced cyber security, and increased government efficiency through widespread use of portal and smart card–based government services. This is particularly important for subsistence programs such as welfare. It's a long list, but cities the world over are using IoE technology to accomplish all of these tasks.

THE INTERNET OF EVERYTHING, AND EVERYONE

When the possibilities presented by digitizing city functions materialized, it became evident to the author and his teams that a strategic, macroeconomic conception of urban growth was an essential part of the technology industry's future, and that much of the thinking, the experimenting, and the implementing was happening in emerging countries, reversing some of the earlier patterns of West-East transfers of technology innovation.

To be part of this global effort to use technology to make modern city living more sustainable, healthier, greener, and more productive has been exhilarating, educating, and formative. The way people live—whether in cities, small towns, or villages—will be better or worse depending on how they decide to use a vast array of new interactive tools.

In the emerging and emerged world, there can be no better use of the Internet of Everything than enabling middle-income innovation and growth. Small and medium businesses will thrive when supply chains are digitized, and they can produce goods and services and go to market while bypassing the oligarchic monopolies that dominate much of the emerging world. As residents gain technology and utilize their improvisational abilities, there can be enormous direct and residual benefits.

Cities as diverse as Cairo and Songdo can promote entrepreneurship, build stronger local communities, and help write new manuals that explain what IoE should be used to accomplish. Perhaps most important, by seizing this nascent technology now, India, Egypt, and other nations can skip several developmental steps and rearrange the global playing field. China has set a powerful example here. With even the basic improvements described earlier, it's conceivable that a nation like Egypt's GDP could grow by an additional 2 to 4 percent annually—sufficient growth to spark a virtuous cycle of investment and return the country to a much stronger regional position.

In the twenty-first century, the Internet of Everything will be our primary prosperity tool. We must continue to explore it and find its essential usefulness.

[1] "Cairo traffic is much more than a nuisance," World Bank, August 21, 2012, http://www.worldbank.org/en/news/feature/2012/08/21/cairo-traffic-much-more-than-nuisance.

[2] Moody's rating action, April 7, 2015, https://www.moodys.com/research/Moodys-upgrades-Egypt-to-B3-with-a-stable-outlook--PR_320392.

[3] "Egypt's tech innovators seize opportunity from turmoil," BBC.com, September 25, 2013, http://www.bbc.com/future/story/20130925-egypt-innovation-from-turmoil.

[4] "Muslim Publics Divided on Hamas and Hezbollah," Pew Research Center, December 2010, http://www.pewglobal.org/2010/12/02/muslims-around-the-world-divided-on-hamas-and-hezbollah/.

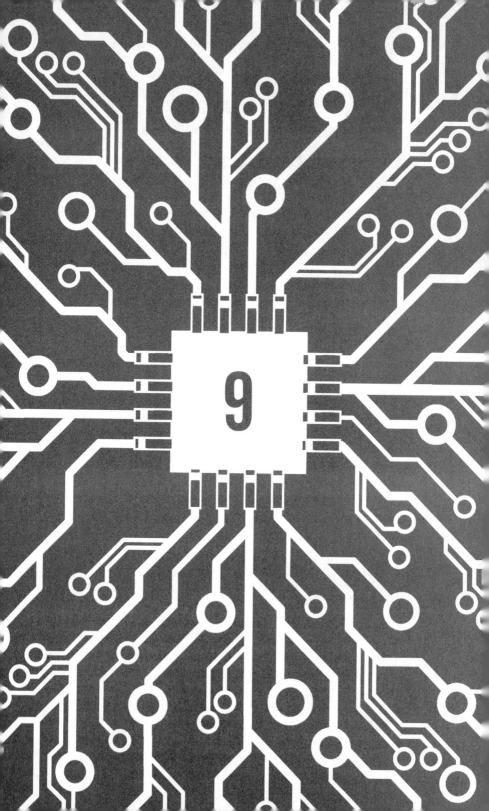

THEORIES ON SMART CITIES: SUSTAINABILITY IN A CROWDED WORLD

T HERE ARE MANY REASONS to be optimistic about civilization today. Optimism rarely makes news, but it is a fact that more people are living life free of hunger, conflict, and disease than at any other point in history. How many more will be raised out of desperate poverty in the coming decades? And how many of them will live in cities?

The first question is beset by debate. The economic strategies of southern Asia are predicated on growth. The potential of their markets has proven irresistible to multinational corporations that anticipate the gain that comes with pulling millions out of poverty and into their client base. The World Bank and other leading institutions are forecasting slowed growth for East Asia and Pacific nations for the next several years. China, so long dependable for high single or double-digit growth, is readjusting its goals to reflect the reality of decreasing demand and a need to restructure some of its more unwieldy holdings. The Chinese people are encouraged to expect a "new normal," in which runaway growth is not the key to prosperity. Nevertheless, growth is still a primary objective. Although by some estimates the nation's annual GDP gain, now hovering around 7 percent, could drop to 6 percent by 2020, China is still intent on becoming the world's leading economy. Growth still defines the twenty-first century model.

Meanwhile, millions of Chinese who already have better living standards—to say nothing of millions more who hope to be enfranchised by improving national fortunes—will expect their gains to be sustainable. Indeed, Beijing has often promoted the growth strategy as a means to curb social unrest. The basis for that growth is consumption: Chinese people are expected to buy more cars, more expensive homes, more furnishings, more electronics, more of the trappings of the Western world.

Not everyone believes this scenario is desirable, or even realistic. The ascendancy of China and the growing power of India and other southern Pacific nations has been undeniable, but as anyone who has traveled in Asia knows, there is far more poverty in each of these nations than many leaders care to admit. Meanwhile, the need for more infrastructure is so great, and the strain on both economic drivers and natural resources so severe, that the distance between today and the abundant, twentieth-century Western living standard for Asia seems very great indeed, so much so that some skeptics are calling for a halt to all the rhetoric.

Chandran Nair, founder of the Global Institute of Tomorrow (GIFT), an independent pan-Asian think tank, has been something of an iconoclast among Eastern business leaders and consultants over the last decade. He advocates for Asia's leading thinkers to take center roles in the ongoing globalization debate. While he is not at all averse to Asia's growing economic power, what worries him is the method. Nair is adamant that a consumption-based growth model in Asia is based on deliberate misinformation or an indifferent, shortsighted reading of some disturbing datasets. The thesis of his 2011 *Consumptionomics* is an exposition on a very basic question: What if Asians—Chinese and Indians in particular—began to live like Americans, consuming the same amount of resources, producing equal amounts of pollution, and, perhaps most importantly, expecting their leaders to endorse and protect this way of life?

Nair proposes that economic and political leaders who embrace Western-style consumption as the best means for growth are eliding over the fact that the resources for this growth simply do not exist, at least by the standards of our present technology. If the "American Way" is synonymous with "having it all," he believes the truth is simple: Asians, beyond a sliver of the elite, can't have it. Consumption at that level for emerging Asia economies likely would wreck the climate and deplete already strained resources to dangerous levels. Nair is very much an advocate for raising living standards in this region, but *Consumptionomics* is a lightning rod for the sort of skepticism that looks critically at the profits of multinational corporations and governments that enable them.

At face value, it would seem that Nair is at variance with the corporate mission of multinationals that are betting heavily on the expansion of the Asian economies. This is especially so when one considers passages like the following:

> By their very nature, companies devour resources in order to meet their production needs. So to expect them to come up with any meaningful solutions for resolving the resource depletion and environmental degradation they create is to mistake what they do.
>
> That Asia might threaten such a model is the kind of thought that companies prefer to ignore. That its sheer size and already overstressed environment may make it impossible to continue using resources in ways that the twentieth-century world could only just cope with is an issue most executives find it easier simply not to address. Instead, the sheer size of its population, and the potential this offers for growth, silences all doubts.[1]

It is difficult to fault Nair for pointing out that, even now, increased consumption already includes some unfortunate byproducts that have plagued Westerners in recent generations. Obesity is on the rise in Malaysia, China, South Korea, and India; China is now stricken with the world's second-highest obesity rate, and the numbers are climbing, especially for children.[2] Vegetarian diets, generally less noxious for the environment and healthier for the human system, are giving way as meat consumption rises. The incidental expenses of processing, shipping, and storing meat-based products will increase across supply chains, and so will the resulting pollution. Resource and food wastage will also increase. For companies that sell products to the upwardly mobile classes in Asian nations, these facts are likely difficult to swallow when growth is the singular imperative.

Nair's book was meant to identify this enormous problem. He also takes to task the unquestioning belief that markets will create solutions as they are needed. His thesis contends that such a belief is the stuff of a "dream world," based on a model for development that simply cannot be sustained in Asia. But what are the alternatives?

THE SMART AND CONNECTED CITY MODEL AND SUSTAINABILITY

Tomorrow's cities' needs are as different from the last century's as are Nair's views of economic development. The emergence of the Asian economies is a source of great promise and opportunity, but it is not contradictory to simultaneously acknowledge the hazards and need for careful planning. Moreover, the inapplicability of the Western experience to Asia is an important premise of the discussion, although many citizens of both the East and West are unaware of or not inclined to acknowledge it.

The last decade's development of smarter, more efficient cities point to the fact that these projects, rather than enhancing the dangerous contradiction Nair identifies, can actually be agents to reverse it. Smart and connected cities can promote growth simply through the amenities they provide. Reliable networks, cloud services, and communications will be the backbone of any prosperous city of the future. Relying on an elite framework for information delivery does not require citizens to consume the resource-intensive and pollution-producing goods that defined commerce in twentieth-century cities. Of course, not every city can organize around finance or information; some cities will continue to organize around the production of goods. But even in these cases, smart technology can mitigate environmental degradation through greater efficiency and reduce the strain on resources by streamlining the delivery of energy and services. No one feature of the Internet of Everything will prove to be the catalyst in a new formula for growth. But when combined with smart policy, willing participation of citizens and businesses, and a chain of accountability, IoE technology will be an essential component to sustainable improvements in Asia, and the rest of the world as well.

The growth enabled by smart services might be precisely the middle way that consumption critics such as Nair (who remain steadfast advocates for Asia's ascendance) are seeking. If Asian nations can continue to develop the technology master plans advocated in this book, tangible quality-of-life benefits can reach many of the millions projected to move to cities in the next two decades. Their lifestyles, due to the constraints imposed by population density and resource depletion, will be hard-pressed to match twentieth-century standards of luxury. This is precisely the point for Chandran Nair and other thinkers who advocate a clean break with those same standards and expectations. There is a need, however, for bridges between a future that enfranchises impoverished citizens of Manila and Mumbai without crushing the economies of those cities with the concurrent demand for services and goods. The political stability of Asian nations will depend on these bridges; they must be constructed based on excellent plans and with deliberate care. They must not, in other words, result in a host of new slums and resource shortages that grow worse over time. Instead, they must lead to communities that have a technological infrastructure that can adapt over time and enable citizens and municipal leaders to shape their communities in ways that will best work for them.

The second question that began this chapter—whether the majority of the newly enfranchised will live in cities—is easier to answer on the face of things. The world is becoming more urban; indeed, many thinkers, such as Harvard's Edward Glaeser, believe that high concentrations of population are essential to innovation and productivity. It is almost certain that cities will become more affluent over time, but the benefits of better living need not be confined to cities. Initiatives like Digital India will raise many boats as government kiosks, broadband, and Wi-Fi hotspots bring interconnectivity and information to even the most remote villages. These services alone will not guarantee higher living standards: No one would argue the astonishingly rapid proliferation of cell phones over the past fifteen years has eradicated poverty. But as information and the maintenance of information technology becomes more valuable, we can expect residual benefits for even those far away from urban centers.

WHO MAKES THE CITY SMART?

There has been considerable criticism of the role of technological leaders moving into the role of city planning. Thanks to its prominent role in Songdo, Cisco has borne the brunt of much of this criticism. Some of it is inevitable, since news cycles move more quickly than business cycles. But there are more fundamental theories that train a skeptical eye on the more ambitious city-building projects, which are worthy of discussion.

Anthony Townsend, in his 2013 book *Smart Cities*, defines a fundamental tension between the methods that can be employed to create a city. He champions the "one app at a time," bottom-up creation and adaptation of city services. In so doing, he contrasts citizen-based development with that of "cookie-cutter," top-down city plans cooked up by a combination of autocratic civic leaders, digital technology experts, and real estate developers. Songdo is presented as the textbook case of city building powered by multimillion-dollar contracts and investments in the billions. Noting the city's rapid construction and abundant automated features, Townsend remains underwhelmed. "Songdo," he writes, "seems intent on engineering serendipity out of the urban equation." Still under construction, the place to him looks "inauthentic," its intelligence difficult to perceive on the street level or from the top of the NEATT Tower.[3] These observations fuel his criticism of engineered cities and their direct contrast to the virtuous, citizen-based innovations he champions throughout his book. Of key importance is an argument presented in the book's introduction:

> *These bottom-up efforts thrive on their small scale, but hold the potential to spread virally on the Web. Everywhere that industry attempts to impose its vision of clean, computed, centrally managed order, they propose messy decentralized and democratic alternatives.*
>
> *It's only a matter of time before they come to blows.*[4]

This is a tidy summation, but the experiences gained in Asia, and elsewhere suggest the following: While "decentralized and democratic alternatives" may be keys to the success of Western cities, they will not, on their own, create new cityscapes in Asia, Africa, and South America. A new slum is the far more likely result of free-form development than if there is a master plan to guide new construction. San Francisco, New York, and other hotspots for bottom-up innovation already work off of an essential infrastructure that has been upgraded over time. To be sure, these cities also will experience massive infusions of new technology and information delivery in coming years. But it is difficult to compare them to the cities waiting to be built, or those with populations likely to double or triple in the next decade.

"Managed order" and "decentralized and democratic alternatives" are not, by their nature, hostile and mutually exclusive options for city building. Managed order is especially useful when the service delivery platform of a city is being laid down for the first time. Songdo may well prove to be exceptional, in that its rapid progression from raw landfill to habitable cityscape will be hard to duplicate without financing from a nationwide, governmental fund with deep reserves. It is hard to imagine that any one city of India or, to an extent, China will be the focus of national ambition as Songdo was, but they will need the strong backing of motivated—and invested—institutions. Institutional muscle cannot be separated from the process of building a city.

As demonstrated in previous chapters, the work of Cisco and other technology companies has focused on anticipating the trouble spots in a delivery platform that must sustain huge amounts of traffic and access points. Both multinational companies and governments can bring a huge concentration of resources to these industrial-scale problems. With thousands of engineers and business consultants on hand, technology companies make excellent partners to governments during the primary tasks of breaking ground, putting down cables, and erecting buildings. This does not mean that, in turn, they present a hostile face to the messy innovation that can follow once the infrastructure is in place. On the contrary; once smart infrastructure and a city platform are in place, technology companies actively encourage startups by providing innovation centers, seed money, and even just space. But for Songdo, Dholera, KAEC, or Chengdu to achieve the interconnectivity standards of Seoul, Barcelona, or San Francisco, a streamlined, tight partnership with existing political leadership is much closer to an ideal than the disjointed work of citizens and business leaders.

Townsend does make points about the challenges a city faces as it tries to define itself. Experimentation and sharing of information will be critical to the success of twenty-first-century cities. But these are secondary challenges in many of the city plans discussed in this book. Nonetheless, in Dholera's planning process, for example, citizen engagement can be part of the process from the outset. It is also clear that China and other nations will need to continue to find ways of making business and citizen services more transparent if they expect their cities to thrive not just as hubs of industry but also as destinations for talent. San Francisco is one example of a collaborative, innovating environment, while a city such as Singapore demonstrates that a strong government need not stand in the way of technological progress.

An excellent means of redefining Townsend's observation about the bottom-up and top-down technological planning is to see these definitions as separate phases of development. All the applications in the world mean little without a service delivery platform on which they can proliferate, be shared, and be improved. Transparency at City Hall will come much easier once the essential components of access and delivery systems are in place. To be sure, citizens ideally can have oversight of the process, but planning citywide service platforms is complicated enough with a relatively limited circle of stakeholders.

Townsend's *Smart Cities* points out that "computing is no longer solely in the hands of big companies and governments. The raw material and the means of producing a smart city—smartphones, social software, open-source hardware, and cheap bandwidth—are widely democratized and inexpensive. Combining and recombining them in endless variations is cheap, easy, and fun."[5] This is true, but the work of ripping out existing infrastructure to lay down new cables and sensors, or envisioning a brand-new system, is neither cheap nor easy. Until it is, technology companies will have a vital role to play in the process of bringing intelligence to our most populated areas.

So who makes a city smart? In emerging and emerged countries, there is no replacement for the Central Party in China, the DMIC Corporation in India, and other centralized institutions and well-funded developers. No other concerns can generate the necessary revenue and materials to help new or expanding cities leap over the dirty, disorganized twentieth-century model of the city and land in the twenty-first. After that, residents will be vital contributors of urban, creative, and functional touches that distinguish one city from the next. Still, citizens will need the partnership of innovative governments that are willing to embrace new uses of technology and think strategically about the future. Strong leaders of pragmatic mindset will continue to be essential to channeling the institutional muscle to get technological upgrades in place.

Author Benjamin R. Barber, for one, is convinced that those leaders will be essential to future prosperity. But he doesn't expect to find them at the national level. His 2013 book, *If Mayors Ruled the World*, argues that civic leaders are the best hope for implementing policies and solutions with the potential to counteract (or at least protect against) climate change, maintain social stability, and foster productive interdependence between disparate cultures. These are tasks at which Barber judges nation-states to be failures. He profiles ten mayors from cities such as Singapore, Lagos, London, and Palermo who have provided the sort of leadership that will be needed in an uncertain future. "A new global space of flows is replacing an old nation space of places," he writes.[6]

This is somewhat hyperbolic. The complex interplay between New York City and Albany (to say nothing of the Port Authority and federal agencies) is just one example of a complex interplay between layers of government that will not be dismantled easily. Nor are all nation-level governments failing to this extent. The Modi government in India, in fact, has been criticized for exercising too much influence over the affairs of cities and ceding responsibility to monolithic structures such as the DMIC Corporation. While leaders such as Bo Xilai have demonstrated how much power regional authorities can wield, his downfall is testament to the oversight of central authorities. The level of dysfunction can only be evaluated case by case, and many developments will need years to be evaluated fairly. But when considering the role played by the Korean government in the rise of Songdo, it is difficult to judge national action as hopeless.

Barber does not pass a final judgment on the success of smart cities, since the IoE technology behind the concept is so new and the full effects remain to be seen. He raises skeptical questions; among the most pertinent to this discussion is perhaps the bluntest: "Smart Cities: Dumb and Dumber or Better than Ever?" The focal point of his question concerns the civic component of urban life; like Townsend, he expresses concern that Internet technology has not delivered on its promise (one proof point is that e-government services have been touted since the 1990s, and yet most municipalities have yet to scratch more than the surface of IoE potential when it comes to their functions and services). The press releases announcing better city services via IoE capability strike him as overheated, but Barber also points out that the civic component of the Internet—and social media in particular—hasn't quite fostered community that leads to public engagement. Chat rooms are full, but public squares are still too often empty.

Barber's book is a showcase for municipal initiatives, and indeed some are technical in nature. But civic leaders, in his estimation, must also take some blame for lack of progress. "Technology can both facilitate and compromise what cities are doing to enhance their interdependence, but way too often, those employing it don't know the difference. Nor do they necessarily grasp what it means to partner with powerful private-sector corporations."[7]

What does that partnership mean? Like Townsend, Barber focuses on the billions of dollars the urban technology business represents to the shareholders of technology multinationals. The implication here is that the IoE solutions devised by corporations need not be aligned with a city's needs or interests, so long as there are profits to be made. This is not an unreasonable argument, but it should be noted that technology companies have invested in smart cities to make money and to adapt to changes in their markets. The teams that worked on the projects described in this book have been shaped by the lessons of IoE technology and smart city solutions, just as they have shaped the emerging future.

A technology corporation that served only investors would make a poor long-term partner for a city (or a nation). The success of smart city business models depends on making cities more interdependent, smarter, and better places to live for a wide variety of people. This will require a balance of priorities. Civic leaders must also balance out what city officials need with what their citizenry wants. The difference between safety and surveillance or troubleshooting and troublemaking often depends on how long that balance can be sustained.

It is important to recognize that all stakeholders in the modern city are living through a paradigm shift in real time. Mistakes will be made; some revenue sources will not deliver and some services will be unpopular. A mixed record is the cost of doing business in a laboratory. But it is the only way—most cities do not have the luxury of time when it comes to preparing for the challenges that are certain to arrive. Under these conditions, the companies that become and remain vital forces in urban technology development will be those that achieve not just reliable connectivity, data storage, analysis, and services; they will also be the best partners for the most innovative leaders. The smartest tech companies will be those that realize shareholder value is a metric of limited value if it is not mirrored by tangible results for urban clients.

Barber does make note of Cisco's collaboration with Barcelona and the resultant City Protocol initiative, but questions "whether putting best practices and innovative policy initiatives on a web feed that goes directly to member cities actually alters the urban landscape." This underscores the fact that information providers and facilitators do not operate in a vacuum. Enabling City Protocol and other instruments for exchanging and improving solutions yields benefits only when there is active participation. These initiatives require input from many sources: government functionaries, academics, business leaders, and citizens. Finding the means to encourage and facilitate that participation is an ongoing process. Companies with vital experience in IoE implementation and thought leadership are essential to modern, information-driven cities. If indeed mayors come to rule the world, they will still be partnering with technology companies to refine the vision of how information technology undergirds and fuels the urban landscape. Ultimately, a corporation's responsibility is to these dynamic leaders and their constituents, for they control a large portion of the smart city market.

THE IMPORTANCE OF TRANSPORT—AND A HUB

In Dubai, over the last ten years, a most improbable story unfolded. A modern city has expanded at an astonishing rate in an inhospitable climate, which at first glance might seem incapable of sustaining a host population, to say nothing of millions of visitors. But Dubai continues to grow in importance as a transportation node and as a destination. It's easy to conclude that oil—and oil alone—fueled this unprecedented growth in the desert. But Dubai's role as a trading hub likely predates recorded history, and transport is key to its present success. Of course, evidence of those ancient trade routes is barely perceptible. This is a twenty-first-century city that is the preeminent example of the symbiosis between city function and its transportation network.

Dubai is what author and air commerce expert John Kasarda calls an *aerotropolis*: a city defined by the functionality and attractiveness of its airport and surrounding neighborhoods. Work takes many residents in and out of Dubai constantly, and the international airport's lounges and walkways are as familiar as their own home. For many who live here, life is a sequence of homecomings and departures, yet there is no question as to whether Dubai has established a distinctive presence. Anyone who has traveled here (even just for a layover) would have to be quite jaded not to perceive the many ways Dubai accommodates visitors and residents alike. Despite serious economic troubles following the global financial downturn of 2008 and the expected depletion of its oil reserves, somehow Dubai has managed to survive as a business hub, destination, and trade locus, while coming to define new high standards for air travel. It is an unlikely combination of economic drivers, but still impressive because the city is the product of a vision.

Kasarda ranks Dubai as the first aerotropolis of the century, but thanks to the foresight of Rashid bin Saeed Al Maktoum, vice president and prime minister of Dubai (as well as father to Dubai's current leader, Mohammed bin Rashid Al Maktoum), the city's metamorphosis began earlier. Dubai has focused on trade since the creation of a deep-water port and the Jebel Ali Free Zone (JAFZA) in the 1970s and '80s. Oil revenues financed the infrastructure, but this city played things smart long before the implementation of sensors and IT revolutionized that description. Not only did the leadership recognize that the time to develop alternate economic drivers was brief, it chose to develop those that worked together and reinforced each other. Dubai is an excellent example of making use of the best a city has to offer.

As Kasarda and his cowriter Greg Lindsay note, "Dubai discovered after 9/11 that its greatest asset wasn't oil but *geography*, defined not by the contours of any map but by the flying times of modern airliners."[8] Like Songdo, a huge slice of the world's population can be visited with a day's flight or less from Dubai. With no personal income taxes and a waiver of corporate taxes for fifteen years, JAFZA is a lightning rod for expats and international meetings and transfers. The gaudy, air-conditioned recreation of the city and its architectural triumphs, such as the twisting spiral of the Burj Khalifa (the world's tallest building, although Dubai will be lucky to retain that honor by 2020), have made Dubai into something of an urban Disneyworld, needing to be seen to be believed. Even the journey to this United Arab Emirates (UAE) city is distinctive. Emirates Airlines, which is government-owned, is ordering more of the modern Airbus A380 jets than any of its competitors. Disembarking from one of these modern aircraft into the $4.5 billion Terminal 3 in Dubai, it is hard to reflect favorably on the aging, warren-like confines of many American and European airports.

Kasarda's thesis was instrumental to much of the thinking behind the city plans developed for King Abdullah Economic City, Knowledge City, Dholera, and other cities attempting to leap directly to the forefront of the twenty-first century urban experience. He recognizes that the aerotropolis itself has some curious antecedents, which may have settled too deeply into daily experience to be noticed, such as Dulles Airport and Northern Virginia. Ronald Reagan (formerly National) Airport, much closer to the center of Washington D.C., has never been able to land large, transcontinental aircraft, which hamstrung business leaders, military contractors, and others who made regular visits, often with cargo.

By strict definition, Washington D.C. is not an aerotropolis; rather, the communities that surround Dulles Airport comprise an "invisible city" that is wealthy, expanding, and intricately tied to the freight and passengers traveling through its gates. With a functional, large airport, the entire world can be invited in to do business. This is the same thinking behind Dubai, and will likely be essential to the plans of new cities in Asia and China in the coming years.

But there is a critical next step. Competition has improved air travel in the affluent but still developing world. The travel hubs of Singapore, Hong Kong, South Korea, and other Asian locales are proof points for a new standard for air travel. But luxury and glitter are only part of the equation. Most business travelers are not interested in the contents of Dubai International's high-end shops.[9] What matters is how easily they can move about, the punctuality of their scheduled flights, and the security of their person and luggage. In short, what interests them is the intelligence of this aerotropolis. The smart aerotropolis will be yet another component of the future of urban development, one that can be used to distinguish between top-tier cities and backwaters.

In the race to develop smart infrastructure, no one should bet against Dubai. The government has proved to be aggressive in its intention to keep the city on the cutting edge of technology. The goal of becoming a "Smart City of the Future" was spelled out by Sheikh Mohammed bin Rashid Al Maktoum in 2013. It was also the host city for Cisco's Internet of Things World Forum in December 2015. Few cities are better suited to a presentation of IoE applications and goals.

BUT MUST WE HAVE SMART *CITIES?*

J ohn Kasarda's coauthor Lindsay admits that the argument for the necessity of aerotropoli is far from over. Many planned cities do not have enviable track records, as critics of Brasilia and Abu Dhabi's Masdar City will claim. Kasarda believes people must "consciously choose to live in cities built in globalization's image" or face serious consequences. Those consequences, for the most part, are outside the scope of his book, but they are familiar to most who are worried about the sustainability of living standards on a hotter, drier, more populated planet. It is worthwhile, however, to explore the benefits of cities, which often can be obscured when the bad news crowds out the good. But Kasarda is hardly alone in his willingness to champion the modern city. Edward Glaeser, a Harvard economist, provides perhaps the most uncompromising defense for high-density, skyscraping living in his book, *Triumph of the City*. This is essential reading for critics who point fingers at China's "ghost towns" or another set of stalled city building plans. Glaeser provides illuminating historical context and parallels that find common lessons in the circumstances that gave the United States a "Motor City" in Detroit, India an electronics and technology hub in Bangalore, and Dubai an aerotropolis. Although his book is not immediately concerned with the implementation of IoE technology, it is nonetheless important validation for many of the aspirations for city life that technology companies have attempted to refine.

Glaeser has a knack for distilling his arguments into phrases that, while simple, contain much food for thought. Singapore is contrasted favorably with Mumbai; the former is "tall and connected," while Mumbai, like much of India, is burdened by building height restrictions that require its slums to spread out and increase commuting time and congestion. He also makes the point that basic infrastructure should come first: "One curse of the developing world is that governments take on too much and fail at their core responsibilities. Countries that cannot provide clean water for their citizens should not be in the business of regulating currency exchanges."[10] By the same token, a reliable Internet service delivery platform is an essential component of green- or brownfield development. Because IoE technology has the capability to deliver resources and services with greater efficiency, it should be designed and implemented as a primary tool for providing those "core responsibilities."

Glaeser also champions a less tangible but essential component to urban planning: flexibility. Like individuals, cities must be ready to adopt new economic drivers, welcome disparate industries, and adjust to the demands of the global economy. Detroit is singled out as a city so defined by automobile production that it was crippled by the downturn in the U.S. auto market. "Like skilled people, skilled cities also seemed to be better at reinventing themselves during volatile times."[11] Dubai, once again, is an excellent example. A strong Internet platform and connectivity is imperative to the flexible city of the twenty-first century. In terms of economic competitiveness, it is nearly as important to provide a data network and security features as it is to provide clean water. Meanwhile, much of the flexibility of cities will depend on their ability to provide and manipulate information.

By Glaeser's thinking, the city is the best vehicle for smart services, simply because it provides the density we need for innovation and to counteract the twentieth-century, mostly American, predilection for sprawl, suburbs, car culture, and other sources of environmental degradation. There is a clear link between his thesis and Chandran Nair's; both would argue vehemently against the creation of U.S.-style suburbias in China or India. Glaeser, providing a rosier counterpoint to Nair's warnings, couches his argument in the benefits of living in greater density.

Beyond the benefits to the environment, Glaeser provides an excellent rationale for why Internet technology is in fact an enabler of human connectivity and innovation, rather than the father of the "inauthentic" vistas of Songdo described by Anthony Townsend. In multiple examples (including Silicon Valley), Glaeser demonstrates how living in proximity to others who share interests, business, and goals brings forth much of the best humanity has yet offered.

Cities, beyond the shared streets and infrastructure, are hives for ideas. It has often been argued that the Internet expands the space between people and will "make urban advantages obsolete." Yet practical experience is demonstrating otherwise:

> One might think that better information technology would reduce the need to learn from other sources, like face-to-face meetings in cities. But . . . all those electronic interactions are creating a more relationship-intense world . . . and those relationships need both email and interpersonal contact. Better connections between people create far-ranging opportunities for trade and commerce.[12]

This explains why aerotropoli can thrive, as well as why a brand-new city, utilizing telepresence and other interactive devices, can actually promote rather than hinder the best exchanges among people, the exchanges that make money for partners, resolve neighborhood problems, and keep traffic flowing. Not coincidentally, the interests of young people, who are so essential to the vitality and influence of a city, are also well served by IoE technology. Rather than being a hindrance or replacement to the sorts of interactions we prefer, Internet technology so far has proven to be an enabler of those interactions.

LESSONS LEARNED

The thoughts of these authors give perspective to the arduous, modular process of implementing cities with connected technology. After listening to endless questions about when Songdo's NEATT building would open its doors, it is refreshing to discover, via Glaeser, that the Empire State Building did not reach maximum occupancy until the post–World War II boom, more than a decade after its completion.[13] The growth and distinguishing of new cities is a process that takes years, if not decades. On occasion, smart city technology is compared to the rise of the railway in the nineteenth century. Prototypes of the steam engine, barely functional and of little practical use, appeared intermittently during the 1820s, '30s, and '40s. The Transcontinental Railroad, a symbol of the technology's triumph over a continent, was not finished until 1869. If railway technology is used as a standard for comparison, smart cities are still in the early phases.

Having said that, technology development has accelerated. The best evidence of the efficacy of the Internet of Everything may be the human mind and its capabilities for collective action.

Urban planning today, as this small survey of authors demonstrates, is a multifaceted discipline that requires the expertise of many specialists. Thinkers such as Glaeser and Nair can provide useful guidelines, but it is up to those who are actually tasked with building out new cities to create something that works and can survive the next technological leap forward. A potent combination of thinkers, dealmakers, and tech expediters is needed to make new cities into vehicles for change. But as Nair points out, they also must serve as loci for sustainable practices that are in accord with what our stressed environments can bear in the long term.

It is a difficult balancing act that will take time to master, but less time than many people think. The following lessons, explored in the work of these thinkers, have been learned by the people working on the projects covered in this book:

- **Action is needed now.** The population trends are incontrovertible in China, India, the Middle East, Africa, South America, and elsewhere. Cities, for most of us, are the future. There is a tremendous opportunity to create smarter, more efficient cities in the next few decades, but the opportunity is not open-ended. Inaction carries the peril of a lack of economic growth and condemns city dwellers to the worst of urban life rather than some of the best.

- **Making ideas is better than making things.** There is nothing wrong with people who have lived on little for centuries living on more. It is difficult to blame any Chinese citizen, who is used to saving nearly all of his pay, for being pleased with the opportunity to spend more. But consumption has its limits. Cities will need to be centers for collaboration and information, and will need to provide means to monetize those pursuits.

- **Population density contributes to the making of good ideas.** The hive mind is an attractive place for those who are eager to collaborate, and these people tend to be young. With so many nations facing the challenge of employing populations that are growing younger (and, presently, underemployed), cities are the best opportunities.

- **Rather than discouraging social interaction, Internet technology seems to encourage it.** The smart city, with modern communication techniques, is not filled with millions of isolation tanks outfitted with screens. Rather, evidence suggests Internet technology *enhances* human interaction and collaboration, rather than limiting it.

- **To globalize is to fly.** As a corollary to the prior point, it is quite clear that air travel will be essential to our future cities, rather than an anachronism from the twentieth century. Airports and transportation systems will be essential components to every smart city. They will need to be supported with best-practice technology infrastructure to remain competitive, even desirable, destinations.

If all these lessons are put into practice, what will be the result? What will the smart and connected cities of 2030 or 2040 look like? Will they be recognizable to people living now? The next chapter will explore a vision of that future.

[1] Chandran Nair, *Consumptionomics: Asia's Role in Reshaping Capitalism and Saving the Planet* (John Wiley & Sons, 2011), p. 66.

[2] "Obesity: A Growing Threat to Health in China," *The Lancet*, Volume 384, No. 9945, p. 766–781, August 2014. See also editorial in same issue, http://www.thelancet.com/journals/lancet/article/PIIS0140-6736(14)61421-5/fulltext.

[3] Anthony Townsend, *Smart Cities: Big Data, Civic Hackers, and the Quest for a New Utopia* (Norton, 2013), p. 28

[4] Ibid, p. 9

[5] Ibid, p. 9

[6] Benjamin R. Barber, *If Mayors Ruled the World: Dysfunctional Nations, Rising Cities* (Yale University Press, 2013). The space of flows, the brainchild of sociologist Manuel Castells, is a concept that defines not just the information packets that travel our technological infrastructure but the infrastructure itself. Beyond that prosaic definition, Castells emphasizes that human perception of space and time are directly affected by the space of flows. See Castells, "An Introduction to the Information Age."

[7] Ibid, p. 246.

[8] John Kasarda and Greg Lindsay, *Aerotropolis: The Way We'll Live Next* (Farrar, Strauss and Giroux, 2011), p. 295.

[9] Graham Boynton, "The New Jet Age," *Vanity Fair*, July 2014, http://www.vanityfair.com/news/business/2014/07/dubai-international-airport-emirates-airbus-a380. *Vanity Fair* magazine applied a thick layer of gloss to a feature on Dubai International and the Emirates' Airbus fleet. Imagining the advent of a new age of glitter, the article describes planes outfitted with showers and a lively bar area that add to "the allure of the voyage" to the Mideast desert.

[10] Edward Glaeser, *The Triumph of the City* (Penguin US, 2011), p. 158.

[11] Ibid, p. 29

[12] Ibid., pp. 248, 37–38

[13] dIbid., p. 143. For contrast, it is notable that one current tenant of the Empire State Building is leasing space near the observation deck for $832 per square foot, thought to be the highest price for any rental in the city above ground. See Adam Pincus,"Empire State Building: A buyer's manual," *The Real Deal*, September 2013, http://therealdeal.com/issues_articles/empire-state-building-a-buyers-manual/.

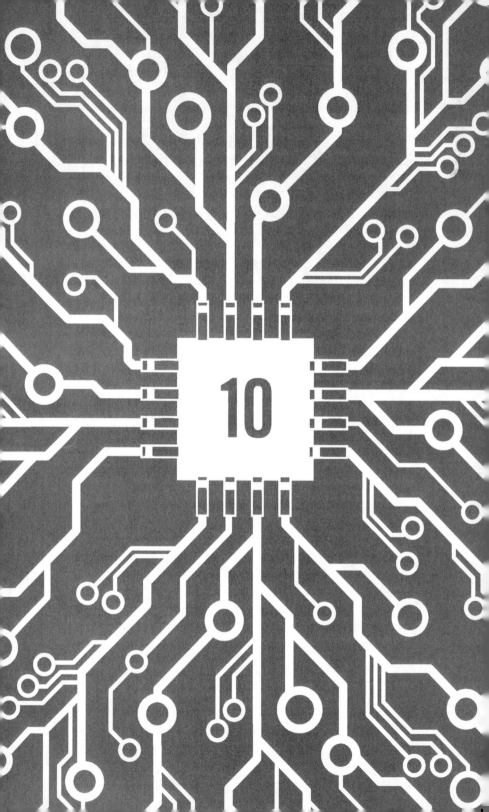

BEYOND SONGDO AND THE FUTURE OF THE CITY

B Y 2014, TELEPRESENCE (TP) technology had rolled out in selected business-to-business conditions in Songdo. U-Life Solutions developed a home network system that would, in time,
bring TP to the population at large, but it remained an open question
whether residents would take to the technology at all. It had tested poorly at the outset, with many potential residents considering
a two-way screen to be an extravagance or an invasion of privacy.
Some skeptics wondered if TP would ever develop beyond restricted
business-use cases.

This was an urban engineering impasse. So many of the proposed
elements of a smart city are predicated on digital communication.
TP's impact on education, health care, and social networking had
been, for the most part, researched but not enacted. Was this to be
another example of engineers presenting the impractical? It was a
question that lingered in Songdo well after its status as a pioneering
smart city was established.

In January 2015, building projects were still everywhere. Cranes
dotted the horizon; to the east, there were still many empty blocks
divided by a network of roads. In the cold of winter, the city was
quiet but not lacking for activity: 55 percent of Songdo's building had
been completed (another 5 percent is in process), and the population
had risen to 86,000 by December 2014 (about 20 percent of whom
were foreigners). Maxing out at $115 USD per square foot, residen-
tial real estate was expensive and demand was high.

The city had come a long way since the first ICT master plan was
completed. The first tech teams brought in by Cisco, for example,
were housed in a pitiful building near the Sheraton Incheon that
lacked air conditioning or sufficient desk space. The company offices

now occupy several floors in one of the two Posco Towers that stand at the southeastern edge of the central park. Songdo had not met its initial development forecasts, and one Gale official described his company's involvement as more "a labor of love" than a source of profit.[1] Nevertheless, the indicators point in the right direction. Songdo by now has "established residents"; their opinions—and decisions—will decide Songdo's fate going forward.

Telepresence's status is curious. In late 2014, the first 1,400 residents had units installed in their homes. Meeting some of these early adopters to gauge their level of interest, there was no question of them accessing all its potential at once. There are legal hurdles to medical professionals providing even basic services remotely, and the educational system in Songdo (indeed, most of the world) has not yet reached forward to meet these citizens. In other words, the "creators" of Songdo are not yet positioned to supply the benefits outlined in marketing material, or the Big Brother intrusions dreamed up by Songdo critics. Rather, the residents were left to their own devices and were free to adapt TP to their own preferences and needs. Far from "engineering serendipity out of existence," Songdo's residents were improvising in the same spirit of curiosity as citizens of San Francisco, New York, or any other city championed by bottom-up development proponents such as Anthony Townsend.

In Songdo, TP is a social media tool. It's proved helpful in establishing relationships between new arrivals, especially the foreigners who often arrive with no connections beyond quick interactions at schools and restaurants. One woman, who is active in a local church, has used TP to organize meetings and introduce new members to parts of the congregation. "It wasn't so much about need," she reported. "I took to it because it was fun." Relatives who visited were eager to install their own units at home to increase the quality of long-distance communication. More important was an aside about a teenaged son: "The children use it all the time, to talk, do homework together. They're better with it than I am." But new arrivals are using it too. Spouses home with young children, especially multinationals still dealing with the shock of the new, have learned to appreciate this intimate but noninvasive means of meeting other people.

Anecdotal though these examples are, they demonstrate a core principle of smart city engagement. Early curiosities become essentials precisely through this soft adaptation process. How strange will it seem to these children to work with a tutor from Seoul, or Bangalore, in a few years? Convinced of the reliability and security of connection, how awkward will a consultation with a trusted medical professional be? It seems certain that Songdo's residents will continue to embrace telepresence. The city's advanced features are proving to be popular. As prices come down (and the affluent early adopters arrive in greater numbers), this test run of technology can become the standard. Songdo is becoming known for its quality of life. Residents are also beginning to sense the potential for greater usage. There is little connection between neighborhoods, one said, while another noted that the local university is an ideal place for TP expansion.

The residents whose opinions are sampled here had been living in Songdo for up to four years. They were impressed by the rate of change, particularly in the last year. These were people who had lived in other nations, owned their own businesses, exhibited the typical South Korean fluency with technology, and had high standards for life quality. No one wanted to leave. They had the feeling of finding a good thing early in its development. Compared to their former residences in crowded Seoul or its outliers, Songdo already provided a high quality of life for them.

Songdo's modernity has provided many perks, but these residents singled out security as a primary benefit. In part this is due to Songdo's relative low-density, wide, well-lit streets and high price tags, but here again, smart technology plays a vital role. The automated features of apartment complexes—RFID features that recognize vehicles, lights that turn on before the owner enters the apartment—make residents feel secure. And while the business community and trendsetters might deride Songdo as a "sleepy" place, the slower pace and openness are just what has helped to keep families here and attract more. The same features that define suburban Connecticut and Westchester County, features that have pulled workers out of New York City for generations, are playing a role in Songdo today. The difference is that security in the twenty-first century can be had in a small city, and it is far more technical in nature.

There is much to do, but people in Songdo are not living with hardship. They see their lives as full of potential (and enviable increases in their real estate's value). Of course, the empty blocks need to be filled; the ambitious system to reuse waste and grey water is not yet fully operational; the city's green features, like the rest of the world's, are still working toward capacity. But according to those who live there, Songdo works. One can see the future when visiting, and it is much easier to imagine life in a smart and connected city here. Still, there is much left to the imagination. What will Songdo look like in 2035? Will India have a dense network of "connected villages"? What innovations might we expect? What headaches?

These are reasonable questions to consider. Cisco, like any other company, makes calculated bets on the future; its research and expertise narrow the margins, but ultimately no one can predict which aspects of city life will prevail in the coming years.

It is possible, however, to predict that the general concept of a city is due to be irreversibly overhauled and expanded in the coming years. Cities will become smarter, and in turn they will support tools that make their citizens happier, more efficient, and safer. The rest of this chapter explores how these changes might come to pass, the benefits that might accrue, and the challenges engineers and planners will face. By no means will the list be exhaustive; there is no way to consider all the facets of modern life that will be affected by the expanse of digital technology. But it may be possible to discern the largest trends and most obvious changes to human life and today's civilization.

IN DEFENSE OF CONDITIONAL OPTIMISM

Peter Diamandis, the author of *Abundance: The Future Is Better Than You Think*, has been a lightning rod for both hope and praise and unbridled criticism. As an entrepreneur and CEO of the X Prize Foundation, he is an unapologetic advocate for technology and its benefits to humanity. Reading his book is a superb antidote to arguments that condemn civilization to irreversible disaster, either from climate change, food and water shortages, civil unrest, or, likely, a terrible combination of them all. To accept his interpretation of data and breakthrough inventions does, in fact, require the reader to embrace a view of humanity that is at least in part optimistic and complimentary. Some facts he presents are incontrovertible: Solar panels have dropped historically in price, as have robotic, 3-D printers and many other elements of IoE technology that are critical to a better future for more people. But in other instances, Diamandis and his cowriter, Steven Kotler, have been criticized for glossing over very real challenges to implementation, challenges that could still derail many technological advances for non-technological reasons. It is one thing to propose digital urban infrastructure, another to find a government with the means and intent to build it.

For instance, there may be many unforeseen (or obvious) impediments to reducing the cost of the "Slingshot," a prototype machine that can purify 250 gallons of water per day for a few dollars worth of energy. This is a remarkable breakthrough, which its inventor Dean Kamen believes can be the type of game-changer that could end water-borne diseases that kill two million people a year. But at present, each unit costs $100,000. It will be an uphill climb to achieve the economy of scale necessary to bring a Slingshot to every village in Africa. An innovator and his team have provided the world with a great technological advance, but it remains to be seen if global markets and political calculations will help in the creation of necessary supply chains.[2] The "smart villages" of India, which must overcome the severe water shortage in that nation, will depend on exactly this sort of problem-solving.

As for cities, the pursuit of a smart water delivery system is in the works in many of them, and it takes many forms. Some will rely on sensors to restrict waste. Others are exploring smart metering, which can more efficiently deliver water to agricultural and urban centers.

Reading Diamandis and other thinkers who see the potential for exponential growth of technological solutions can drive away years of bad news. But is this "techno-optimism at its worst," as one reviewer of *Abundance* complained?[3] Probably not. The future will not be a particularly orderly place. The technology of the new smart cities will solve a great many problems, but it will introduce many new ones as well.

Abundance makes extensive reference to the Internet of Everything, but Diamandis does not look at the smart city as a distinctive, technological advance, although many of the improvements and breakthroughs he discusses may well be found in urban environments. What is most familiar about his work is the unspoken sense—or fear—that the future either will be utopian, in which everything works perfectly to humankind's benefit, or dystopian, to the point where humans are "scrubbed out" by machines that are smarter than they are.

When imagining the city of 2035, one should not anticipate perfection. It will be a place where more things work for more people, where the engines run on less fuel, less energy and resources are wasted, the people use less power and exploit far greater computational power with a flick of a switch than today's sophisticated programmers do in a day's work. But for humans and machines, twenty years is not an equal unit of measurement. Even if Moore's Law[4] does reach its fundamental limit in that time, computers, sensors, and the data they harness will be as foreign to people today as NASA's 1969 mainframes. Humanity, however, needs more time to evolve. That is both a check on Diamandis's enthusiasm and a source of hope for the doomsayers who fear the end of privacy and spontaneous living.

The differences in twenty years will be impressive enough without hyperbole. In contrast to today's current best standards, the following list, nowhere near comprehensive, details some of what can be expect of Smart City 2035. Rest assured that there is another side; after looking at the benefits of this modern cityscape, this chapter will talk about the challenges—and threats—its citizens will reckon with on a regular basis.

Taller, denser, and stronger. Smart cities of 2035 will go up. The race to climb above will continue, and even accelerate. The Burj Khalifa in Dubai will be dwarfed by structures that likely will top out at a full mile above the landscape. These will be exceptions, of course; super skyscrapers are more ornamental than practical drivers of new city growth. But the benefit of using aerial space to restrict sprawl will continue to push average building heights beyond what we have seen. Density, when it is based on a plan, does not create slums and dysfunction; rather, it encourages collaboration and economies where the proximity of competitors drives progress and innovation. City populations will trend younger; even in countries where populations are stable or declining, the urban zones will continue to attract the best, most eager talent.

Building materials will be "greener" in that they will be chosen for their durability. There is a clear need to reverse decades of reliance on ever cheaper, disposable construction material, given the long-range inefficiency of this model. Then there is the resultant environmental degradation to consider. The new model will trend toward buildings that endure for generations. This, too, will be a function of improved master planning. Buildings that encompass sustainable, modern technology and smart features will be easier to design and build than working around cumbersome legacy structures. They will be flexible, built to adjust to changes in building codes and technology and thus prolong their usefulness.

Doing more with less in a green, efficient way. Sensor systems will track the flow and use of electricity, heat, and water to the point where waste of these essentials is practically unheard of. End users will rely on increasingly sophisticated appliances that adjust their function to suit their preferences and needs. Instead of these appliances sporting a lengthy menu of presets, consider the possibility of intelligence. A refrigerator with its own IP address, comprehensive sensor system, and computational power an exponent beyond today's laptop is not just the latest gizmo; it becomes an essential component of a household, helping to keep down costs, suggesting recipes based on current supplies, and saving time. Programmable thermostats can still monitor temperature, but also the humidity, lighting, color, and musical accompaniment. What is more, these conditions can be set remotely and automatically. Rather than waiting for apartments to become warm, cool, brightly lit, or covered in artistic murals, residents of smart cities will equate home with the proper mood and temperature.

The key here is to imagine more function embedded in a single device. The smart office and apartment of 2035 will work off a single control panel, much as today one can track business, personal communications, and household expenditures with interactive software. As more processing power is pressed into smaller and smaller space, the control rooms may well shrink to the size of a single screen.

Cities will do more with less energy. Solar panels will be ubiquitous, as will charging stations for solar-powered batteries. Grey and wastewater will routinely be processed and repurposed; droughts may still put strain on agriculture, but water renewal technology will ensure clean drinking water for almost everyone. More farming will move into cities as well—rooftop gardens and greenhouses that utilize the same climate controls as residences and businesses will be generating a growing percentage of food requirements. With more localized production of food, transport costs will drop and supply chains will contract. The first few advanced metropolises will have become energy and food self-sufficient. They literally will not rely on any other state, nation, or city for the essentials of life.

Shortages may occur, but urban populations will be insulated from doomsday scenarios by making the most of what is available. This will not be a triumph exclusively of technology or human adaptability. Both will be needed for effective response to potential crises.

The Internet of People. Miniaturization has led to uncounted advances in medical imaging and diagnostics. Sensors will continue to shrink in size as they become more sophisticated and sensitive. Data that presently can be compiled only by expensive, large, onsite equipment will be generated through sensors that will provide readouts of a person's vital signs and mapping scans at any given moment. The implications for human health and lifespan are beyond the context of this book; suffice to say that the patient of 2035 will have access to more refined preventative and palliative care than the best of today's healthcare can provide. And it will be constant, as the body's sensors talk with data analysis engines that serve each patient individually.

Surgery and long-term care will be automated more often (although not exclusively). Care for the swelling population of elderly citizens will be managed in great part by machines that can dispense proper doses of medicine, provide locomotion (Dean Kamen has also invented the iBOT, a motorized wheelchair),[5] perform surgeries, and, through future generations of telepresence and other communication technology, keep their trusts in regular contact with their families. Human error that leads to deaths will have dropped significantly. Air-quality sensors will help identify bacteria and reduce airborne illnesses. Hospitalization or long-term care will be far less common events, which will help enable care providers to refine and specialize the experience.

Short-term travel is a special occasion. Before the advent of the railway system, long-distance travel was either a luxury or a tedious, frequently dangerous undertaking. Most people either avoided or could not afford it. In 2035, it will be short-range travel that is uncommon, but not because there is any great premium of money or danger to be paid. It simply will not be necessary. "Commuting" will not have the same connotation, and the term "rush hour" may well become obsolete. Trends toward remote-site work will continue and extend. Travel avoidance will exist on such a scale as to drastically impact the use of cars and other transportation. The savings in energy and work hours will be enormous. Cleaner air and more open space for parks will foster a healthier environment; the polluted cities of the twentieth century will be nothing more than a bad memory for those old enough to recall them.

Meanwhile, long-range travel, thanks to many new aerotropoli and safer, connected air flight, will be yet more affordable for many. Globalization will make the connections between cities more critical than before. Political differences will take more than a generation to resolve, but the economic interdependence of the most advanced cities will continue to increase.

The "office" as we know it may disappear. An executive traveling in 2035 likely will not have a foreign office to visit. Rather, he or she will have office space designated for their visit; at its conclusion, another executive or team may occupy the same space for a shorter time. Why will companies need to purchase or rent expensive, energy-intensive sites when onsite meetings are much less frequent and telepresence and cloud services allow for routine virtual interaction? In the morning, the signage throughout an office complex might read Cisco, only to be replaced by GE or Siemens in the afternoon. The fluid, interactive nature of Cisco's Bangalore will no longer be an innovative anomaly. The drudgery of cubicles will have been replaced by multivaried, nonrepeatable schedules that change with the nature of business and daily tasks. The static worksite will become a rarity, superseded by one that changes due to need, circumstance, or even personal preference.

Freed from dull patterns, innovation and creativity will be encouraged. New technologies can provide a sudden reconfiguration of humankind's approach to problems, exposing weak points in the established way of doing things that once seemed unchangeable. The Internet of Everything is helping to show that some givens in life, such as office life, rush hours, and the compounding stress of work, in fact might be ephemeral.

Education remains recognizable. Online learning is a booming business for universities and colleges. The software that brings sophistication to online curricula, through steady refinement, will undergird a healthy exchange between experts and students the world over. Education at all levels and for all ages will be readily accessible. DIY instruction and demonstration will be encouraged, and the cloud will expand to cover even the most remote areas with libraries' worth of information. So long as digital platforms remain in place, there will be no reason for children and adults who live away from major educational centers to be disenfranchised. The price of two-way screening will have dropped to the point that all a community will need to bring top-notch education to its children will be personal commitment.

But there will still be vibrant, elite universities; most of them will be in smart cities. Students will continue to benefit from the density and community that have made colleges into coveted destinations for generations. The globalization and city-centric trends of today will have accelerated to the point where the best institutions are truly international; students from the West will more frequently travel East to study and make connections. The bloodlines between these universities and the professional spheres will grow stronger. Insigma's relationship to Zhejiang University will be seen in many industries as competition for talent intensifies. The concentration of opportunity will fuel the continuing migration to cities from towns and villages. Sprawl will reduce as young people continue to find professional and social benefits to city life. Even the need to "escape" to greener places will be affected. The tendency of the affluent to escape city life for quieter, calmer, and cleaner environs originated in times when cities were hot, polluted, crime and disease-ridden, and poorly designed. Smart cities that incorporate expansive parklands and green spaces, such as Songdo, will prove to be habitable and pleasant year-round. As a result of greater human concentration, more wild spaces will remain truly wild, subject to destination travel and ecosystem protection. This balance between development and preservation will continue to be delicate; debates between conservationists and builders will rage on. But well-planned, intricately connected cities will have a beneficial effect on the debate nonetheless.

More connections afford more protection. Surveillance systems are easy to disparage—until they are needed. The most refined security networks will belong to the cities that see the advantage in connecting everything and creating a video record of the most streets, buildings, and public spaces. They will have the most signage, and they will be capable of broadcasting important messages from more endpoints than any city currently in existence.

As an example, consider the response in 2035 to another tsunami generated by violent seismic activity somewhere along the Pacific Rim. A modern coastal city is among the most vulnerable locations. But many years before, a sophisticated disaster awareness network has been implemented; alerts from national authorities reach the city within minutes of the tsunami's generation, with accurate estimates for its time of landing. Residents of the city are advised of the danger in every direction. The faces of tall buildings broadcast the warning and evacuation information. Personal phones show the best evacuation route based on each device's proximity to transport; as with regular traffic patterns, the city's roadways are monitored and congestion points are pinpointed. Alternate routes are highlighted by lights colored to indicate the easiest way to safety. Responders read through a database of homebound residents and are dispatched through a sequence that preserves order and exploits routes left clear by the evacuation pattern.

Are all citizens saved in time? We can't expect that level of efficiency in twenty years. But compared to a disaster on the level of the 2004 Indian Ocean tsunami, which killed more than 350,000 people, smart communities and networks will perform at a level of efficiency that, by today's standards, will seem miraculous.

Day to day, the sensor systems and analytic tools available to law enforcement agencies will make crime ever harder to perpetrate. Population density has often been associated with high crime rates; in slum conditions, where police either are unable or disinclined to exercise oversight, the correlation is based in fact. But as Sherlock Holmes noted, more than 120 years ago, "the lowest and vilest alleys in London do not present a more dreadful record of sin than does the smiling and beautiful countryside."[6] The sleuth emphasized that the "pressure of public opinion"—the enforcement of common expectations and rules among those who live close together—maintains order even better than the police. Data has supported Conan Doyle's insight, which will apply to Smart City 2035 just as it did to Victorian London. Criminal behavior will lack incentive in a smart city. If a neighborhood is vibrantly, densely populated; if it is outfitted with sophisticated surveillance technology; if the technology links to an effective, responsive system of analytics that relies both on human oversight and the algorithmic power of computers, it simply is not a climate that is conducive to crime. Again, a virtuous loop of conditions will favor the cities that exploit the best of technology. Safety will attract more residents, who in 2035 simply will expect that the neighborhoods in which they live are pleasant to explore and outfitted with requisite protection from both people and machines.

With all these elements synthesized, what is the result? Will the smart city be antiseptic, too planned, lacking serendipity and the essential spark that is rarely anticipated but always found in a dynamic urban space? While possible, this seems unlikely. It is worthwhile to point out that humanity's track record is decidedly jagged, full of failures, natural disasters, and enough "end of times" to have snuffed out all life, not just our own. Yet humans are still here, in a world where more people live longer, healthier lives than ever before. The average city of 2035 will be an improvement on the best of 2015, even as overpopulation and climate conditions exert pressure on people's livelihoods.

Utopia? Far from it. There will be many difficulties to overcome, some longstanding, some brought forth by new technology.

There are other concerns. It is natural to fear the unknown. In the interest of encouraging governments and citizens to embrace IoE technology and have confidence that this will lead to a superior quality of life, it is worthwhile to consider these concerns from a rational standpoint.

Privacy in a modern city. Revelations of domestic surveillance programs, to say nothing of the operations of twentieth-century totalitarian regimes, have bred a deep fear that everyone is being watched. The fear is greatest, perhaps, in the memories of countries that suffered under oppressive governments. Today, when former NSA contractors reveal that enormous caches of data, emails, and phone records are routinely swept up by federal agencies, it is easy to assume that the details of people's lives are being "jealously scrutinized," as George Orwell imagined in *1984*. Will this dragnet stretch wider and deeper in a smart and connected community? How can privacy survive in a world where there is more data, more collection points, and a more powerful network through which data can flow and be analyzed?

Those who have served in intelligence organizations have many opportunities to see how important information is utilized once collected. Much of the time, it isn't. While movies and recruitment ads give the impression of precision and calculated action within armies and police stations, the fact is that collecting, sorting, and employing data are three distinct functions. Most agencies or services currently collect more data than they can manage. But even if IoE technology and Big Data allow governments to effectively sort through information recorded in people's daily lives, it does not automatically follow that they will or are able to employ it.

Many of the details of people's lives are mostly forgettable, even for the individuals themselves. In a crowded world, the daily routines, and even private behavior, of normal citizens simply do not justify scrutiny. Government agencies will be overtaxed, even in 2035, maintaining a lookout for active criminals. In fact, many conditions must apply for any personal correspondence to stand out from the billions generated every day. When it comes to the attention data receives, there is great safety in numbers.

The real problem will lie with data management. Already cities can generate the equivalent of data sewers: overflows of information that are never analyzed or stored properly, if they make it to the data centers at all. The future will give rise to data storage at the edges of networks. Today, solutions like Data Virtualization and Connected Analytics are the best options for managing that flow. The coming tsunami of data will require innovation and reinvention for years to come.

By 2035, expect that the analytic and storage solutions will be keeping up with the data generated by our cities. But there will still be little time for government agencies to keep up with the average citizen. What is more, citizens will be armed with increasingly sophisticated security systems that allow them to keep records of who explores their data, and when.

There will be insufficient security. Perhaps violent crime and burglaries will be rarities in the smart city, but what about cybercrime? With a massive proliferation of endpoints, is a correlating spike in security breaches inevitable?

Perhaps. What "security" is, what it requires, and whether it is there (or not)—these are open-ended subjects that will continue to evolve. Cutting-edge security in the Roman era meant the London Wall: a strong fortification to keep out hostile enemies. As the nature of the city changed, a wall was insufficient. By 1829, London was vast and complex enough that unpaid constables could no longer investigate and prevent crime effectively. A paid police force was then introduced. Today, London, as a vital financial center, has one of the most sophisticated surveillance and security systems in the world. While conditions change, the tension between safety and danger remains, the outcome of the conflict always somewhat in doubt. Today, the gravest threats to safety require little more than a computer and knowledge put to bad ends, and the stakes of the conflict remain high.

At present, data generated by a closed system can be compromised by insufficient encryption or hacker ingenuity.[7] As the endpoints proliferate, so will the need for firewalls, ever more sophisticated encryption methods, and oversight from both people and machines. It may be that the criminal mind, which can take the time it needs to study the defenses of a society, will always find a way through. Security forces will respond, correct, and analyze the breach in an attempt to find a future solution. There is a silver lining to this age-old conflict: Innovation is always required. Human ingenuity will always come as a premium, so long as there are ingenious humans who are unwilling to respect society's fabric.

But innovation and vigilance do not belong just to the network experts. Private citizens and businesses will have to become adept at securing the Internet equivalent of their back doors and windows. Just as city dwellers have learned to be alert on unfamiliar streets, citizens in 2035 will take more precautions to protect privacy of their web cams, devices, and accounts.[8] Mistakes will be inevitable; tragedies still will be possible. But it is irrational to believe that in a future of billions more ingress points and vast networks, the bad guys must win.

Our tools will replace us, or destroy us. The melding of machines and humans has fascinated people for generations now, but as we move closer to the event of singularity, or automated intelligence, unease is spreading. Robotics and automated functions will continue to impact the world economy and do some jobs better than people. But will this trend continue to the point where humans are stripped of purpose, excepting a few at the apex of technological and financial pyramids? This seems unsustainable. Unless the cities and nations of the world were able to find the resources to house, feed, and entertain billions made idle by automation, there would be no stability. Even if the funds could be procured, it presumes the idle would be content to stay that way. This seems highly unlikely. We have always been inventors, explorers, and above all an industrious species. It is difficult to believe that our children, who will be young adults in 2035, would accept a world in which there simply was no way to earn, create, or participate in society. They, like millions of young people today, will want more.

Market forces might make this difficult. It is reasonable to assume that without proactive efforts to place limits on what humans allow machines to do for us, they may "take over" many of the functions humans need to feel purposeful and engaged. Even so, it is difficult to imagine that algorithms will do a better job interpreting law, writing books, or closing business deals. They will not supplant political leadership or the intuitive thinking that is needed to adjust to rapidly changing circumstances. But that does not mean market forces might not shift the balance of jobs away from people to machines. Industries that might support a human workforce at slightly higher cost than machines will need to engage in sophisticated analysis that measures not only return on investment but also the benefits to the consumer base and economic ecosystem. Governments may need to pass legislation that restricts the level of automation within an industry as a protective measure against high unemployment and social unrest. A government-based solution may seem unrealistic to Americans and others who believe in the primacy of markets. But residents of Indonesia, Egypt, and other nations with populations trending younger have a different perspective. In these places, government intervention may be the only way to ensure that the majority of future generations have any chance whatever of holding a job.

There also are the perceived existential threats of singularity. Thinkers as sophisticated as Stephen Hawking and Bill Gates have expressed concern that artificial intelligence, through an extended process of redesigning itself, could find humanity to be an imperfect pattern, and replace it. As cities become smarter, we are counting on the emergence of machines of astonishing algorithmic power. If they can "think" faster, and more efficiently, than humans, will they escape the conclusion that everything would run better, and all the threats to the network removed, if malfeasance and error were rooted out at the source?

Dave Evans, cofounder of Stringify, a company that offers an app designed to connect the Internet of Things, makes a valid point. "We are biased by our own beliefs," he wrote in 2015. "Many assume that because computers will become intelligent, they will 'think' just like we do. We are projecting our own belief system onto technology."[9] Considering humanity's record of violence and dysfunction, it is not surprising that one can't imagine smart machines without humankind's less admirable traits infecting their programming.

It is never easy for us to face the unknown. Irrationality can cloud our vision, magnifying threats and minimizing our strengths. Whether the concern is that computers will steal too many jobs or plot the end of our species, it is easy to overlook the exceptional abilities of the human mind and spirit. The essential spark of humanity, its soul, will not be replicated in any man-made machine. Humans will meld with their machines. Artificial organs and implants will prolong lives and keep people connected to networks, but a full human brain cannot be fabricated. The essential element that keeps humans human will remain elusive, and preserve free will.

Ultimately, many questions about what is and is not a machine will belong to ethics, not engineering. But until artificial intelligence is a reality, people will continue to face choices, and will need to be engaged in a collective evaluation of what the connected world is going to look like.

SMART CITIES, TOWNS, AND VILLAGES

Most people who have lived in cities remain committed advocates of the quality of life they present. There is sometimes a tendency among city dwellers to dismiss rural or small-town life as inferior. But cities are not the destiny for all. As India's Connected Villages initiative makes clear, life in small communities is still valued by those who can make it work. Unfortunately, the number who can is dwindling: 2035 will not sustain the same numbers of livestock and water-intensive crops, and more effort will be placed on keeping forests and wetlands intact as humans are forced to reckon with the results of too much carbon in the atmosphere.

The Internet of Everything will incorporate the world's small communities as the means of connectivity to the cities and richer human resources improve. Telepresence and other flexible interfaces will continue to appear outside of cities—perhaps India in 2035 will set the goal of one TP kiosk per village, countrywide. Agriculture and small businesses, already benefiting from data and smart delivery of resources, will become yet more dependent on the Internet to stay operational and efficient. Wealthier citizens will continue to enjoy second homes away from their normal, busy city lives, and tourist destinations will continue to attract visitors and support local economies. Unless there are enormous, drastic changes to water supply or energy delivery systems, smaller communities will survive; some will thrive. Gandhi's vision of 70,000 villages embracing an ascetic approach to life may not survive the great migration toward cities, but nations that value rural traditions will be able to sustain them, should they take steps to provide and maintain the necessary IoE connections.

But the future belongs to cities. The development of new metropolises will become more formulaic, based on the experiences in Asian nations, which will separate out sustainable, repeatable growth policies and practices from the misfires. Mayors and municipal agencies will continue to concentrate power over economic levers and strategies. The Internet of Everything will be considered a utility, as fundamental as electricity itself, and most of the time, it will be taken for granted. There will be outages, service disruptions, and, unfortunately, more frightening upsets created by security breaches or widespread attacks on primary systems. The unexpected will never be factored. Still, urban life will continue to improve through alertness, improvisation, and well-constructed strategies.

The human ability to surprise cuts both ways. But if the right combination of governments, companies, and citizens can support the best opportunities for successful connection today, the city's future already looks brighter.

---

[1] In-Soo Nam, "South Korea's $35 Billion Labor of Love," *Wall Street Journal*, December 6, 2013, http://www.wsj.com/articles/SB10001424052702304579404579236150341041182. Gale has recouped its initial investment, but the 2008 shock to global finance is one of several factors that negatively impacted profits and delayed construction.

[2] There are promising signs for Slingshot, notably Kamen's partnership with Coca-Cola. With supply chains and delivery systems that have already conquered the world, the company pledged 2,500 "Ekocenter" kiosks on three continents by 2015; each will contain a Slingshot. Still, the enormity of the water issue is borne out by the numbers. One Slingshot can provide a year's water for about 300 people. The World Health Organization stated in 2014 that 1.8 billion people rely on contaminated water sources, and that half of the world's population will live in a "water-stressed" area by 2025. Among all the threats to human progress, clean water shortages are the least discriminating, affecting the city and village alike. See also Rececca Borison, "The Guy Who Invented the Segway Is Working with Coca-Cola to Bring His Water Distilling Invention to Third World Countries." *Business Insider*, June 2014. http://www.businessinsider.com/segway-inventor-coke-spread-clean-water-2014-6.

[3] Timothy Ogden, "Techno-Optimists Beware," *Stanford Social Innovation Review,* Summer 2012, https://ssir.org/book_reviews/entry/techno_optimists_beware1.

[4] Moore's Law is cofounder of Intel Gordon Moore's 1965 supposition that the number of transistors per square inch on integrated circuits will double every year into the foreseeable future.

[5] The challenges facing the implementation of technology are illustrated by iBOT's declining fortunes. Although it was designed to help U.S. veterans who had been injured in combat, the prototype lost support and has not been manufactured since 2013.

[6] Quoted from "The Adventure of the Copper Beeches," Arthur Conan Doyle, 1893.

[7] Independent researchers have demonstrated how devices such as smart meters and traffic sensors are vulnerable in the event of improper programming and encryption, human error, or taking advantage of the sheer number of devices that must be protected throughout a network. See Nicole Perlroth, "Smart Technology May Be Vulnerable to Hackers," *New York Times*, April 21, 2015, http://bits.blogs.nytimes.com/2015/04/21/smart-city-technology-may-be-vulnerable-to-hackers/. Dan Kaplan, "Black Hat: Assessing Smart Meters for Hacker Footprints, Vulnerabilities," *SC Magazine*, July 25, 2012, http://www.scmagazine.com/black-hat-assessing-smart-meters-for-hacker-footprints-vulnerabilities/article/251947/.

[8] In addition to Cisco's dedicated focus on security, there are many independent groups highlighting the vulnerabilities of devices and how consumers can protect themselves, e.g. "Abusing the Internet of Things: Blackouts. Freakouts. Stakeouts," (Blackhat.com; https://www.blackhat.com/docs/asia-14/materials/Dhanjani/Asia-14-Dhanjani-Abusing-The-Internet-Of-Things-Blackouts-Freakouts-And-Stakeouts.pdf), which describes how several household devices can be compromised.

[9] Dave Evans, "End of the Human Race?" LinkedIn, May 8, 2015, https://www.linkedin.com/pulse/end-human-race-david-evans

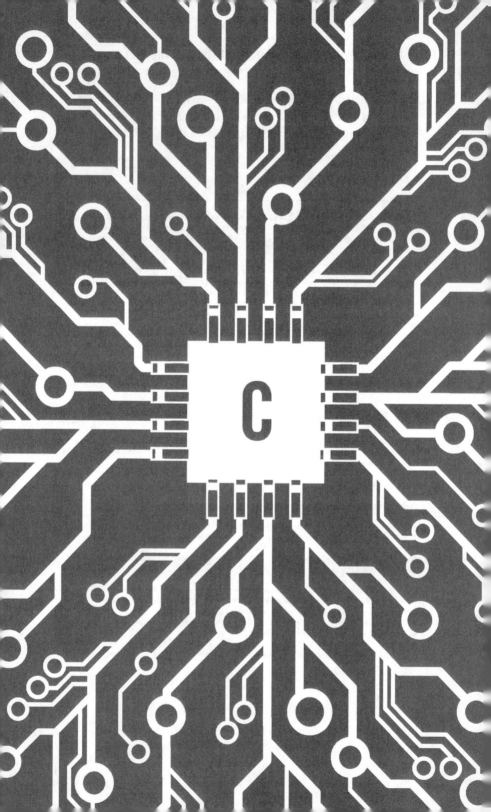

CONCLUSION

AS THE AUTHOR THINKS BACK on a decade of work and its implications for the future of digital cities, there is the inescapable fact that very few details remain in place for long. By the end of this decade, the plans for the landscape of a modern, digitally driven city will have changed in ways we are only just now discerning. The underlying themes of this book are of greater importance, and they can continue to instruct us as we make our way under some circumstances we can predict and many others we cannot. Three of those themes stand out.

First, there is the story of technology and its evolution, from a product-centric organization to a menu of services consumed via a digital platform, with the smartphone as a linchpin device. When the author and his team first designed the idea of a "smart" city in Saudi Arabia in 2006–2007, digital technology was the "fourth utility," and an afterthought to the developers and decision makers investing billions of dollars in roads, buildings, ports, and all the rest of the physical infrastructure of a greenfield development, the "economic city." It is the nature of the tech world, especially in global corporations, to continuously create and promote new buzzwords to reenergize their market capitalization. So the evolution of city technology has been stamped with many labels—smart + connected, smart, digital, IoT, IoE, and so on. But underneath the layers, the basic facts remain: Physical things connect, via the Internet, and create the layer of Internet of Things IoT. In Saudi Arabia, and then, to greater success in Korea, the team developed a menu of IP-based services, which employed data generated by connected things to serve both citizens and city managers. These services allowed citizens to navigate the city more efficiently and safely, while city and building managers could provide safer, more cost and energy-efficient spaces for residential and commercial purposes.

Pioneered at scale in Songdo and Macau, these services are now common to the deployments of city-wide platforms. But what is obvious today would not have been possible without the initial push for the concept of smart services rather than smart *products*. As a bundle that can be adapted to the needs of each individual group of municipal stakeholders, these services have become the core of the smart and digital city, and of the smart and digital nation.

The second theme concerns entrepreneurship in a big organization. The California cliché of a start-up in a garage, brilliantly innovating on a shoestring budget, lives on at the heart of many tech success stories, and probably it will never die. But this fable masks the many ideas, planning and labored execution of business plans of employees whose contributions cannot be so easily summarized. Good ideas that grow out of a global corporation of many thousands have founding fathers, champions, and detractors, just like the original Big Ideas of the start-up phase. The service menu and its smart city application was one such good idea. What made it resilient in the face of initial setbacks, and ultimately successful, was the culture of determined innovation that was, and still is, the hallmark of any successful business. The author and his peers had an opportunity only global companies can give: to experiment ambitiously in many of the most exciting, growing, technology-friendly markets simultaneously. After an initial setback in Saudi Arabia, the group needed a new place to continue the digital city experiment; South Korea was ready to engage and take the idea further. In China, the team found scale; in India, digital nation building. All the while, the parent corporate structure allowed the author and his peers to experiment, while demanding accountability, progress, and the application of lessons learned. This culture that fosters ambition, risk tolerance, and collaboration with new partners is critical to the success of future city-building projects.

The third and most personal theme is linked directly to the second: facing failure, which is an inevitable byproduct of engineering on the scale of cities. There is a corollary need to recognize success that goes beyond the surface or real time. Too often in corporate hierarchies—and politics—failures are dressed up as successes, and real successes are not understood or exploited, since the big organization feels the need to move to the next market or opportunity. Taking responsibility when things are not working, understanding the underlying causes, and developing a genuine success (that works for multiple stakeholders), and absorbing unflattering feedback are difficult experiences. But ultimately, they are among the most rewarding in life.

These three themes combined—much like the combination of processes and technologies that we know as Internet of Things—create a greater, basic truth. It is human nature to fear the technology we create, even as we pursue its benefits. Some concern is justified, and good governance of the technology is not guaranteed. But ultimately, it is the author's conviction that the cities of tomorrow will, thanks in great part to the technology we are building out today, bring better life to millions. And rather than heading toward a dystopic future in which machines control us, we stand to reap the promise of the sensors, networks, algorithms, and data collection that will continue to redefine what a city is and what it does. If we can continue to act on our boldest and best ideas, the smart city will be, at its essence, a *good* city.

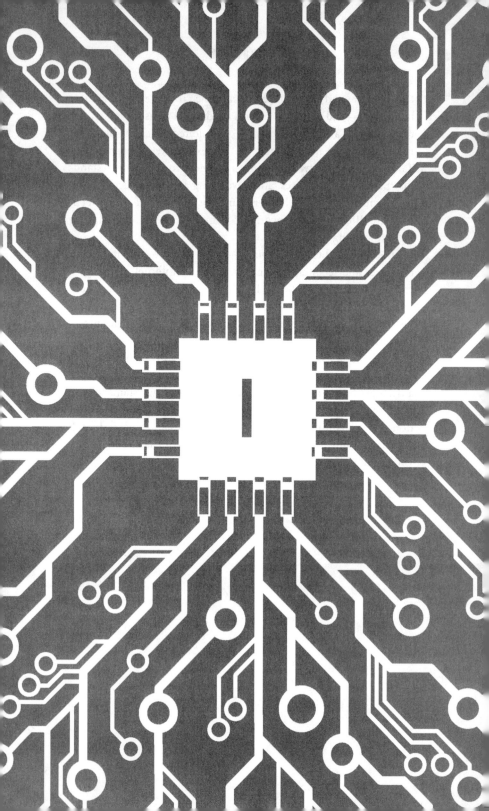

INDEX

A

Abdullah, King, 43–44, 46, 55
Abe, Shinzo, 135
Abu Dhabi, United Arab
    Emirates, 185
Aerotropoli, 65, 182–85, 187,
    201
Afiat Healthpark, 149, 150
Albany, New York, 179
Al-Dabbagh, Amr, 44, 47, 50,
    51, 55
Alexandria, Egypt, 165
Al Maktoum, Mohammed bin
    Rashid, 183, 184
Al Maktoum, Rashid bin Saeed,
    183
Al-Yamani, Ahmed, 55, 56
Amsterdam, 34
Artificial intelligence, 208–9
Arup, 95
Australia, 154–55

B

Bangalore, India, 124–31, 185
Barber, Benjamin R., 179–81
Barcelona, Spain, 17, 23, 110,
    148, 151–53, 181–82
Beijing, 102, 117, 148, 171
Big Data, 37
Bilbao, Spain, 23
Bo Xilai, 108, 109, 110–11, 112,
    113, 119, 180
Brasilia, Brazil, 45, 185
Brazil, 22.
    See also individual cities
Brownfields
    challenge of, 164
    decision making for, 27
    importance of, 34
    Internet of Everything and,
        34–35, 147–60, 164
    needs of, 36–37
    as smart cities, 34–35
Burj Khalifa, 183, 198

C

Cairo, Egypt, 45, 163–68
Chambers, John, 11, 23, 51, 58,
    69, 70, 84, 93, 97, 117, 124,
    125
Changsha, China, 95
Chengdu, China, 101, 102–7,
    112

Chicago, 45
China. *See also individual cities*
  Cisco and, 87–88, 91–120
  consumption in, 171–73
  economic zones of, 101
  GDP growth of, 22, 62, 95,
    101, 171–72
  Internet "Plus" initiative, 26
  lessons learned from, 116–20
  multinational interest in,
    87–88, 91, 117–18, 133
  new cities in, 19, 23, 33, 94
  obesity in, 173
  urban population growth of,
    16, 19, 91–92
Chongqing, China, 101, 102–3,
  107–13
Cisco
  in Australia, 154–55
  in Brazil, 157
  in China, 87–88, 91–120
  criticism of, 82, 176
  in Ecuador, 157
  expertise of, 51
  in greenfield and brownfield
    projects, 26
  in India, 124–33, 136–44
  in Malaysia, 149–50
  role of, 17, 22
  in Saudi Arabia, 41, 47–59, 61
  in South Korea, 61–62, 67–87,
    193–94
  in Spain, 151–53, 181–82
Cities.
  See also Smart cities
  benefits of, 185–87, 188

building new, 33, 45, 48–49
future of, 196–211, 213
mega-, 27, 101, 164
population growth of, 15–16,
  20–21, 22, 33, 39, 175
predicting health of, 85–86
as a process, 31–33
small communities vs.,
  209–10
upgrading existing, 34
varied perspectives on, 15
City of Dreams, 98–100
Connected Cloud International
  (CCI), 114, 119
Cotai Strip, 98
Crime, 204, 206

D

Dalian, China, 108
Data
  agnostic nature of, 19, 32
  "Big Data," 37
  capturing, 32
  growth of, 15–16, 18, 37
  in ideal smart city, 32
  management, 206
  networks, 35–36
Delhi-Mumbai Industrial
  Corridor (DMIC), 126, 127,
  132, 134–39, 149
Detroit, 185, 186
Dholera, India, 33, 136–41, 178,
  184
Diamandis, Peter, 196–98
Digital India, 175

Doyle, Conan, 204
Dubai, United Arab Emirates,
    41, 47, 148, 182–84, 185, 186,
    198
Duisburg, Germany, 113
Dulles Airport, 184

E

Education, 202–3
Egypt, 45, 163–68
Elfrink, Wim, 61, 124, 143
Emaar Properties, 45, 49
Emaar, the Economic City, 45,
    52, 53, 54, 55, 57
Empire State Building, 187
Entrepreneurship, 168, 214
Ericsson, 56, 58, 59, 61
Evans, Dave, 209

F

Failure, facing, 214–15
Fogg, B.J., 82–83

G

Galaxy Entertainment Group,
    98
Gale, Stan, 72, 95
Gale International, 62, 65–68,
    70–73, 75, 78, 79, 82, 84, 85,
    87, 95–96, 194
Gandhi, Mahatma, 140, 141,
    210
Gates, Bill, 41, 66, 208

Gaudí, Antoni, 151
Glaeser, Edward, 175, 185–87,
    188
Global Institute of Tomorrow
    (GIFT), 172
Greenfields
    definition of, 33
    examples of, 33
    service delivery platforms in,
    36
    as smart cities, 34
Guayaquil, Ecuador, 17, 23, 34,
    148, 155–58, 159

H

Hacking, threat of, 18, 206–7
Hamburg, Germany, 17
Hangzhou, China, 34, 113–16
Hawking, Stephen, 208
Hewlett Packard, 110
Hikvision Digital Technology,
    110
Hong Kong, 65, 97, 110, 184
Huawei, 96, 117

I

IBM, 117
Incheon Free Economic Zone
    (IFEZ), 62, 64–65, 69, 70, 71,
    75, 82, 93, 136
Incheon International Airport
    (ICN), 63, 64
India.
    See also individual cities

Cisco and, 124–33, 136–44
consumption in, 172–73
as economic ally of Japan, 133–36
GDP growth of, 22, 132
new cities in, 19, 23, 33, 94, 135
obesity in, 173
as opportunity, 132–33, 143–44
politics of, 123–24, 179
problems of, 124, 131–32, 133, 140–44
urban population growth of, 16, 19, 91, 131–32, 133
water in, 197
Indonesia, 22, 28
Insigma Corporation, 113–16, 119, 203
Intergraph, 110
Internet of Everything (IoE)
in brownfields, 34–35, 147–60, 164
definition of, 23–24
effect of, on daily life, 37–39, 160
efficacy of, 188
engineering challenge of, 24
infancy of, 24–25
as Internet of Everywhere, 95
as prosperity tool, 168
small communities and, 210
smart cities and, 32–33
value of, 17–18
Internet of People, 200–201
Internet of Things (IoT)

definition of, 17
future of, 19
history of, 77, 124
Internet "Plus" initiative (China), 26
Iskandar, Malaysia, 34, 149

J

Jakarta, Indonesia, 28
Japan, 22, 62, 133–36
Jazan Economic City, Saudi Arabia, 46
Jebel Ali Free Zone (JAFZA), 183
Jeddah Economic Forum, 44

K

Kamen, Dean, 197, 201
Kansas City, 23, 147
Kasarda, John, 65, 182–84
King Abdullah Economic City, Saudi Arabia
Cisco and, 41, 47–59
as early test bed, 17
grand opening of, 55–56
as greenfield development, 33
lessons learned from, 57–59
site of, 53
vision for, 45–46, 49, 184
Knowledge Economic City, Saudi Arabia, 46, 52, 184
Kohn Pedersen Fox, 76, 95
Kotler, Steven, 197
KT Corporation, 75

L

Lagos, Nigeria, 179
Las Vegas Sands Corporation, 98
LEED (Leadership in Energy and Environmental Design) certification, 78
Lee Myung-bak, 69, 84
LG CNS, 75, 82
Lindsay, Greg, 67, 183, 185
London, 45, 179, 204

M

MacArthur, Douglas, 71
Macau, 97–98, 214
Malaysia, 19, 34, 149–50, 173
Manila, Philippines, 28
Masdar City, United Arab Emirates, 185
Medina, Saudi Arabia, 46
Meixi Lake, 95–96
Melco Crown Entertainment, 98–100
Mexico, GDP growth of, 22
Mexico City, 164
Microsoft, 62, 66–67, 117
Modi, Narendra, 123, 132, 140, 179
Moore's Law, 198
Morgan Stanley Real Estate, 72
Mubarak, Hosni, 164
Mumbai, India, 133, 185.
  See also Delhi-Mumbai Industrial Corridor

N

Nair, Chandran, 172–75, 186, 188
Nebot, Jaime, 157
New Cairo, Egypt, 45, 165, 166
New Songdo International City Development (NSIC), 75, 77
New York, 34, 110, 177, 179
Nicklaus, Jack, 84
Northeast Asia Trade Tower (NEATT), 83, 187
Nusajaya, Malaysia, 148–50

O

Orwell, George, 205

P

Palermo, Italy, 179
Pan Yunhe, 114
Peking University, 93
Population growth, 15–16, 20–21, 22, 33, 39, 175
POSCO E&C, 67, 71, 72, 73, 75, 82
Prince Abdulaziz bin Mousaed Economic City, Saudi Arabia, 46
Privacy, 205–6
Prodam, 156

R

Resource scarcity, 20–21, 28
Rio de Janeiro, Brazil, 28, 45

Robots, 207–8
Ronald Reagan Airport, 184

S

Salvador, Xavier, 156
San Francisco, 34, 177, 178
San Jose, California, 125, 128
Sao Paolo, Brazil, 23, 45, 156–57
Saudi Arabia.
    See also individual cities
    demographics of, 19, 41,
        42–43
    employment in, 43
    multinational interest in, 41,
        51–52
    new cities in, 19, 23, 33,
        44–47, 50, 57
    oil and, 42
    reform in, 43–44, 46
Saudi Arabia General
    Investment Authority
    (SAGIA), 44, 47, 48, 49, 51,
        53, 54, 55–56, 57
Schneider Electric, 153
Security and Facilities
    Operating Center (SFOC),
    129
Sentilo, 152, 153
Seshadri, Roger, 99, 100
Shanghai, China, 92–93
Singapore, 148, 149, 150, 178,
        179, 184, 185
6th of October City, Egypt, 45,
        165, 166
SK Telecom, 61–62

Slingshot, 197
Smart cities
    benefits of, 26–28, 37–39, 85,
        160, 189
    brownfields as, 34–35, 164
    challenges of, 17, 25
    criticism of, 176–82
    data and, 32
    fluid definition of, 17, 23,
        31–39
    future of, 27–28, 196–211,
        213
    Internet of Everything and,
        32–35
    map of key projects, 12–13
    necessity of, 20, 188
    planning and, 176–82
    resource scarcity and, 20–21,
        28
    sustainability and, 174–75,
        185, 199–200
Snowden, Edward, 116
Songdo, South Korea
    Cisco and, 67–87, 193–94
    criticism of, 176
    as early test bed, 17, 70, 87,
        214
    economics of, 79–81, 83
    entrepreneurship in, 168
    features of, 81–84, 193–96
    as greenfield development, 33
    LEED certification and, 78
    lessons learned from, 85–88
    Microsoft and, 66–67
    success of, 25, 84–85, 91
    vision for, 65–66, 76–78

South East Queensland, Australia, 153–55
South Korea.
See also individual cities
free economic zones in, 64–65, 75
GDP of, 62
multinational interest in, 63–64
new cities in, 19, 23
obesity in, 173
urban population growth of, 19
Streetline, 152
Success, recognizing, 214–15
Surveillance systems, 110, 111, 117, 203–4, 205–6
Sustainability, 174–75, 185, 199–200

T

Telepresence (TP), 55, 77, 83, 193–95, 210
Tianfu Software Park, 104–6
Tomorrow City, 67–68
Townsend, Anthony, 66, 176, 178, 180, 186
Transcontinental Railroad, 188
Transport, importance of, 182–84, 189
Travel, future of, 201–2
Trias, Xavier, 151
Tsunami warning systems, 203–4

U

U-Life, 71, 73, 75, 79, 81–82, 193
United Arab Emirates, 41, 47, 183.
See also individual cities
U.S. Green Building Council, 78

W

Wang Lijun, 112
Washington, D.C., 184
Water, 197
Worksites, remote, 166–67, 201–2
World Bank, 171

X

X Prize Foundation, 196

Z

Zhejiang University, 114, 203
ZTE Corporation, 117

ACKNOWLEDGMENTS

T HE IDEA FOR THIS BOOK was born out of my desire to tell the story of building smart cities from the perspective of a small group of men and women in a multinational company. An idea and value proposition developed and incubated by a small team in Saudi Arabia and Dubai in 2005–2006 has since swept the globe and become a large industry, setting the standard for a better, more sustainable urban future. There are many across the Middle East, Asia, China, and the Americas to whom I am indebted for making this story possible. As I look back now at my experience during a time of unprecedented human and technological progress across a part of the world that emerged and continues to emerge at breathtaking speed, I am struck by just how many incredible people I have worked with. To them, the real heroes of this story, I dedicate this book.